New Perspectives in History

Bosses and Reformers

New Perspectives in History

Bosses and Reformers
Urban Politics in America, 1880–1920

Edited by

BLAINE A. BROWNELL
and
WARREN E. STICKLE
Purdue University

Houghton Mifflin Company · **Boston**

Atlanta · *Dallas* · *Geneva, Illinois* · *Hopewell, New Jersey* · *Palo Alto*

Printed in the U.S.A.
Library of Congress Catalog Card Number: 72-4798
ISBN: 0-395-14050-1

Contents

Preface

The terms *bosses* and *reformers* are burdened with more than their share of subjective overtones. *Boss* immediately conjures up the image of a rather unprincipled character who exploits the public to enrich himself. *Reformer*, on the other hand, usually denotes a disinterested, honorable, and forward-looking citizen who seeks change and progress. The story of urban politics in the years between 1880 and 1920 has all too often been perceived, by journalistic muckrakers and academic historians alike, as a ceaseless struggle between bosses and reformers, with the reformers winning out in the end.

The major view expressed in this book is that this boss-reformer dichotomy is not valid; political leaders and their organizations, ideas, and goals simply do not fit into the rigid framework that such a notion imposes on the incredibly complex reality of urban politics. It is equally clear, however, that historians are still far from agreement about the precise character of this reality. Scholars have demonstrated the limitations of older conceptions without—as yet—fully replacing them with newer terminology and interpretations. Thus, we use the terms *boss* and *reformer* not to support the notion of the boss as villain and the reformer as hero, but to aid students in seeing the falseness of the dichotomy and to expose them to a different angle of vision.

Although historians may disagree about the nature of the challenges and transformations that America experienced in the forty years after 1880, virtually all would agree that these challenges were momentous and that they were first confronted in the nation's cities. An examination of urban politics in these years, therefore, seems to us to be an especially appropriate means of grasping—in the hard reality of specific historical situations—the fundamental importance of the socioeconomic forces of the "Gilded Age" and the "Progressive Era," and the political responses to those forces.

The selections in this book include writings of professional historians and a political scientist, as well as the testimony of participants in the drama of urban politics and affairs of the period. Though carefully chosen, these selections represent but a small sampling of the material that could have been reprinted, were space available. We have thus attempted in our introductory essays to place the selections in historical perspective by relating them to the important events of the time.

We have also attempted in the general introductions to place the selections within the context of the historical debate over the nature of "reform" and over the roles played by various so-called bosses and reformers during these years. We have not, however, sought to offer any final, ultimate answers to these problems, but rather to assemble a set of readings that will enable the student to consider the basic issues involved and to make up his own mind.

We owe a great deal to our teachers George E. Mowry and J. Joseph Huthmacher, respectively, for introducing us to the historical study of urban politics, though they will not agree with all we have written. We also gratefully acknowledge the many suggestions and observations of our friends and colleagues Donald J. Berthrong and Floyd J. Fithian. We have also benefited from the comments of Joel A. Tarr of the Carnegie-Mellon University. Any errors of fact or interpretation that remain are, of course, our own.

B. A. B.
W. E. S.
West Lafayette, Indiana

Introduction

"We must face the fact," Professor Edward A. Ross of Stanford University lamented in 1898, ". . . that the *community*, undermined by the stream of change, has caved in, carrying with it part of the foundations of order." Indeed, whether expressed in terms of the movement from country to city or from old-time religion to new scientific ideas, the late nineteenth and early twentieth centuries of American history were dominated by socioeconomic and cultural flux and transformation. Intellectuals sought to understand the tides of change not only in the various areas of scholarship but also in the nation at large. Social and political commentators took note of technological innovations and new forms of popular protest, while millions of average citizens simply tried to cope with the most immediate of the pressing problems forced upon them. Like many others, the philosopher Josiah Royce was troubled by the implications of transformation and by the apparent incapacity of the country to meet new challenges. The United States appeared, he wrote in 1908, "a country so ripe at present for idealism and so confused . . . by the vastness of . . . its social and political problems." It was bound to be a time of concern and confusion, for an older America was dissolving and a newer nation was in the process of being born. In many ways the years from 1880 to 1920 were the gestation period of modern America.

In the mid-nineteenth century America was a nation of relatively isolated, nearly autonomous communities, provincial in temper and confident in purpose. The security, certainty, and self-sufficiency of such communities began gradually to erode, however, under the impact of industrialization, technological innovation, immigration, and the centralization of business and government. By 1880, Americans were already engaged in efforts to preserve older values while at the same time reaching reluctantly for new means of providing order and stability. As the rate of change increased, the need for order grew more desperate. Slowly, a new scheme began to replace the old, a scheme in its largest dimensions "derived from the regulative, hierarchical needs of an urban-industrial life. Through rules with impersonal sanctions, it sought continuity and predictability in a world of endless change."[1]

The changes that induced such hopes, fears, and frustrations in the last half of the nineteenth century were indeed impressive in both scope and depth. Industrialization increasingly removed millions of Americans from agricultural pursuits into the new regimen of the factory, from dependence on the forces of nature and the informal patterns of community life to dependence on unprecedented and ill-defined economic imperatives. The creation of consolidated business enterprises heralded the appearance of industrial concentration and vast financial empires. Power and authority in both business and government were more and more centralized and bureaucratized, and economic and political problems that had once been manageable now seemed hopelessly complex. Periodic panics and depressions served to augment the sense of helplessness many individuals felt in a society grown larger and far more difficult to understand.

Technological innovation alone would have been sufficient to reshape the character of American society. By 1880 the railroad had already done its share in reducing the isolation of individual communities and in transforming older ways of doing business, and these same trends were incalculably accelerated by the advent of the telegraph, the telephone, the streetcar, and eventually the automobile. New industrial processes and new methods of communication shattered comfortable relationships of space and time and distance. In a society that liked to measure its quality in quantitative terms, these developments were generally welcomed. But there were growing fears, too, that the ultimate consequences of such changes might not be entirely beneficent.

Perhaps the most disturbing new development of the period for many native Americans was the tide of foreign immigration that swept over the nation following the Civil War. In the forty years after 1880, more than twenty million immigrants entered the country, about a third of them arriving in the single decade between 1900 and 1910. Unlike most of the foreign immigrants before 1880, the great majority of these "new" arrivals hailed from southern and eastern Europe, and from ethnic and religious backgrounds that seemed alien to those who classified America as a Protestant, white man's country. Significantly, the new wave of Italians, Austro-Hungarians, Poles, Russians, Greeks, Turks, Lithuanians, and Finns, many of whom were Roman Catholic or Jewish in religion, began to congregate in the cities. In 1900 about two-thirds of the foreign immigrant population lived in American urban areas.

Even though most of the migrants to American cities in these years were rural natives, the addition of new urban foreign populations was a spectacular demographic phenomenon. By 1900 there were more than 9.6 million foreign-born people living in American urban centers, and they constituted from one-third to one-half the populations of the major cities in the Northeast and Midwest as early as 1890. Many "Newer Americans," as well as those who came from American rural regions, lacked the skills required in an industrial society, and the majority were not only poor but also increasingly confined to the overcrowded urban slums. Many native Americans feared that the very character of the nation was being threatened, and the spectre of the congested immigrant districts in the larger cities evoked visions of strange, foreign habits and ideas and the threat of lower-class revolution.

A variety of movements and organizations appeared during the period, all dedicated in one way or another to the elimination of economic, social, and political inequities. The Knights of Labor eventually gave way to the American Federation of Labor as organized workingmen sought security in shorter hours, higher wages, and the principles and practice of collective bargaining. The Populists of the 1890s were the chief political expression of widespread agrarian discontent with economic exploitation by railroads, banks, and other large corporate monopolies. And the "Progressives," a tremendously diverse group of largely urban citizens, began to emerge from the struggles over the character and quality of municipal government in the 1890s to become thoroughly involved in state and national affairs by the first decade of the twentieth century.

Whatever the differences between these various groups and organizations —and they were many—all were responding in some way to the real and suspected consequences of industrialization, economic expansion and centralization, technological innovation, and foreign immigration. Nowhere were these forces more profound or their consequences more apparent than in the larger cities. Indeed, urbanization was itself a highly significant factor in these years. In 1860 slightly less than 20 per cent of all Americans lived in incorporated municipalities of 2,500 or more people; by 1920 more than half the nation's population could be classified as urban. By 1880 there were only twenty American cities that contained 100,000 or more people, whereas forty years later there were sixty-eight such urban areas and three cities—New York, Chicago, and Philadelphia—that together accounted for more than 10 million persons. The urban population almost quadrupled in the same period, from 14,129,735 to 54,157,973, and the population in cities of 250,000 or more rose from 4.5 million to almost 21 million.

With the impact of industrialization, technological innovation, and immigration, the last half of the nineteenth century witnessed the advent of the industrial metropolis, spread over a large territory, spatially divided into specialized industrial, commercial, and residential districts, and fragmented along ethnic and class lines. Streetcars shattered older urban boundaries horizontally, and the electric elevator made possible a considerable vertical expansion by means of the skyscraper. New and complex systems of communication rendered the larger cities into vast capitals of industry, commerce, finance, and far-flung economic enterprise, while urban newspapers and magazines carried the outlines of city habits, ideas, and lifestyles throughout the country.

The prevailing socioeconomic trends of the time not only were most palpable in the cities, but they also called for an almost immediate response in urban areas. Rural areas and small towns could afford to delay in dealing with new challenges, but in the city these demands were both sudden and pressing. Thus, it was in the nation's urban areas that the confrontation with the realities of modern America first occurred. Certainly before 1900, the federal government and the two major political parties responded only slowly and haphazardly to transformations in the social and economic fabric. State legislatures, largely dominated by rural representatives, were in many ways even less prepared to provide effective remedies for a wide range of urban problems. Millions of urban Americans therefore turned increasingly to local movements, organizations, leaders, and agencies to resolve their difficulties.

If the theme of the period was indeed a "search for order," as Wiebe suggests, then surely the quest was nowhere else more necessary or profound than in the cities. Charles Horton Cooley, a sociologist at the University of Michigan, observed in 1899:

Our time . . . is one in which, old structures having gone to pieces, we are slowly and tentatively building up new ones. In the meantime the social process is at once intensified by the extraordinary call upon it and somewhat confused and demoralized by the failure of the structures which normally control and direct it. Our cities, especially, are full of the disintegrated material of the old order looking for a place in the new: men without trades, immigrants with alien habits and traditions, country boys and girls who have broken loose from their families and from early ties and beliefs, college graduates ignorant of the intellectual progress of the past fifty years, young theologians whose creeds the world has ceased to believe, and so on.

The city was not in all respects, of course, a perfect microcosm of American life, but it was unquestionably the most significant arena both for change and for the responses to change.

The search for order in the city took, at least in a political sense, two very broad forms. The first was the growth of the urban boss and the political machine which combined many of the newer immigrant communities and some prominent urban business interests into a well-organized and successful political base. The second was the rise of what historians have usually termed "urban reform movements," dedicated to the principles of "good government" and the democratic process, and firmly opposed to corruption and immorality. As the following selections demonstrate, both the boss and those who sought to depose him responded in varying ways to the challenges of the times, and both helped, consciously or unconsciously, to provide some direction and order in the increasingly complex, multifaceted urban environment.

In terms of contemporary political rhetoric, the struggle between "bossism" and "reform" usually appeared as a direct clash between the forces of good and evil, between corruption and purity, venality and morality, darkness and light. The realm of urban politics was, however, considerably more complex, and can hardly be explained in terms of rigid dichotomies. The great variety of ideas, groups, and individuals within the "reform movement," especially after 1890, and the emergence of urban bosses like Hazen S. Pingree of Detroit and Samuel ("Golden Rule") Jones of Toledo, who erected powerful political machines devoted to substantial social change, suggest not only that the categories of "bosses" and "reformers" are by no means mutually exclusive, but also that our definitions of these terms are probably inadequate for the perception of historical reality.

The first of the following three sections deals with the urban boss, focusing particular attention on the origins and functions of the "traditional" city political machine in the years between 1880 and 1920. The second section takes up the question of "urban reform movements" which, from a myriad of emotional and ideological perspectives, sought to end the corruption, inefficiency, and immorality that many associated with the city boss. Finally, an examination of the contributions of the political machine to urban stability, and in some cases to considerable social, economic, and political change, is presented in the third section.

Neither "bosses" nor "reformers" were uniquely urban in habitat, of course; strong state and local party leaders had certainly appeared by the eighteenth century, and reformers of one kind or another could be found in small towns and rural areas throughout American history, especially in the Midwest and South. But, by 1900, politics in the city became the most significant area for gauging the development of modern America.

It is therefore quite possible that the reexamination of bossism and reform in American cities in the late nineteenth and early twentieth centuries will lead eventually to revisions of what many historians have concluded with regard to local, state, and national politics, and about the "Progressive Movement" in general. The following selections should suggest, at the very least, the complex, variegated nature of America's adjustment to the demands of a new and challenging age. In this respect, as in so many others, the city was the frontier.

NOTES

[1]Robert H. Wiebe, *The Search for Order, 1877–1920* (New York: Hill and Wang, 1968), p. xiv. Wiebe's study is recommended as the best single historical survey of the period.

I The City Boss and the Urban Political Machine

The urban political boss has traditionally been examined from the muck-raker's perspective. Corruption, inefficiency, immorality, and waste were the features usually associated with bossism, and the services provided by the political machine were deemphasized if not ignored entirely. In reevaluating the role of the urban boss, however, a number of scholars have recently concluded that, although urban political machines often offended middle-class sensibilities and engaged in manipulations of the ballot box and the public treasury, their overall contributions to American life were not limited to corruption and venality. As a result of these new investigations, we have come to know a great deal about the "boss" and his "machine" that does not fit the muckraker's interpretation, and we have gained new insights into the complex reality of urban America in the years from 1880 to 1920.

Neither a product of a European-type class consciousness nor a group welded together by ideology, the urban political machine of the late nineteenth and early twentieth centuries was a uniquely American institu-tion, tightly disciplined, pragmatically oriented, seeking power, influence, and stability in the urban chaos of the post–Civil War period. The federal, state, and local governments and the stalemated and equilibrated national parties did not respond adequately to the changing urban environment created by the transportation, communication, technological, and industrial revolutions. As the cities absorbed the influx of immigrants from abroad and from American rural areas, the enlarged electorate overwhelmed the traditional leadership of the gentry and created a power vacuum which competing political factions sought to fill. The demands by these newcomers for municipal services multiplied more rapidly than they could be met. In addition, demands of an expanding business community often went unanswered. The lines of political authority were lost in the bureaucratic scramble of boards, councils, and commissions that characterized nineteenth-century city government. Frequent elections, perhaps even annually, the lack of defined responsibilities, and the emergence of city officials with limited, "private" constituencies (due to direct election) resulted in government inefficiency, duplication, stagnation, and a lack of cooperation between officials and lack of continuity between administrations. Lincoln Steffens once asked Richard Croker, "Why must there be a boss, when we've got a mayor and—a council—?" "That's why," interrupted the Tammany boss. "It's because there's a mayor *and* a council *and* judges *and*—a hundred other men to deal with. A Government is nothing but a business and you can't do business with a lot of officials, who check and cross one another and who come and go, there this year, out the next."[1] The political boss and his urban machine were simply better equipped than most "reformers" to create lines of order and stability within the chaotic city.

By centralizing the lines of authority and power which had been dispersed throughout governmental institutions, and by coordinating power within the city in much the same way that successful reformers did, the urban political boss could mediate the needs of diverse subgroups, respond to the changes in urban life, and construct a coalition of self-interested supporters. The boss was a political broker who provided services, both legal and illegal, for his constituency in return for political and sometimes economic remuneration. He was not totally reactionary, but rather, pragmatic, and he often successfully adapted his machine to the changing desires and needs of his constituents. The urban boss was, in fact, perhaps more responsive to the problems of the urban environment than many "reformers," and certainly to a greater extent than many contemporaries or scholars have realized.

The real source of the boss's political power was the ability of his organization to control the primaries, the nomination process, and to get out the vote. Indeed, the most effective organization of the period was not the business corporation, the farm cooperative, or the labor union—but the urban political machine. By eliminating "private" constituencies, the organization developed a chain of command which reached down into the precinct and even block levels. Some congested slums even boasted tenement captains. To maintain the support of his organization and the rank and file of the electorate, the boss was required to perform a number of complex functions which frequently differed from city to city.

Differences between bosses were in fact almost as great as the similarities. Some, like Richard Croker of New York's Tammany Hall, Tom Pendergast of Kansas City, and Frank Hague of New Jersey, not only dominated their local urban machines and at times the state government, but also were important figures in the national councils of the Democratic party. Others, like George Washington Plunkitt of New York, concentrated their efforts within a specific city and only indirectly influenced state and national affairs. Chicago, for example, saw a number of mayors, Democratic and

Republican, come and go in the years between 1890 and the mid-1920s; but the ebullient "Bathhouse" John Coughlin and the crafty Michael "Hinky Dink" Kenna were the dominant powers in the city's downtown First Ward throughout most of the period. Protecting the gambling, saloon, and prostitution interests along the notorious "levee," Coughlin and Kenna played a crucial role in electing some mayors (including a few known as "reformers") and in defeating some others, but their own political fortunes were only slightly affected by personalities and events at the national, state, and even city-wide levels.

City political machines were also organized in a myriad of ways. Some bosses built tightly-knit organizations through the force of their own personalities. Other machines were no more than relatively loose coalitions of ward bosses held together by the immediate prospect of electoral victory or financial gain. Some ward bosses were so popular that they were rarely challenged and never resorted to stuffing ballot boxes or buying votes. Others, like Coughlin and Kenna in Chicago, found it necessary to import hoards of vagrants and floaters at election time, proffer them with beds, free lunches, and a regular fee for their votes, and herd them to the polls. On occasion, armed hoodlums were hired to literally demolish the opposition forces in open street warfare. Even though the differences between urban political machines were often pronounced, there were recurrent patterns in the function of these organizations that should be noted.

A major function of the boss was to minister to the immediate needs of his constituents by providing food, bins of coal, funeral expenses, a place to stay in case of eviction, and—probably most important—jobs. Often confronted with grinding poverty, frustration, and loneliness, the new arrivals to the city—both foreign- and native-born—were not so much concerned with abstract principles of right and wrong, or with complex issues like the tariff, as with the immediate socioeconomic problems of their urban neighborhoods. The needs for jobs, education, or a new bathhouse for a precinct or ward demanded the kind of personal attention that, all too frequently, only the boss's agent could provide. The boss also mediated between the city government and his constituents by securing bail and reduced sentences, eliminating fines with a kind word to the judge, interceding with building and fire inspectors, and securing licenses for pushcarts and saloons. He extended friendship and sympathy in areas of the city where these were rare commodities, aided immigrants in the process of social integration into the ways of a new urban environment, and frequently advanced the sense of ethnic identity among newcomers that provided them with some feeling of community and recognition. The survival of the urban political machine depended, in the final analysis, on those ward bosses who cultivated their constituents on a day-to-day basis, not from the remote corridors of city hall but on the streets and in the barrooms of their respective districts. Martin Lomasny, a Boston ward leader, told Lincoln Steffens: "I think that there's got to be in every ward somebody that any bloke can come to—no matter what he's done—to get help. Help, you understand; none of your law and justice, but help."[2]

The urban political machine also served as a broker for various financial interests. Businesses required fire and police protection, adequate streets, the efficient disposal of industrial waste, and sometimes freedom from the strict enforcement of safety ordinances and building codes. Many companies sought profitable franchises for public construction and for the operation of public utilities—gas, water, electricity, sewage, and transportation. Businessmen desired political "favors" that could enable them to stabilize markets and maximize profits, while the boss was seeking favors that business could provide—jobs, financial contributions, and "honest" and "dishonest" graft, to borrow Plunkitt's phrase. Thus, the relationship between the boss and legitimate business was a unique alliance predicated on mutual self-interest. It should also be noted that this relationship led most frequently to the bribes and "boodling" for which the boss was condemned by many reformers, and for which legitimate business was often equally responsible.

In addition, the boss provided services for illegitimate businesses such as gambling, prostitution, and illegal liquor operations, in return for financial support. Not only did crime, vice, and rackets usually constititute a significant portion of the urban economy, but such illegal goods and services were also frequently demanded by the machine's supporters and at least tolerated by some "respectable" elements in the community who realized that gambling, prostitution, and free-flowing liquor brought money and customers into the city. The boss's protection usually consisted of political pressures on the police department to avoid enforcement of the law in vice districts, and of his readiness to provide bail and legal defense for those constituents who were arrested. In many cases, his protection was, quite frankly, regarded as a "public service" by the residents of his ward. On the other hand, the boss's protection and encouragement of "immorality" was what stamped him, more than any other of his diverse activities, as undesirable in the eyes of most middle- and upper-class reform groups. But it was only when organized crime began to conduct its operations behind legitimate business "fronts" in the twentieth century that the boss's protection of these activities became less necessary or pronounced.

The principal emphasis in this section is on the character and functions of the city boss and the urban political machine, and the reader should be particularly alert to several points which suggest the role of the boss in the emerging American metropolis. The city boss has been criticized for mercilessly exploiting a large, docile, ignorant mass, and for relying almost exclusively on the support of lower-class ethnic and immigrant groups. Futhermore, most scholars have tended to stress the corruption and graft of the urban political machine. Are these criticisms valid? Were those who supported the urban political machine unable to intelligently identify and seek their own interests? Did the boss, in other words, primarily shape the opinions and desires of his constituents, or did he merely reflect them? Were successful city-wide political machines totally dependent on lower-class ethnic votes, or did they also require the support of middle- and upper-class elements? Finally, was the urban political machine substantially more corrupt than other major institutions of the period—and, in any event, should the city boss and his organization be judged mainly by their graft and questionable methods or by the benefits they provided, or by some other criteria? The answers to these questions can obviously tell us not only a great deal about the city boss and his machine but also provide considerable perspective on the reality and meaning of the complex, multifaceted American urban experience in the late nineteenth and early twentieth century.

NOTES

[1]Lincoln Steffens, *The Autobiography of Lincoln Steffens* (New York: Harcourt, 1931), p. 236.
[2]*Ibid.*, p. 618.

ELMER E. CORNWELL, JR.

Bosses, Machines, and Ethnic Groups

Elmer E. Cornwell, Jr. is professor of political science and chairman of the department at Brown University. His essay, reprinted below, not only provides a classic analysis of the relationship between the boss and urban ethnic groups and a lucid examination of the functions and purposes of the political machine in this period, but also poses some crucial questions with regard to city politics of the present day. Since Cornwell's interpretation has been accepted by a number of scholars, it is appropriate that we begin our reevaluation of urban politics here, where many of the major issues are raised and discussed. The reader should focus his attention on the principal thesis—is it valid? does it apply to the majority of cities? what does it suggest of the realities of urban America?—and also measure it against the suggestions and interpretations in the selections which follow.

Though the direction of the causal relationship may be difficult to establish, the classic urban machine and the century of immigration which ended in the 1920's were intimately intertwined phenomena. This fact is not always recognized as fully as it should be. Much of the literature on bosses and machines, beginning with the muckrakers, but not excluding more recent studies with less overt moralistic flavor, carries the implication that such factors as the dispersal of power in urban government—under weak mayor charters and through rivalries among state, county, city and special district authorities, all plowing the same field but none with full responsibility for its cultivation—invited the machine's extralegal reconcentration of power. It is also true that attitudes engendered by a business society whose prime movers characteristically had their eye on the "main chance"—and specifically on traction franchises and the like—also fostered the growth of the essentially entrepreneurial role and amoral attitude of the boss.

RELATION OF MACHINE TO IMMIGRATION

When all this has been said, however, the fact still remains that the classic machine would probably not have been possible, and certainly would not have been so prominent a feature of the American political

Reprinted by permission from *The Annals of the American Academy of Political and Social Science* (May, 1964), 28-39.

landscape, without the immigrant. Essentially, any disciplined grass-roots political organization rests upon a docile mass base which has in some manner been rendered dependable, predictable, and manipulable. The rank and file of the Soviet Communist party is disciplined by a combination of ideological allegiance, fear, and hope of reward. The average party supporter in a liberal-democratic society cannot be so disciplined under ordinary circumstances, at least not for long. The newly arrived immigrant was a special case, however. He was characteristically insecure, culturally and often linguistically alien, confused, and often in actual want. Thus, even if he had valued the franchise thrust upon him by his new political mentors, its careful exercise would have taken a low priority in his daily struggle for existence. In most cases, he did not value or even understand the political role into which he was being pushed.

Thus, it was the succeeding waves of immigrants that gave the urban political organizations the manipulable mass bases without which they could not have functioned as they did. And, until immigration dried up to a trickle in the 1920's, as one generation of newcomers began to espouse traditional American values of political independence, there was always a new group, often from a different country of origin, to which the machine could turn. As long as this continued to be possible, machines persisted, and once the immigrant base finally began to disappear, so did most of the bosses of the classic model. In a very real sense, then, the one phenomenon was dependent on the other.

The argument can be made that there were other machines that clearly were not immigrant-based in this sense. All generalizations, especially those in the social sciences, are but proximate truths. At the same time, machines based on white, Protestant, "old stock" clienteles were not wholly unrelated in their motivation and operation to the factor of immigration. Platt's smooth-functioning organization in New York State[1] and Blind Boss Brayton's contemporary operation in Rhode Island[2] were both based, in the immediate sense, on what Lincoln Steffens called "the good old American stock out in the country."[3] And yet recall that both of these states were highly urbanized even in the 1890's and early 1900's when these two worthies flourished and had ingested disproportionate numbers of immigrants. As of 1920, when 38 per cent of the total United States population was foreign born or of foreign parentage, the corresponding percentages for New York and Rhode Island were 64 and 71.[4] These facts alone suggest what the political history of both makes clear: these rural "old stock" machines existed largely as means of political defense against the newcomers and doubtless would not have existed had there been no immigrants.

The point, then, is that, whereas in the cities the immigrants sold their political independence for the familiar currency of favors and aid, their rural native cousins were sometimes prompted to do the same, in part out of desire for cultural-religious as well as political, and perhaps at times economic, self-protection. Recollection of the Know-Nothing era of militant nativist activity a half-century earlier suggests that this kind of cultural-religious antagonism can be a very potent political force indeed. An analogous explanation could even be offered for the existence of machines in the South like that of Harry Byrd in Virginia, by simply substituting the perceived Negro threat for the danger of engulfment by foreigners in the North. And, curiously enough, the two examples of reasonably thoroughgoing machine-like organizations that flourished in the otherwise inhospitable English soil—Joseph Chamberlain's Birmingham caucus[5] and Archibald Salvidge's "machine" in Liverpool[6]—also were at least indirectly related to the problem of Irish home rule, and, in Liverpool, to actual rivalry with Irish immigrants over religion and jobs.

In short, whatever else may be said about the conditions and forces that spawned the classic machine, this kind of disciplined political entity must rest at bottom on a clientele which has felt it necessary to exchange political independence—its votes, in a word—for something seen as more essential to its well-being and security. In general, such a group will be the product of some kind of socioeconomic disequilibrium or cultural tension which finds its members in an insecure or seriously disadvantaged situation. Thus, the immigrant was willing to submit to the boss in exchange for aid—real or imagined—in gaining his foothold in the new environment, and the old-stock machine supporters, North or South, submitted in part for protection against swarming aliens or a potential Negro threat to white dominance.

THE CLASSIC MACHINE IN OPERATION

It cannot be assumed that the process of machine exploitation of succeeding groups of newcomers was a smooth and simple operation. Any formal organization, political or otherwise, must maintain a continuing balance among a series of often contradictory forces.[7] Its very existence rests on the success with which it achieves its objective—in the case of a political party, the winning of elections and, thus, power. In the long run, this success depends on the organization's continuing ability to tap fresh sources of support as time goes on and old reliances dwindle and may at times depend on keeping newly available resources away from its rival or rivals. For the machine, this has meant wooing each new ethnic contingent. Yet this process of growth and renewal will inevitably threaten the very position of many of the proprietors of the organization itself by recruiting rivals for their roles. Any organizational entity must not only achieve its corporate goals but, to survive, it must also satisfy the needs and desires of its members as individuals. If it fails in this, its supporters will vanish and its own objectives remain unattainable. Specifically, for the machine, this fact of organizational life often tempered missionary zeal and tempted its members to protect even an eroding *status quo*.

Usually the machine did yield in the long run to the political imperative that all groups of potential supporters must be wooed, if for no other reason than to keep them from the enemy. The short-term risk to the present leadership often must have appeared minimal. The plight of the newcomers was so pitiful, their needs so elemental, and their prospects of achieving security and independence so problematical in the foreseeable future that they must have appeared like a windfall to the machine proprietors. Thus, after initial hesitancy, the Irish were taken into Tammany and found their way into the ranks of the clientele of other big city party organizations.

The ways in which immigrant political support was purchased are familiar and need no elaborate review here. They had at least three kinds of needs which the ward heeler could fill on behalf of the party leadership. Above all, they needed the means of physical existence: jobs, loans, rent money, contributions of food or fuel to tide them over, and the like. Secondly, they needed a buffer against an unfamiliar state and its legal minions: help when they or their offspring got in trouble with the police, help in dealing with inspectors, in seeking pushcart licenses, or in other relations with the public bureaucracy. Finally, they needed the intangibles of friendship, sympathy, and social intercourse. These were available, variously, through contact with the precinct captain, the hospitality of the political clubhouse, the attendance of the neighborhood boss at wakes and weddings, and the annual ward outing.[8]

As has often been noted, these kinds of services were not available, as they are today, at the hands of "United Fund" agencies, city welfare departments with their platoons of social workers, or through federal social security legislation. The sporadic and quite inadequate aid rendered by the boss and his lieutenants thus filled a vacuum. Their only rivals were the self-help associations which did spring up within each ethnic group as soon as available resources allowed a meager surplus to support burial societies and the like. The fact that the politicians acted from self-serving motives in distributing their largess, expecting and receiving a *quid pro quo,* is obvious but not wholly relevant. At least it was not relevant in judging the social importance of the services rendered. It was highly relevant, of course, in terms of the political power base thus acquired.

Some of the later arrivals following the pioneering Irish were in at least as great need of aid. The Irish did speak English and had had some experience with political action and representative institutions at home. This, plus the fact that they got here first, doubtless accounts for their rapid rise in their chosen party, the Democracy. The groups that followed, however, usually did not know English and bore the additional burden of a cultural heritage that had less in common with the American patterns they encountered than had been the case with the Irish. And, too, almost all groups, the Sons of Erin included, differed religiously from the basic Protestant consensus of their Anglo-Saxon predecessors.

As group followed group—not only into the country but into the rickety tenements and "river wards" reserved, as it were, for the latest arrivals—the processes of absorption became more complex. The Irish ward politicians doubtless had, if anything, more difficulty bridging the cultural and language gap to meet the newcomers than the "Yankees" had had in dealing with themselves some decades earlier. Also, while it may well be that the Yankees gave up their party committee posts fairly willingly to the Irish, because politics was not essential to their well-being either economically or psychologically, the Irish were in a rather different position when their turn came to move over and make room.[9] They had not fully outgrown their dependence on politics for financial and psychic security. Thus, the conflicting demands of the machine for new sources of support versus the reluctance of the incumbents to encourage rivalry for their own positions, produced tension. In the long run, however, most of the new ethnic groups found their place in the party system. In some cases, as with the Italians, the Republicans, generally less skillful in these arts, won support by default when the Irish were especially inhospitable.

THE MACHINE AS SOCIAL INTEGRATOR

There is another side to the coin of machine dependence on the continuing flow of immigrants. The "invisible hand"—to use an analogy with Adam Smith's economics—which operated to produce social benefits out of the *quid pro quo* which the ward heelers exchanged for votes was at work in other ways, too. Henry Jones Ford noted in the 1890's, while discussing the role of party:[10]

This nationalizing influence continues to produce results of the greatest social value, for in co-ordinating the various elements of the population for political purposes, party organization at the same time tends to fuse them into one mass of citizenship, pervaded by a common order of ideas and sentiments, and actuated by the same class of motives, This is probably the secret of the powerful solvent influence which American civilization exerts upon the enormous deposits of alien population thrown upon this country by the torrent of emigration.

Again, in other words, the selfish quest by the politician for electoral support and power was transmuted by the "invisible hand" into the major force integrating the immigrant into the community.

This process has had several facets. In the first place, the mere seeking out of the immigrants in quest of their support, the assistance rendered in getting them naturalized (when it was necessary to observe these legal niceties), and so forth were of considerable importance in laying the foundation for their more meaningful political participation later. In addition, the parties have progressively drawn into their own hierarchies and committee offices representatives of the various ethnic groups. The mechanics of this process were varied. In some cases, there doubtless emerged leaders of a particular group in one ward or neighborhood who, if given official party status, would automatically bring their followings along with them.[11] On other occasions, new ethnic enclaves may have sought or even demanded representation in exchange for support. Perhaps prior to either of these, the machine sought to co-opt individuals who could speak the language and act as a cultural bridge between the party and the newcomers. Depending on the situation, it probably was essential to do this and impossible for precinct captains of a different background to develop adequate rapport. It is at this point that ethnic group rivalry in the organization becomes difficult. Gratitude to the boss for initial admission into the lower ranks of the hierarchy would be bound to change in time into demands, of growing insistence, for further recognition of the individual and his group.

These general patterns can to some extent be documented, at least illustratively. The tendency for the urban machines to reap the Irish vote and later much of the vote of more recent arrivals is well known. The process of infiltration by group representatives into party structure is harder to identify precisely. With this in mind, the author did a study of the members of party ward committees in Providence, Rhode Island, the findings of which may reflect trends elsewhere.[12] Analysis of committee membership lists or their equivalent going back to the 1860's and 1870's showed initial overwhelming Anglo-Saxon majorities. For the Democrats, however, this majority gave way, between the 1880's and 1900, to a roughly

75 per cent Irish preponderance, while the Republican committees stayed "Yankee" until after the First World War. Then, in the 1920's, both parties simultaneously recruited Italian committeemen to replace some of the Irish and white Protestants, respectively. Today, both have varied, and roughly similar, proportions of all major groups in the city population. In other cities, the timing of shifts and the ethnic groups involved will have differed, but the general process and its relation to local patterns of immigration were doubtless similar.

It is incredible, viewed now with hindsight, how reckless the American republic was in its unpremeditated policy of the open door and the implied assumption that somehow, without any governmental or even organized private assistance, hundreds of thousands of immigrants from dozens of diverse cultures would fit themselves smoothly and automatically into a native culture which had its own share of ethnocentrism. The fact of the matter was that the process did not operate smoothly or particularly effectively. There were tensions and incidents which accentuated cultural differences and engendered bitterness. These ranged, chronologically, all the way from the abuses of the more militant Know-Nothings to the Ku Klux Klan activity of the 1920's.

Economically, most occupational doors that did not lead to manual labor jobs were closed to the Irish and later arrivals and were only gradually pried open after much time had passed and many lasting intergroup enmities had been engendered. Here again, the party organizations represented one of the few mechanisms, public or private, that lubricated a process of integration which, in its very nature, was bound to generate enormous amounts of friction. Besides drawing group representatives into its councils, party work also was one of the few career ladders available to the immigrant and his ambitious sons. Here, status could be achieved, as well as a comfortable income, one way or another, when few other routes were open. This became not just status for the individual but a measure of recognition and acceptance for the group as a whole through the individual's success. In fact, not only did the newcomer use this alternative career ladder, but he carried over into the political sphere some of the "Horatio Alger" quest for success and other aspects of an essentially pragmatic, materialistic American culture as well.

Politics for the machine politician never was an ideological enterprise or a matter of beliefs and principles. As someone once said, the boss had only seven principles, five loaves and two fishes. Rather, politics was an entrepreneurial vocation like any other business. Banfield and Wilson have written: "A political machine is a business organization in a particular field of business—getting votes and winning elections. As a Chicago machine boss once said . . . it is 'just like any sales organization trying to sell its product.' ''[13] The politician's aim was and is so to invest his supply of capital—jobs, favors, and the like—as to earn a profit, some of which he will take as ''income'' and the rest reinvest in quest of larger returns. In other words, the immigrant political leader took the one vocation open to him, politics, and made it into as close an approximation as he could of the more valued business callings in the society, from which he was effectively barred. He acted out the American success story in the only way open to him.

Obviously, the foregoing is not designed to portray the machine as a knight-errant rescuing American society from its willful folly. In the first place, the folly was not willful, and perhaps not folly. In the second, the boss's contribution toward making the melting pot melt should not be overrated. At the same time, many have testified—as does the record itself—to the almost unique ability of party as organization to bring people together across cultural and similar barriers. As Glazer and Moynihan have written of New York City:[14]

> . . . political life itself emphasizes the ethnic character of the city, with its balanced tickets and its special appeals. . . . For those in the field itself, there is more contact across the ethnic lines, and the ethnic lines themselves mean less, than in other areas of the city's life.

Ticket-balancing, or United Nations politics, as it is sometimes called, is perhaps symbolic of the ultimate step in the process of granting group recognition and confirming the fact that something approaching intergroup equality has been achieved. Either, as with the Manhattan Borough presidency and the Negro group, certain prescriptive rights become established to a particular office or to one place on a city-wide ticket or ethnic allocation is made using the background of the head of the ticket as point of departure.

In short, the classic urban machine rested upon the immigrants, while at the same time it fostered their integration into American life. It also made, in the process, a major contribution to the over-all American political style. It is true that politics as a pragmatic entrepreneurial vocation owes much in America to the contributions of Burr, Van Buren, Weed, Marcy (to the victor belong the spoils), and, in a sense, to Andrew Jackson himself. Thus, Richard Hofstadter's attribution of one of the two central systems of political ethics in America to the immigrants is only partially valid.[15] He is clearly correct, however, in suggesting that a political style which stressed ''personal obligations, and placed strong personal loyalties above allegiance to abstract codes of law or morals''[16] was congenial to the machine politicians and their followers, and they made it their own, developing its full implications in the process. At the same time, the immigrant versus old stock cultural cleavage prompted the latter to espouse the more vigorously the typically middle-class, reformist style which stresses honesty, impartiality, and efficiency. These two styles or ethics, since the late nineteenth century, have, by their interaction, shaped both the evolution of urban politics and the machinery of urban government.

THE DECLINE OF THE MACHINE

The decline and fall of the boss as a political phenomenon has often been chronicled and explained. It is argued, *inter alia*, that reforms like the direct primary, nonpartisan systems of election, voting machines and tightened registration requirements, and city-manager schemes often dealt crippling blows. In the aggregate, they doubtless did, though many exceptions can be found to prove the rule. One particular contribution of the reformers which has had unquestioned importance—though circumvention has not proven impossible—was the elimination of patronage with the installation of civil service based on the merit principle. And, generally, educational levels have risen, and occupational levels and incomes have risen as well. Even where patronage remains available, the latter develop- ment has rendered it less attractive, and to fewer people. Finally, and most often cited, there was the impact of the New Deal. Its installation of publicly sponsored welfare programs eliminated many of the rough-and-ready welfare functions of the precinct captain, though the more imaginative recouped part of their loss by helping to steer constituents through the bureaucratic maze, claiming credit for the benefits thus obtained.

Granting the importance of all of these developments, in the long run, the decline of immigration doubtless proved the most important blow to the traditional machine operation. New arrivals had been entering the country at a rate in excess of four million each half decade up to the First World War. The rate averaged barely more than one third of that between 1915 and 1930 and dropped to a mere trickle for most of the period down to the present. Sharply restrictive legislation passed in 1921 and 1924 was responsible. Obviously, the impact on the machines came in the form of a delayed reaction, but most of them gradually withered. The few that survived did so through shrewd adaptation to changed condi- tions, specifically through judicious self-administered doses of reformism, as, for example, with the Daley organization in Chicago.

Thus ended an era. Immigration may not have called the boss into being, but the two in most cases were closely linked. Two questions remain to be dealt with. What contemporary counterparts are there, if any, of the immigrant influx of yesteryear and how are the parties dealing with them? And what can be said of the current political behavior of the children and grandchildren of the former immigrants?.

THE PARTIES AND THE NEW IMMIGRATION

There are, of course, two major groups that do represent close parallels with the earlier influx and at the same time carry important differences. These are the Negroes who have been migrating in increasing numbers from the South to northern urban centers since the First World War and the Puerto Ricans who began coming to New York City, for the most part, after the Second World War.[17] Both resemble their alien predecessors in the magnitude of their numbers, their basic and important cultural differences from the population into whose midst they are moving, an almost invariable need of assistance in adjusting to a new environment, and their potential impact on the political balance of forces.

The major points of difference are also worth noting. Both come bearing the credentials of American citizenship, which was not the case with the earlier groups. Though this factor should make for easier adjustment, other group characteristics operate to make acceptance more difficult. For the Negro, there is the fundamental problem of color, coupled with cultural characteristics which, though acquired ostensibly in the American environment, operate to make assimilation more difficult. These include all the long deposit of servitude and enforced inferior status: loose marital ties and correspondingly weak family ties generally, a poverty of leadership potential, low literacy and skill levels, and the like. For the Puerto Ricans, there is language, plus differences of culture, and a partial color barrier which operates to cause at least some Spanish Americans to be classified—against their will—as Negroes. On balance, it is probably true that, so far as these two groups are concerned as groups, they face higher barriers to integration into American life than almost any earlier group save, possibly, the orientals.

But the society itself has changed enormously from the society to which the Irish, Italians, and Jews sought entrance. Urban areas are now equipped with facilities to which the newcomer can turn for aid that counterbalance to some degree the particular hostilities which members of these two groups arouse. There are now elaborate public welfare programs, there is Aid to Dependent Children for the many fatherless families, there are numerous private agencies and charities which stand ready to help, and, in the case of the Puerto Ricans, their land of origin has taken a unique interest in the welfare of its emigrants. There have been legislative efforts to ban the discrimination in housing or employment which they encounter.

Though these facilities stand ready to ease aspects of the economic and social integration of these latest immigrants, there still remains the question of political absorption. Here, too, the situation today sharply differs from the past. The political parties now have neither the incentive nor the means with which to perform the functions they performed for the earlier immigrants. The machine in most affected areas is gone beyond recall, and there remain in its place party organizations that are hollow shells of their former strength and vigor. Party in general, given the proliferation of both public bureaucracies and the mass entertainment industry, has been pushed to the fringes of the average citizen's attention span and often to the fringes of the governing process itself. The debilitating impact of reform legislation contributed to the same end, needless to say. Thus, in general, the new immigrants can look to the parties for little of the former assistance they once provided in gaining entrance and leverage in the political processes of their new homes.

There are partial exceptions here, as there are to all the foregoing generalizations. Mayor Daley's modern Chicago version of the old-style machine has been mentioned earlier. Within his over-all Cook County Democratic organization, there is the "sub-machine" comprising the Negro followers of Representative William E. Dawson.[18] Dawson, a former maverick Republican, shifted parties in 1939 and joined forces with Mayor-boss Kelly. Some twenty years later, he had put together a combination, under his leadership, of five or six Negro wards. This "organization within an organization" appears to bargain as a unit through Dawson and his lieutenants for patronage and other kinds of preferment in the gift of Mayor Daley and in turn tends to exert a moderating influence on the more aggressive elements in the Negro community. Trends suggest that this is not destined to be a permanent arrangement. The population of the Dawson-controlled wards has been declining as the more prosperous Negroes manage to settle in more desirable locations, and as Dawson and his associates grow older, they become more conservative. Whether or not this latter is partly an illusion produced by the rapid rise in Negro militancy since 1954 would be hard to say. It is probably true that leaders of the Dawson type will get more "out of phase" with the civil rights movement as that movement gains further momentum.

New York City, almost by traditional right, is *the* locale for the study of the behavior of American parties in relation to the immigrant. The 1960 census reported just over a million Negroes in New York City and somewhat more than 600,000 Puerto Ricans. In broad terms, it can be said that, since the days of Al Smith and Boss Murphy, New York politics have been long on confusion and fragmentation and short on centralized, disciplined organization. There was, therefore, little possibility that a relationship such as Representative Dawson worked out with his Negro clientele on the one hand and the leaders of the Cook County Democracy on the other could be developed in New York. Especially in Manhattan—which we shall take for analysis—one finds exemplified the more typical contemporary party situation: no dominating borough-wide authority save that in the hands of the mayor himself, hence a series of local feudal chiefs who are rarely willing to exchange their relative independence for the rather meager supplies of patronage available, and the whole system wracked periodically by factional feuding.

The Negro in New York, in apparent contrast to the Chicago situation, has been more fragmented in his political organization, has found little boroughwide structure with which to associate, but has made more spectacular symbolic gains in the party and city government. Representative Adam Clayton Powell, the rather erratic champion of the city's nonwhites, reaps vastly more national publicity for his espoused cause than the publicity-shy Congressman Dawson.[19] How much this means in concrete benefits would be hard to determine. More significant is the fact that in 1953 a Negro, Hulan Jack, was elected for the first time to a major office in the city, that of Borough President of Manhattan. Powell had a major role in this, though he later broke with Jack. Since then, this position has become an accepted Negro prerogative. Other high positions have been filled by Negroes in the city administration in recent years.

REPRESENTATION ON PARTY COMMITTEES

A somewhat more useful basis for judging the reality of ethnic or racial group political absorption and power position than possession of some of these "commanding heights" (in Lenin's phrase) would be an analysis of the extent to which they had gained footholds in the lower and intermediate levels of the party organization. The ethnic proportions among Providence ward committee members cited above are a relatively accurate reflection of the nationality power relationships in city politics. For example, the fact that the Irish Democrats have held onto about half of the ward committee seats after yielding some places to Italians reflects the fact that they still have the dominant voice in the party. The rise of the Italians on the Republican side to the status of the largest single ethnic group also reflects their growing power.[20]

Table 1 shows the approximate percentages of ethnic/racial representation in the total New York City population and, in the second column, the background of the Manhattan Democratic Assembly district leaders and coleaders insofar as these could be determined.[21] There are sixteen Assembly districts, but most are divided into two or three parts with a leader and coleader for each. There were some vacancies at the time the data were obtained. It can be seen that the Negro has done quite well by this measure of political integration in that the group has considerably more than the share of district leadership positions it would be entitled to on a strict population basis. The bulk of these Negroes preside over districts in or around Harlem, as might be expected—the 11th, 12th, 13th, 14th, and 16th Assembly districts. Of the eighteen occupied positions in these five Assembly districts, they hold twelve. There are two Negroes, one each in the 5th and 10th, to the west and east of Central Park, respectively, but none to the south of the Park at all.

In passing it might be noted that the other groups on the Table each have something approximating their proportionate share of the leaderships. The Jewish contingent is disproportionately large, due in considerable

Table 1–Comparison of Ethnic Proportions in Population with Democratic District Leaders in Manhattan

	Approximate Percentage of New York City 1960 Population[a]	Percentage of Democratic Assembly District Leaders (N = 66)
Negroes	14	21
Puerto Ricans	8	6
Jews	25 ±	38
Italians	17 ±	11
Irish	10 ±	9
Others	26 ±	15[b]
	100	100

[a]Population percentage estimates are from Nathan Glazer and D. P. Moynihan, *Beyond the Melting Pot* (Cambridge: Massachusetts Institute of Technology and Harvard Press, 1963). Only figures for Negroes and Puerto Ricians were given in the 1960 census. It was impossible to get ethnic group percentages for Manhattan alone.
[b]Includes Anglo–Saxon Protestants and others of unidentified background.

measure to the fact that three-fifths of all the anti-Tammany "reform" leaders come from that part of the city population. True to what one knows about their situation in other cities, the Italians appear to be under-represented. The Irish, however, even in view of the extreme difficulty in guessing their share of the city population, have far fewer positions than the prevailing myth of continuing Irish dominance of urban Democratic politics would suggest.

Turning now to the Puerto Ricans, they offer the best opportunity for assessing the ability of at least the Manhattan Democratic organization to absorb a genuinely new ethnic group. In Table 2, the backgrounds of the district leaders in the areas of heaviest Puerto Rican population are tabulated. Also included, in the last two columns, are figures on the personnel of the lowest level of "grass-roots" party organization, the election district captains. Out of the twelve district leader positions occupied at the time the data were obtained, four were held by Puerto Ricans, giving that group representation in three of the six most heavily Puerto Rican districts. Though only firsthand knowledge would indicate how effective these individuals are in representing their ethnic group and bargaining on its behalf, there is indication here of rather significant infiltration into the party structure. The figures for election district captains, where these could be obtained, point to the same conclusion. Except for the lower east side, where the proportion is smaller, roughly half of these captains are also Puerto Rican, casting further doubt on common assumptions that the party in Manhattan is lagging seriously in making room for this latest group to arrive.

In general, both Table 1 and Table 2 suggest that the Puerto Ricans have secured, in the relatively short time since their arrival in large numbers, party offices roughly commensurate with their share of the population overall and in areas of high concentration. In addition, there are three state assemblymen from this group (two from East Harlem and one from the Bronx) and four or five with high positions in the city administration.[22]

These achievements, obviously, as well as the district leaderships themselves and election district captaincies, can only be taken as rough indicators of the political progress of the group as a whole and are doubtless far less significant than they could have been viewed in the political setting of forty or fifty years ago when parties were central to the governing process and urban life generally. At the same time, they must be evaluated in light of the fact that New York State will not accept literacy in a language other than English (such as Spanish) as qualification to vote, and, thus, only some 150,000 to 175,000 of the total Puerto Rican group are on the rolls.

Table 2–Areas of Heavy Puerto Rican Population[a]

AREA	ASSEMBLY DISTRICT	DISTRICT LEADERS	ELECTION DISTRICT CAPTAINS	
			Total	Puerto Ricans
Lower East Side	4th, South	2 Jewish	29	7
East Harlem	10th, North	1 Puerto Rican and 1 Negro	16	9
	14th, South	2 Puerto Ricans	17	8
	14th, North	2 Negroes	—[b]	—[b]
	16th, South	1 Italian and 1 Puerto Rican	—[b]	—[b]
Upper West Side	13th, South	1 Italian and 1 Negro	52	23

[a]Puerto Rican population location was determined by plotting location of census tracts with at least 15 per cent Puerto Ricans and coloring these in according to density. There are scatterings in a few other parts of Manhattan as well.
[b]Data could not be obtained.

Returning for a moment to the current status of descendents of earlier immigrants, the assumption that significant cultural distinctions and tendencies toward common political attitude and behavior would disappear in two or three generations has proven erroneous. Ticket-balancing, for example, in ethnic or religious terms is as prevalent, perhaps, as it ever was and shows few signs of disappearing in the immediate future. The election of an Irish Catholic President in 1960, if anything, enhanced the importance of such balancing tactics, as the discussion in early 1964 of Democratic vice-presidential candidates indicated. In psychoanalysis, it is well recognized that problems have to be clearly recognized and frankly made explicit before they can be eliminated. The same may in a sense be true of ethnic factors in American politics. Only the frank recognition of the once-potent barrier to a Catholic in the White House paved the way for the Kennedy election. At the state and local level, it is probably also true that only after various groups have achieved and enjoyed the recognition they feel they are entitled to and have done so for a long enough period to transform a privilege into a quasi right will it become possible, gradually, to choose candidates without these criteria in mind. The unfortunate thing is that American parties have decayed as organizations to the point that they can make far less contribution to this process of adjustment than they could and did in the past.

NOTES

[1] See Harold F. Gosnell, *Boss Platt and His New York Machine* (Chicago: University of Chicago Press, 1924).

[2] See Lincoln Steffens, "Rhode Island: A State for Sale," *McClure's Magazine*, Vol. 24 (February 1905), pp. 337–353.

[3] Lincoln Steffens, *Autobiography* (New York: Literary Guild, 1931). p. 367.

[4] E. P. Hutchinson, *Immigrants and their Children* (New York: John Wiley, 1956), p. 27.

[5] See J.L.Garvin, *The Life of Joseph Chamberlain* (3 vols.: London: Macmillan, 1932–34).

[6] Stanley Salvidge, *Salvidge of Liverpool* (London: Hodder and Stoughton, 1934).

[7] For an elaboration of this approach to the internal dynamics of the machine, see James Q. Wilson, "The Economy of Patronage," *Journal of Political Economy*, Vol. 69, pp. 369–380.

[8] One of the most readable depictions of these machine functions is to be found in Edwin O'Connor's novel *The Last Hurrah* (Boston: Little, Brown, 1956).

[9] See the author's "Some Occupational Patterns in Party Committee Membership," *Rhode Island History*, Vol. 20 (July 1961), pp. 87–96.

[10] *The Rise and Growth of American Politics* (New York: Macmillan, 1911), p. 306.

[11] *Ibid.*, p. 307.

[12] "Party Absorption of Ethnic Groups," *Social Forces*, Vol. 38 (March 1960), pp. 205–210.

[13] Edward Banfield and James Q. Wilson, *City Politics* (Cambridge: Harvard and M.I.T. Presses, 1963), p. 115.

[14]Nathan Glazer and Daniel Patrick Moynihan, *Beyond the Melting Pot* (Cambridge: Harvard and M.I.T. Presses, 1963), p. 20.

[15]Richard Hofstadter, *The Age of Reform* (New York: Knopf, 1955), pp. 8 ff.

[16]*Ibid.*, p. 9.

[17]Two recent books are especially useful discussions of these groups: Glazer and Moynihan, *op. cit.*; and Oscar Handlin, *The Newcomers: Negroes and Puerto Ricans in a Changing Metropolis* (Cambridge: Harvard Press, 1959).

[18]This discussion of the Dawson organization draws particularly on James Q. Wilson, *Negro Politics* (Glencoe, Ill.: Free Press, 1960), pp. 50 ff. and *passim*.

[19]A useful source on Powell is David Hapgood, *The Purge that Failed: Tammany v. Powell* (New York: Holt, 1959).

[20]"Party Absorption of Ethnic Groups," *op. cit.*

[21]Thanks are due the author's former student, Edwin Cohen, now active in Manhattan politics, and to George Osborne, himself a district leader, for tracking down the leadership data used.

[22]Layhmond Robinson, "Voting Gain Made by Puerto Ricans," *New York Times*, November 23, 1963.

WILLIAM T. STEAD

Mr. Richard Croker and Greater New York

William T. Stead was an English journalist who published, in 1893, a sensational expose of urban corruption, prostitution, and institutional decay entitled *If Christ Came to Chicago*, which enjoyed a wide and immediate success. "The boodling aldermen," Stead concluded, "are indeed the swine of our civilization. . . ." His revelations accounted in part for the formation of the Chicago Civic Federation, a group of "respectable" citizens who set out to end the evils of bossism, and he maintained an interest in American politics until his death in the Titanic disaster of 1912.

On a voyage to England in 1897, Stead held an extended interview with Tammany Hall's Richard Croker, who later in the year was destined to become the first leader of a "Greater New York" that joined Manhattan, Brooklyn, and a number of other districts to form a single city of 318 square miles and three million people. Whereas Boss Plunkitt, in the following selection, preferred to focus on political methodology, Croker took this occasion to wax eloquent on the larger social contributions of the city machine in an argument that even William Stead found convincing. This interview not only reveals a great deal about Richard Croker, but also affords an unusual opportunity to compare the boss of Tammany Hall with the polished English journalist who voiced the concerns and ideas of a large number of American urban "reformers."

From William T. Stead, "Mr. Richard Croker and Greater New York," *Review of Reviews*, 16 (October, 1897), 342-347, 349, 353-354.

The man, Richard Croker, has been a kind of veiled prophet, a modern Mokanna to those who have lived under his sway. Even among those who have headed revolts, and successful revolts, against his rule, there are many who would not recognize him if they met him in the street. Lord Salisbury carries to a great length the doctrine that it is not expedient for men of opposing parties to meet each other in private, and incidentally it came out that he had only once in all his life set eyes on Mr. Parnell. There are many in New York who have never set eyes upon Richard Croker. The chasm between parties, if not between classes, is far wider in New York than it is in London, and social contempt intensifies the estrangement which political bias has begun.

Mr. Croker is not a silk-stocking dude, but he is a gentleman in his bearing and in his conversation. I speak of him as I saw him. To all outward appearing there was no one on board ship who was less exposed to the accusation of vulgarity, forwardness, bad manners, or bad language. He behaved himself as seemly as any one could desire. He vaunted not himself, he talked quietly and intelligently to those to whom he was introduced, and so far as in him lay he contributed as much as any one on board, and more than most, to the amenity of the voyage. Probably half of his fellow travellers felt that from his record they would need a very long spoon to sup with Richard Croker, but none of those who had the good fortune to meet with him in his endless constitutional up and down deck but liked him as a companion and parted with him with regret.

. . .

This is what Mr. Croker said:—"Tammany Hall," he began, "is much spoken against. But unjustly. You will never understand anything about New York politics if you believe all that they write in the papers. They are always abusing Tammany. But the real truth is just the opposite of what they say. Tammany's reputation has been sacrificed by newspaper men, whose sole desire is to increase their circulation, appealing to the itch for change and a malignant delight in the misfortunes of our fellows."

"Do you think the world is built in exactly that way, Mr. Croker?" I asked.

"No sir," he replied with emphasis, "it is not built that way, but quite another way. These things I speak of are temporary; the permanent law of the world and humanity is quite different. You asked me how it was Tammany was overthrown three years ago, and I have told you. But the issue of an election is but an incident. The law that governs has exceptions. The exception proves the rule."

"And what is the rule?" I asked, somewhat curious to know the Boss's theory of the Universe. "What is the underlying fundamental law of the Universe?"

"Sir," said Mr. Croker, speaking with quiet gravity, "the law is that although wrong-doing may endure for a season, right must in the long run come to the top. Human nature is not built so that roguery can last. Honest men must come to their own, no matter what the odds against them. There is nothing surer than that. Lying, calumny, thieving may have their day, but they will pass. Nothing can last but truth."

"Really, Mr. Croker," I exclaimed, "what an optimist you are! I have not found so great faith, no not in Israel," I added, laughing.

"That's right," he replied. "If you put ten honest men into an assembly with ninety thieves, human nature is such that the ten honest men will boss the ninety thieves. They must do it. It is the law of the world. All evil, whether lying or thieving, by its nature cannot last. Honest John Kelly, who was Boss before me, when I first came into politics before he was Boss, always used to tell me that, 'Never mind the odds against you if you are in the right. Being in the right is more than odds. Keep on hammering away and you are sure to win.' And I have always found it so."

"And Tammany," I asked; "is it not down now?" "No, sir," he replied. "In a moment of restlessness, the people put in what they called a Reform Administration, but after three years' experience they have had enough of it, and Tammany is coming out on top once more. It's bound to, for Tammany is honest and Tammany is true. And you have only to go on being honest and true to come out on top—not every time, for we have our reverses; but on the whole, Tammany has come out on top most of the time. And mark my words, you will see that the first election for Greater New York will be the most triumphant vindication of the law that slander may last for a time, but in the long run honest men come by their own."

I felt somewhat like Bret Harte's bewildered hero when he asked: "Do I sleep? Do I dream? Are there visions about?" And then I thought that the Boss was playing it rather low down upon the innocent and confiding stranger. But his countenance was imperturbable, and I do not believe that he was saying a word which in some way or other he had not first convinced himself was gospel truth.

Mr. Croker resumed: "They will tell you that Tammany has ruled New York nearly all the time. And they will tell you true. Do you think we could have done it if we had been the thieves and rogues they pretend we are? I have been in office in New York nearly all my life; do you think the citizens would have been such fools as to elect me and re-elect me if I had been [the] bad man that some people say I am? Things that are rotten do not last. They go to pieces. Thieves are not trusted by their fellow thieves, let alone by their fellow citizens. It is not by the bad in them that institutions and parties last, but by what is good. If Tammany has lasted and triumphed, that is the best proof that what its enemies say is false. And when it carries this next election, with all the newspapers against it, and all the mugwumps, then you will have our vindication.''

"Nothing succeeds like success, I suppose," I replied; "but you have not won yet."

"But we shall," he said, "certain sure. Tammany is honest. Tammany is not corrupt. Tammany is the best, the only permanent hope of real reformed administration. Therefore Tammany will win."

.   .   .

"Politics," he said, "are impossible without the spoils. It is all very well to argue that it ought not to be so. But we have to deal with men as they are and with things as they are. Consider the problem which every democratic system has to solve. Government, we say, of the people, by the people, and for the people. The aim is to interest as many of the citizens as possible in the work—which is not an easy work, and has many difficulties and disappointments—of governing the State or the city. Of course in an ideal world every citizen would be so dominated by patriotic or civic motives that from sheer unselfish love of his fellow men he would spend nights and days in labouring for their good. If you lived in such a world inhabited by such men I admit that there could be no question but that we could and would dispense with the spoils system. But where is that world to be found? Certainly not in the United States, and most certainly not in New York. Look at the facts plainly in the face. There are in our country and in New York a small number of citizens who might reasonably be expected to be responsive to the appeal of patriotic and civic motives. They are what you would call the cultured class, the people who have wealth, education, leisure, the men who have got sufficiently above the common level to be able to hear the appeals which the city or the State makes to the conscience and heart of men. They have received everything, enjoyed everything, learned everything. From them no doubt, and from all citizens on their level, you might think you could meet with such a response to your appeals as would enable you to run the State upon high principles, and dispense with spoils. But if you were to expect any such thing, you would be very much disappointed. What is the one fact which all you English notice first of anything in our country? Why, it is that that very crowd of which we are speaking, the minority of cultured leisured citizens, will not touch political work—no, not with their little finger. All your high principles will not induce a mugwump to take more than a fitful interest in an occasional election. The silk stocking cannot be got to take a serious hand continuously in political work. They admit it themselves. Every one knows it is so. Why, then, when mugwump principles won't even make mugwumps work, do you expect the same lofty motives to be sufficient to interest the masses in politics?''

"And so," I said, "you need to bribe them with spoils?"

"And so," he replied, "we need to bribe them with spoils. Call it so if you like. Spoils vary in different countries. Here they take the shape of offices. But you must have an incentive to interest men in the hard daily work of politics, and when you have our crowd you have got to do it one way, the only way that appeals to them. I admit it is not the best way. But it is for practical purposes the only way. Think what New York is and what the people of New York are. One half, more than one half, are of foreign birth. We have thousands upon thousands of men who are alien born, who have no ties connecting them with the city or the State. They do not speak our language, they do not know our laws, they are the raw material with which we have to build up the State. How are you to do it on mugwump methods? I tell you it cannot be done.''

We were silent for a time. Mr. Croker took a turn or two, and then resumed:—

"People abuse Tammany for this and for that. But they forget what they owe to Tammany. There is no denying the service which Tammany has rendered to the Republic. There is no such organization for taking hold of the untrained friendless man and converting him into a citizen. Who else would do it if we did not? Think of the hundreds of thousands of foreigners dumped into our city. They are too old to go to school. There is not a mugwump in the city who would shake hands with them. They are alone, ignorant strangers, a prey to all manner of anarchical and wild notions. Except to their employer they have no value to any one until they get a vote.''

"And then they are of value to Tammany?" I said, laughing.

"Yes," said Mr. Croker, imperturbably; "and then they are of value to Tammany. And Tammany looks after them for the sake of their vote, grafts them upon the Republic, makes citizens of them in short; and although you may not like our motives or our methods, what other agency is there

by which so long a row could have been hoed so quickly or so well?
If we go down into the gutter it is because there are men in the gutter,
and you have got to go down where they are if you are to do anything
with them.''

"And so,'' I said, "Tammany is a great digestive apparatus, fed with
all manner of coarse, indigestible food, that would give a finer stomach
sudden death. But Tammany's stomach is strong; nothing is too rough
for Tammany's gastric juice, and so you build up the body politic out
of material—''

"That but for us would have remained undigested and indigestible—a
menace to the State, a peril to society. You may carp at our motives
and criticize our methods—we do not complain. All that we say is we
have done the work, and we deserve more recognition for that than we
have yet received.''

I suppose it was because I felt the truth of what he said so forcibly
during my investigations at Chicago that led Mr. Croker to declare, as
he introduced me to some of his "leaders'' on the landing-stage, that
he was quite sure, if only I were a citizen of New York, I should soon
be at Tammany Hall.

Said Mr. Croker, "It was never to Tammany's interest to put bad
men in office, or dishonest men. While I am all for the spoils system,
as you call it, I am as much opposed as you can be to putting bad men
in office and keeping them there. No doubt under any system sometimes
bad men get into office. What we claim is that with a strongly organized
machine we can turn them down when they are shown to be bad. You
assume that there is only one supremely good competent man, and that
he ought to be appointed every time. We say that there are plenty of
good competent men on both sides, and each does right to appoint its
own friends. And why not? No power on earth would ever induce me
to pass over my friend if he was as fit for office as any other man.
Other things being equal, always give your friend the first chance, rather
than the other fellow's friend.''

"But,'' I objected, "do you mean that Tammany has always appointed
the best men?''

"Tammany has appointed good men. For nearly thirty years Tammany
has been a good and honest element in the government of the city. Tammany
was there all the time. Tammany did not vote at an election and then
go home and forget all about it. Tammany watched how its men behaved.
If they behaved ill, Tammany turned them down. And that for the best
reason. Tammany could not afford to be discredited by maintaining bad
men in office. It needs a strong outside political organization to enforce

discipline. It is always to our interest to do so. Every leader has always a dozen men hungry for the post which he can vacate by turning out a bad man. A strong effective party machine is essential to the safe working of popular institutions.''

This brought Mr. Croker by a natural transition to insist upon the peculiar and distinctive virtue of Tammany Hall. If there be one virtue more than incorruptible honesty and an austere regard for the city's welfare, which distinguishes the famous institution which has Mr. Croker as its presiding genius, it is a profound regard for the principle of free popularly elected government. Herein, strange though it may appear to those to whom Tammany is but the embodiment of the principle of Despotism, Mr. Croker was on firmer ground.

"Tammany," said Mr. Croker, "is everywhere spoken against because it is said to be a foreign organization. Tammany, on the contrary, is a distinctively American organization founded on much more thoroughgoing American principles than those which find favour with the framers of the Charter of Great New York for instance. It makes me tired to hear their talk about foreigners. Where would America be to-day without foreigners?''

Mr. Croker's question this time admitted of an easy answer. It would have been in the hands of the Red Indians. From the *Mayflower* downwards the white people of the United States have all been foreigners at first.

Mr. Croker went on: "This discrimination against citizens because of the place of their birth seems to me un-American and unjust. Do not these men pay taxes, found homes, build up states, and do a great deal more in the government of the city than our assailants? They may have been born under another flag. But they forswear their own nationality, they swear allegiance to our flag; they filled the ranks of our armies in the great war; everywhere they fulfill the duties and accept all the burdens of the citizen, and yet we are told they are foreigners. Sir,'' said Mr. Croker, speaking with more earnestness than was usual with him, "in Tammany Hall there is no discrimination against citizens on account of race or religion. We meet on the common ground of one common citizenship. We know no difference of Catholic or Protestant, of Irishman, German or American. Every one is welcome amongst us who is true to the city and true to the party. To me the old sectarian quarrels are absolutely inconceivable. Priests have no voice in the management of Tammany Hall. It is of the people, created for the people, controlled by the people—the purest and strongest outcome of the working of democratic government under modern conditions.''

. . .

"But," I objected, "an eminent Republican fellow-passenger assures me that Tammany differs from all other American political organizations in that it is absolutely under the despotism of the men in office. Other organizations cannot enforce discipline; Tammany rules with an iron hand."

"Now," said Mr. Croker in his most Reineckian vein, "how can that be? You talk of Tammany and those who are in office as if they had an authority whatever beyond the popular vote freely expressed. What is Tammany? I am the Boss, they say. But I hold no office. If I am Boss it is simply because what I may say or think goes with the Executive Committee. You or any man might be a Boss tomorrow if you could convince those who hear you that you are a sensible man who has a sincere regard for the party and the city. They cry Tammany Hall! Tammany Hall! But what is Tammany Hall? It is simply an Executive Committee of the Democratic party of New York, elected annually at primaries or open public meetings held subject to the law, which makes strict provisions against any fraud or wrongdoing. New York is divided into thirty-four assembly districts. Each of these districts holds a public meeting, to which every member of the party resident in that district is free to attend. At these primaries representatives are selected by the free vote of the citizens present. These representatives elect one of their number in whom they have confidence as their leader. This leader becomes their representative on the Executive Committee of Tammany Hall. He may be re-elected year after year. But he can be superseded in twelve months if he cannot retain the confidence of the people in his own district."

"But do they ever get turned out?" I asked.

"Certainly," said Mr. Croker, "they are always changing. Their only authority depends upon their personal influence. You hear a great deal about my being the Boss, as if I were lord and master of Tammany Hall. I hold no office. I have no power, not an atom, except what I can exercise because of the confidence which the people have in me. They know that I am honest, that I am true, that I care for the party and the city, and that is all there is to it. Boss Tweed no doubt was a bad Boss. But we met him in the primaries, and we turned him down, and put honest John Kelly in his stead. When Kelly died there was some discussion as to his successor, I said, let us appoint no successor, or rather let us all be his successors. Instead of one Boss let us all thirty-four be Bosses, and it was agreed. But somehow when people found that what I said went, they got into the habit of saying I was Boss. But I could not help that."

Thus, by slow degrees and in the course of many conversations, I gradually began to perceive, as it were, some glorified image of Tammany Hall and its Boss as he evidently loved to dwell upon them in his dreams, and it was not far from the Kingdom of Heaven. For it was based upon the great principle of human brotherhood; it has as its foundation the doctrine that in Tammany there is neither Jew nor Gentile, Barbarian or Scythian, bond or free; and it has as its habitual rule of life the serving of the Brethren. Instead of being an excrescence upon the State, it was the great digestive apparatus of the Republic, upon whose rude strength and capacity for assimilation depended the health of the Commonwealth. And to-day, while Citizens' Unions and Charter Committees, and all the great and learned and influential of the city are going astray from the true Democratic faith, and seeking to cast out municipal evils by having resort to elective Caesarism, Tammany stands forth fearless and undismayed, the very Abdiel, faithful among the faithless found, in its unswerving allegiance to the pure original principles of free popular elective self-government.

．　．　．

Mr. Croker does not like the title of Boss. He regards it as the most offensive which has ever been devised by mortal men to describe their leader. In every age the title of the Governor and Director has varied. Consul, dictator, emperor, king, duke, doge, general, president—any or all of these titles are universally recognized as more or less honourable. It has been reserved to Americans of these latter days to invent a term for their leader which excites anything but reverence, and is at once familiar, vulgar, and offensive. It is probably the one office in the world which is universally coveted, whose title instead of adding to the dignity of the post, detracts from it. Nevertheless, popular or unpopular, Boss has acquired a permanent position in American nomenclature. Possibly, in time, to be styled a Boss may be held to be as honorific as to be called Consul or Duke, for of all posts and offices accepted in the American Republic, that of Boss is the most distinctively characteristic and unmistakably American. Possibly, a thousand years hence the children of our remote posterity will learn from their school books that at the end of the nineteenth century the United States of America, nominally preserving the shadow of Republican institutions, were really governed more or less despotically by Bosses, thereby reproducing in the Western World the familiar phenomena by which in ancient Rome the shade of the Republic lingered on the Seven Hills long after Augustus had concentrated all power in the hands of the Caesars. Presidents come and go like the phantom consuls in the Roman Empire, but the rule of the Boss remains. An unwritten law forbids the election of a President for the third term of office, but no law interferes with the indefinite prolongation of the rule of the Boss.

. . .

I asked Mr. Croker wherein lay, in his opinion, the secret of his strength.

He replied that he had always trusted the people, and the people trusted him. He had never been crooked, nor would he ever tolerate crooked men in office. If a man became corrupt he was fired out. This was even more necessary in the interests of the party than of the city. The people knew him, and they felt he spoke straight and acted honestly in their interest, and so forth.

But, I said, apart from these general considerations, what did he consider differentiated him as Boss from his predecessors?

He considered a while, and then replied, "Two things. They were both very simple, but they contributed the most to the maintenance and to the strength of my position. The first was the divesting myself of all the patronage which previous Bosses possessed. As soon as I became Boss I terminated at one stroke the system which every previous Boss had acted upon—of keeping all the city appointments in his own hands. The result of that system was the Boss had no time to do anything but fill up offices. I changed all that. I decentralized the whole thing. All the appointments in each assembly district were made over to the leader for that district. Instead of one Boss distributing all the offices, each of the thirty-four leaders on our Executive Council had absolute control over all the patronage in his district. This made them more powerful, and at the same time relieved me of infinite worry and left me free to attend to other business. That was the first change I made. The other was quite as important. No small part of my hold on Tammany, and through Tammany on the city, came from the fact that from the first I always made a point of pushing young men to the front. I had myself come out when young. I favoured young men on principle on a calculation which worked right every time. If you get the young men you get their fathers and their elder relations. That is invariable. It is quite otherwise with the old. If you get the father you probably won't get the son, whereas if you get the son you always get the father. There is no motive," said Mr. Croker emphatically, "which operates more constantly in American life than the desire of every father to secure for his children a better education than he has had himself. That motive, far more than any greed for the dollar, takes most men into politics. They want to see their boys better educated." (Mr. Croker evidently used the term in the wider sense as meaning the educating of the faculties by the training of life rather than a mere college education.) ''And when they see their boy taken hold of and put into place early, they are true to the party that pushes their boy. Another reason why it is good policy is because if you get a reputation for picking out young fellows and giving them a show six or ten years sooner than anybody else, all the smartest lads will crowd round you, and naturally. You are giving them the chance they want to-day, while the other fellows only promise it next week. Nothing gave Tammany such hold as these two things—the decentralization of the patronage and the encouragement of young men.''

If Mr. Croker be not belied, his love for excitement has at times led him into strange adventures. As for instance, when he battled through raging surf off the coast of Florida in order to fish for sharks. Shark-fishing is just the kind of inspiriting amusement strong enough to suit a man who had been Boss of Tammany Hall.

WILLIAM L. RIORDON
Plunkitt of Tammany Hall

George Washington Plunkitt was born in a poor immigrant neighborhood in upper Manhattan in 1842. Though he eventually held a number of political offices, including that of State Senator, his power and fortune (he died a millionaire in 1924) derived from his position as ward boss of the Fifteenth Assembly District for Tammany Hall, New York City's notorious Democratic political machine. William L. Riordon, a writer for the *New York Evening Post,* conducted a series of interviews with Plunkitt and preserved the boss's candid observations for future generations in a little volume published in 1905, *Plunkitt of Tammany Hall: A Series of Very Plain Talks on Very Practical Politics.* . . . The following selections are among the most remarkable in that remarkable book. In the first, Plunkitt distinguishes between "Honest Graft and Dishonest Graft," a distinction that hardly veils what was essentially a blatant conflict of interest and the use of political power for personal economic gain. This is one example of the "corruption" for which the urban boss has been so villified, by critics in his own time and by later generations of politicians and historians.

The power of Tammany Hall and of George Washington Plunkitt, however, did not rest on corruption but on votes. The ward boss, and the city machine

From William L. Riordon, *Plunkitt of Tammany Hall* (New York: McClure, Philipps & Company, 1905).

as a whole, provided essential services to their constituents that no official city agency could effectively perform in this period. In the final section of his book, "Strenuous Life of a Tammany District Leader," Riordon presents a brief look into the world of ward politics, a realm in which George Washington Plunkitt moved with a confidence and élan that many "good government" reformers found not only foreign but even threatening. Whether Plunkitt was a devil or a saint is hardly to the point: the real issue has to do with the role of the urban boss in the exceptionally complex political setting of the emerging American metropolis.

HONEST GRAFT AND DISHONEST GRAFT

Everybody is talkin' these days about Tammany men growin' rich on graft, but nobody thinks of drawin' the distinction between honest graft and dishonest graft. There's all the difference in the world between the two. Yes, many of our men have grown rich in politics. I have myself. I've made a big fortune out of the game, and I'm gettin' richer every day, but I've not gone in for dishonest graft—blackmailin' gamblers, saloonkeepers, disorderly people, etc.—and neither has any of the men who have made big fortunes in politics.

There's an honest graft, and I'm an example of how it works. I might sum up the whole thing by sayin': "I seen my opportunities and I took 'em."

Just let me explain by examples. My party's in power in the city, and it's goin' to undertake a lot of public improvements. Well, I'm tipped off, say, that they're going to lay out a new park at a certain place.

I see my opportunity and I take it. I go to that place and I buy up all the land I can in the neighborhood. Then the board of this or that makes its plan public, and there is a rush to get my land, which nobody cared particular for before.

Ain't it perfectly honest to charge a good price and make a profit on my investment and foresight? Of course, it is. Well, that's honest graft.

Or supposin' it's a new bridge they're goin' to build. I get tipped off and I buy as much property as I can that has to be taken for approaches. I sell at my own price later on and drop some more money in the bank.

Wouldn't you? It's just like lookin' ahead in Wall Street or in the coffee or cotton market. It's honest graft, and I'm lookin' for it every day in the year. I will tell you frankly that I've got a good lot of it, too.

I'll tell you of one case. They were goin' to fix up a big park, no matter where. I got on to it, and went lookin' about for land in that neighborhood.

I could get nothin' at a bargain but a big piece of swamp, but I took it fast enough and held on to it. What turned out was just what I counted on. They couldn't make the park complete without Plunkitt's swamp, and they had to pay a good price for it. Anything dishonest in that?

Up in the watershed I made some money, too. I bought up several bits of land there some years ago and made a pretty good guess that they would be bought up for water purposes later by the city.

Somehow, I always guessed about right, and shouldn't I enjoy the profit of my foresight? It was rather amusin' when the condemnation commissioners came along and found piece after piece of the land in the name of George Plunkitt of the Fifteenth Assembly District, New York City. They wondered how I knew just what to buy. The answer is—I seen my opportunity and I took it. I haven't confined myself to land; anything that pays is in my line.

For instance, the city is repavin' a street and has several hundred thousand old granite blocks to sell. I am on hand to buy, and I know just what they are worth.

How? Never mind that. I had a sort of monopoly of this business for a while, but once a newspaper tried to do me. It got some outside men to come over from Brooklyn and New Jersey to bid against me.

Was I done? Not much. I went to each of the men and said: "How many of these 250,000 stones do you want?" One said 20,000 and another wanted 15,000, and others wanted 10,000. I said: "All right, let me bid for the lot, and I'll give each of you all you want for nothin'."

They agreed, of course. Then the auctioneer yelled: "How much am I bid for these 250,000 fine pavin' stones?"

"Two dollars and fifty cents," says I.

"Two dollars and fifty cents!" screamed the auctioneer. "Oh, that's a joke! Give me a real bid."

He found the bid was real enough. My rivals stood silent. I got the lot for $2.50 and gave them their share. That's how the attempt to do Plunkitt ended, and that's how all such attempts end.

I've told you how I got rich by honest graft. Now, let me tell you that most politicians who are accused of robbin' the city get rich the same way.

They didn't steal a dollar from the city treasury. They just seen their opportunities and took them. That is why, when a reform administration comes in and spends a half million dollars in tryin' to find the public robberies they talked about in the campaign, they don't find them.

The books are always all right. The money in the city treasury is all right. Everything is all right. All they can show is that the Tammany heads of departments looked after their friends, within the law, and gave them what opportunities they could to make honest graft. Now, let me tell you that's never goin' to hurt Tammany with the people. Every good man looks after his friends, and any man who doesn't isn't likely to be popular. If I have a good thing to hand out in private life, I give it to a friend. Why shouldn't I do the same in public life?

Another kind of honest graft. Tammany has raised a good many salaries. There was an awful howl by the reformers, but don't you know that Tammany gains ten votes for every one it lost by salary raisin'?

The Wall Street banker thinks it shameful to raise a department clerk's salary from $1500 to $1800 a year, but every man who draws a salary himself says: "That's all right. I wish it was me." And he feels very much like votin' the Tammany ticket on election day, just out of sympathy.

Tammany was beat in 1901 because the poeple were deceived into believin' that it worked dishonest graft. They didn't draw a distinction between dishonest and honest graft, but they saw that some Tammany men grew rich, and supposed they had been robbin' the city treasury or levyin' blackmail on disorderly houses, or workin' in with the gamblers and lawbreakers.

As a matter of policy, if nothing else, why should the Tammany leaders go into such dirty business, when there is so much honest graft lyin' around when they are in power? Did you ever consider that?

Now, in conclusion, I want to say that I don't own a dishonest dollar. If my worst enemy was given the job of writin' my epitaph when I'm gone, he couldn't do more than write:

"George W. Plunkitt. He Seen His Opportunities, and He Took 'Em."

· · ·

STRENUOUS LIFE OF THE TAMMANY DISTRICT LEADER

NOTE: *This chapter is based on extracts from Plunkitt's Diary and on my daily observation of the work of the district leader.* —W.L.R.

The life of the Tammany district leader is strenuous. To his work is due the wonderful recuperative power of the organization.

One year it goes down in defeat and the prediction is made that it will never again raise its head. The district leader, undaunted by defeat, collects his scattered forces, organizes them as only Tammany knows how to organize, and in a little while the organization is as strong as ever.

No other politician in New York or elsewhere is exactly like the Tammany district leader or works as he does. As a rule, he has no business or occupation other than politics. He plays politics every day and night in the year, and his headquarters bears the inscription, "Never closed."

Everybody in the district knows him. Everybody knows where to find him, and nearly everybody goes to him for assistance of one sort or another, especially the poor of the tenements.

He is always obliging. He will go to the police courts to put in a good word for the "drunks and disorderlies" or pay their fines, if a good word is not effective. He will attend christenings, weddings, and funerals. He will feed the hungry and help bury the dead.

A philanthropist? Not at all. He is playing politics all the time.

Brought up in Tammany Hall, he has learned how to reach the hearts of the great mass of voters. He does not bother about reaching their heads. It is his belief that arguments and campaign literature have never gained votes.

He seeks direct contact with the people, does them good turns when he can, and relies on their not forgetting him on election day. His heart is always in his work, too, for his subsistence depends on its results.

If he holds his district and Tammany is in power, he is amply rewarded by a good office and the opportunities that go with it. What these opportunities are has been shown by the quick rise to wealth of so many Tammany district leaders. With the examples before him of Richard Croker, once leader of the Twentieth District; John F. Carroll, formerly leader of the Twenty-ninth; Timothy ("Dry Dollar") Sullivan, late leader of the Sixth, and many others, he can always look forward to riches and ease while he is going through the drudgery of his daily routine.

This is a record of a day's work by Plunkitt:

2 A.M.: Aroused from sleep by the ringing of his doorbell; went to the door and found a bartender, who asked him to go to the police station and bail out a saloonkeeper who had been arrested for violating the excise law. Furnished bail and returned to bed at three o'clock.

6 A.M.: Awakened by fire engines passing his house. Hastened to the scene of the fire, according to the custom of the Tammany district leaders, to give assistance to the fire sufferers, if needed. Met several of his election district captains who are always under orders to look out for fires, which are considered great vote-getters. Found several tenants who had been burned out, took them to a hotel, supplied them with clothes, fed them, and arranged temporary quarters for them until they could rent and furnish new apartments.

8:30 A.M.: Went to the police court to look after his constituents.

Found six "drunks." Secured the discharge of four by a timely word with the judge, and paid the fines of two.

9 A.M.: Appeared in the Municipal District Court. Directed one of his district captains to act as counsel for a widow against whom dispossess proceedings had been instituted and obtained an extension of time. Paid the rent of a poor family about to be dispossessed and gave them a dollar for food.

11 A.M.: At home again. Found four men waiting for him. One had been discharged by the Metropolitan Railway Company for neglect of duty, and wanted the district leader to fix things. Another wanted a job on the road. The third sought a place on the Subway and the fourth, a plumber, was looking for work with the Consolidated Gas Company. The district leader spent nearly three hours fixing things for the four men, and succeeded in each case.

3 P.M.: Attended the funeral of an Italian as far as the ferry. Hurried back to make his appearance at the funeral of a Hebrew constituent. Went conspicuously to the front both in the Catholic church and the synagogue, and later attended the Hebrew confirmation ceremonies in the synagogue.

7 P.M.: Went to district headquarters and presided over a meeting of election district captains. Each captain submitted a list of all the voters in his district, reported on their attitude toward Tammany, suggested who might be won over and how they could be won, told who were in need, and who were in trouble of any kind and the best way to reach them. District leader took notes and gave orders.

8 P.M.: Went to a church fair. Took chances on everything, bought ice cream for the young girls and the children. Kissed the little ones, flattered their mothers and took their fathers out for something down at the corner.

9 P.M.: At the clubhouse again. Spent $10 on tickets for a church excursion and promised a subscription for a new church bell. Bought tickets for a baseball game to be played by two nines from his district. Listened to the complaints of a dozen pushcart peddlers who said they were persecuted by the police and assured them he would go to Police Headquarters in the morning and see about it.

10:30 P.M.: Attended a Hebrew wedding reception and dance. Had previously sent a handsome wedding present to the bride.

12 P.M.: In bed.

That is the actual record of one day in the life of Plunkitt. He does some of the same things every day, but his life is not so monotonous as to be wearisome.

Sometimes the work of a district leader is exciting, especially if he happens to have a rival who intends to make a contest for the leadership at the primaries. In that case, he is even more alert, tries to reach the fires before his rival, sends out runners to look for "drunks and disorderlies" at the police stations, and keeps a very close watch on the obituary columns of the newspapers.

A few years ago there was a bitter contest for the Tammany leadership of the Ninth District between John C. Sheehan and Frank J. Goodwin. Both had had long experience in Tammany politics and both understood every move of the game.

Every morning their agents went to their respective headquarters before seven o'clock and read through the death notices in all the morning papers. If they found that anybody in the district had died, they rushed to the homes of their principals with the information and then there was a race to the house of the deceased to offer condolences, and, if the family were poor, something more substantial.

On the day of the funeral there was another contest. Each faction tried to surpass the other in the number and appearance of the carriages it sent to the funeral, and more than once they almost came to blows at the church or in the cemetery.

On one occasion the Goodwinites played a trick on their adversaries which has since been imitated in other districts. A well-known liquor dealer who had a considerable following died, and both Sheehan and Goodwin were eager to become his political heir by making a big showing at the funeral.

Goodwin managed to catch the enemy napping. He went to all the livery stables in the district, hired all the carriages for the day, and gave orders to two hundred of his men to be on hand as mourners.

Sheehan had never had any trouble about getting all the carriages that he wanted, so he let the matter go until the night before the funeral. Then he found that he could not hire a carriage in the district.

He called his district committee together in a hurry and explained the situation to them. He could get all the vehicles he needed in the adjoining district, he said, but if he did that, Goodwin would rouse the voters of the Ninth by declaring that he (Sheehan) had patronized foreign industries.

Finally, it was decided that there was nothing to do but to go over to Sixth and Broadway for carriages. Sheehan made a fine turnout at the funeral, but the deceased was hardly in his grave before Goodwin raised the cry of "Protection to home industries," and denounced his rival for patronizing livery-stable keepers outside of his district. The cry had its effect in the primary campaign. At all events, Goodwin was elected leader.

A recent contest for the leadership of the Second District illustrated further the strenuous work of the Tammany district leaders. The contestants were Patrick Divver, who had managed the district for years, and Thomas F. Foley.

Both were particularly anxious to secure the large Italian vote. They not only attended all the Italian christenings and funerals, but also kept a close lookout for the marriages in order to be on hand with wedding presents.

At first, each had his own reporter in the Italian quarter to keep track of the marriages. Later, Foley conceived a better plan. He hired a man to stay all day at the City Hall marriage bureau, where most Italian couples go through the civil ceremony, and telephone to him at his saloon when anything was doing at the bureau.

Foley had a number of presents ready for use and, whenever he received a telephone message from his man, he hastened to the City Hall with a ring or a watch or a piece of silver and handed it to the bride with his congratulations. As a consequence, when Divver got the news and went to the home of the couple with his present, he always found that Foley had been ahead of him. Toward the end of the campaign, Divver also stationed a man at the marriage bureau and then there were daily foot races and fights between the two heelers.

Sometimes the rivals came into conflict at the deathbed. One night a poor Italian peddler died in Roosevelt Street. The news reached Divver and Foley about the same time, and as they knew the family of the man was destitute, each went to an undertaker and brought him to the Roosevelt Street tenement.

The rivals and the undertakers met at the house and an altercation ensued. After much discussion the Divver undertaker was selected. Foley had more carriages at the funeral, however, and he further impressed the Italian voters by paying the widow's rent for a month, and sending her half a ton of coal and a barrel of flour.

The rivals were put on their mettle toward the end of the campaign by the wedding of a daughter of one of the original Cohens of the Baxter Street region. The Hebrew vote in the district is nearly as large as the Italian vote, and Divver and Foley set out to capture the Cohens and their friends.

They stayed up nights thinking what they would give the bride. Neither knew how much the other was prepared to spend on a wedding present, or what form it would take; so spies were employed by both sides to keep watch on jewelry stores, and the jewelers of the district were bribed by each side to impart the desired information.

At last Foley heard that Divver had purchased a set of silver knives, forks and spoons. He at once bought a duplicate set and added a silver tea service. When the presents were displayed at the home of the bride, Divver was not in a pleasant mood and he charged his jeweler with treachery. It may be added that Foley won at the primaries.

One of the fixed duties of a Tammany district leader is to give two outings every summer, one for the men of his district and the other for the women and children, and a beefsteak dinner and a ball every winter. The scene of the outings is, usually, one of the groves along the Sound.

The ambition of the district leader on these occasions is to demonstrate that his men have broken all records in the matter of eating and drinking. He gives out the exact number of pounds of beef, poultry, butter, etc., that they have consumed and professes to know how many potatoes and ears of corn have been served.

According to his figures, the average eating record of each man at the outing is about ten pounds of beef, two or three chickens, a pound of butter, a half peck of potatoes, and two dozen ears of corn. The drinking records, as given out, are still more phenomenal. For some reason, not yet explained, the district leader thinks that his popularity will be greatly increased if he can show that his followers can eat and drink more than the followers of any other district leader.

The same idea governs the beefsteak dinners in the winter. It matters not what sort of steak is served or how it is cooked; the district leader considers only the question of quantity, and when he excels all others in this particular, he feels, somehow, that he is a bigger man and deserves more patronage than his associates in the Tammany Executive Committee.

As to the balls, they are the events of the winter in the extreme East Side and West Side society. Mamie and Maggie and Jennie prepare for them months in advance, and their young men save up for the occasion just as they save for the summer trips to Coney Island.

The district leader is in his glory at the opening of the ball. He leads the cotillion with the prettiest woman present—his wife, if he has one, permitting—and spends almost the whole night shaking hands with his constituents. The ball costs him a pretty penny, but he has found that the investment pays.

By these means the Tammany district leader reaches out into the homes of his district, keeps watch not only on the men, but also on the women and children, knows their needs, their likes and dislikes, their troubles and their hopes, and places himself in a position to use his knowledge for the benefit of his organization and himself. Is it any wonder that scandals do not permanently disable Tammany and that it speedily recovers from what seems to be crushing defeat?

LYLE W. DORSETT
The Roots of Political Control

Lyle W. Dorsett, associate professor of history at the University of Colorado at Denver, provides in his book, *The Pendergast Machine,* an interesting, brief account of the origins and growth of Kansas City's urban political organization. From this beginning, the Pendergast machine eventually became one of the most powerful political forces of its kind in twentieth-century America. When James Pendergast's younger brother Tom assumed direction of the local machine in 1909, it became much different from the earlier organization. He introduced a variety of illegal voting tactics and strong-arm methods, extended the organization's influence into middle-class residential areas, established alliances with local Republicans, attracted support from the business community, and achieved political supremacy in all of Kansas City by 1925. Seven years later he had become the boss of Missouri politics as well, dominating not only city hall but the governor's mansion. The relief programs of the New Deal did shift the sources of welfare and jobs to the federal government, but the Pendergast machine still controlled the distribution of these resources in Missouri. Rather than eliminating the duties of the ward boss and destroying his influence, the New Deal made available new sources of machine power. "Indeed," argues Dorsett, "the Pendergast machine (and probably many others) was actually strengthened by the New Deal." The eventual collapse of the organization resulted not from New Deal programs, but from the election scandals of 1936 that brought to light the entrenched corruption of one of the most successful and notorious political machines in American history.

Our attention in this selection is directed to the origins of the Pendergast machine in the 1890s. What were the sources of its power? What was the nature of its organization and the character of its leadership? What were its purposes? What were the conditions in the West Bottoms and the North End that facilitated the rise of such a political organization? These questions are especially significant because, though political machines and their leadership naturally varied from community to community, the story of James Pendergast's rise to political power in Kansas City is in its major outlines probably as typical an illustration of the development of the urban political machine in late nineteenth-century America as one can find.

James Pendergast was born in the little town of Gallipolis, Ohio, on the banks of the Ohio River, on January 27, 1856. When he was two years old, his Irish parents packed him up with the rest of the family possessions and moved to St. Joseph, Missouri. The second of nine children, Jim Pendergast attended the public schools in St. Joseph. After his twentieth birthday, he left St. Joseph and went to Kansas City, where the opportunities for a young man were much greater.

Pendergast arrived in Kansas City in 1876 with only a few dollars in his pocket. An intense, ambitious young man, he was willing to accept any kind of work. He rented a room in the West Bottoms, and immediately found employment in the packing houses. Physically, Pendergast was well-suited for heavy work. Although not even five feet nine inches tall, he was the picture of strength with his short, thick neck and massive shoulders and arms. But he did not like packing-house work. After a few weeks he took a job as a puddler in an iron foundry.

The life of a puddler did not fulfill Pendergast's ambitions any more than packing-house work had. Thus in 1881, after a horse named Climax paid well at the racetrack, he quit his job and purchased a combination hotel and saloon with his winnings. The Climax, as he named his saloon, was located on St. Louis Avenue in the heart of Kansas City's industrial West Bottoms.[1]

By 1891 Pendergast had become a successful businessman. He soon was able to sell his original saloon and purchase a new one in the same neighborhood. He kept the hotel and he also bought a second saloon in the North End. Pendergast's saloon-keeping career would prove to be extremely advantageous once he became active in local politics.

Kansas City was a spectacle of immense diversity during the three and a half decades that Pendergast pursued his business and political fortunes there. A year before he opened his saloon, the United States Census showed the population of Kansas City to be 55,785. By 1910, just prior to his death, the population had soared to over 248,000. This growing population, composed of both Negro and white native-born Americans as well as German, Irish, Italian, and other foreign-born persons, spread over the city, which was made up of neighborhoods no less diverse than the groups which inhabited them.

The West Bottoms, the neighborhood Jim Pendergast represented in the city council for eighteen years, was bounded on the west by the state line, on the north by the river and railroad tracks, and on the east by exclusive Quality Hill. It encompassed packing houses, railroad yards, machine shops, factories, and warehouses. In many respects this neighborhood changed very little during the years that Pendergast lived there. When he came to the West Bottoms in 1876 it was the heart of the city's industrial district, and it remained so until after his death. Likewise, before he came to Kansas City, the West Bottoms had poor streets, many of which were unpaved or in need of repair. Three decades later mud and dust still covered most of the neighborhood's thoroughfares.

The West Bottom's population, which was composed mostly of low-income Negroes living in the eastern part of the neighborhood, and Irish, German, and native laborers in the remaining portions, did not change its character to any noticeable extent while the neighborhood was Pendergast's political domain. The ubiquitous junk shops and second-hand stores on Ninth Street were patronized by these low-income laborers, most of whom lived in overcrowded tenements and shanties. The perennial problem of open sewers and gutters, coupled with overcrowded living conditions, constantly threatened the inhabitants with disease and added to the unpleasantness of their surroundings.

Immediately adjacent to the West Bottoms on the northeast was the neighborhood known as the North End. In his early political career, "Big Jim," as Pendergast's friends called him, extended his political strength from its matrix in the West Bottoms to every corner of the North End. That neighborhood was not nearly so industrialized as the West Bottoms, but in many other respects the two areas were very similar. The North End did not have as large a Negro population as the West Bottoms, but it was largely inhabited by poor laborers, who lived in dilapidated tenement houses. Most of the city's Italian citizens were housed there in a district commonly referred to as "Little Italy."

Most of the area provided nothing better than crowded tenement housing for its inhabitants. A local newspaper writer, appalled by the living conditions, reported that

for whole blocks of inhabited buildings there are no yards. Tired mothers sit on doorsteps with fretful babies in their arms and children swarm over the streets, dodging electric cars and other vehicles.[2]

The "dingy North End," as it was sometimes called, was lined with old buildings used for small factories and tenements. Most of these four- and five-story buildings were decrepit firetraps, which would have collapsed immediately in the event of a fire. It was here that the city's "red light" districts flourished, and where most of the local underworld activities were born.

Overlooking both the North End and the West Bottoms was the neighborhood called Quality Hill. During the Civil War era this neighborhood on the highest peak of the city's west bluffs began to be settled by Kansas City's elite. By the time Jim Pendergast came to Kansas City in the 1870's, Quality Hill was illuminated by gas streetlights, while much of the West Bottoms and North End remained in darkness. The glow of these lights displayed the pretentious brick houses that decorated Quality Hill, as well as the luxurious hotel called the Coates House, complete with marble swimming pool and copper-roofed towers. But the passing years brought marked changes to Quality Hill. The wealthy social elite gradually moved to the southern and eastern portions of the growing city to make room for the expanding commercial interests. By 1890 business houses dotted many parts of Quality Hill, and the best residential districts were to be found to the east and south.[3]

These diverse neighborhoods, with their motley populations, made up the Kansas City in which Jim Pendergast became a political success. When Pendergast first came to Kansas City in 1876, city politics reflected more chaos than organization. Between 1870 and 1889, none of the wards or neighborhoods showed any political stability. The election returns reported in the newspapers for those two decades show that neither the Democratic nor Republican parties had a consistent majority in any ward or neighborhood. There were many reasons for this, but a marked lack of political leadership and organization played a significant role. The Democratic party, for example, had no permanent Democratic club or organization until 1890, and the Republican party was so dismembered by factional strife that it could seldom work efficiently. Also, neither party had for any period of time, other than immediately prior to an election, more than one or two men who devoted much time to city politics. Party leaders came and went with the annual city elections because many of them were businessmen with only an incidental interest in local politics.

While Kansas City politics lacked the organization of Boss Tweed's New York and Abraham Ruef's San Francisco, it did not lack the color. The city elections which were held each April were often preceded by gala events. A torchlight procession around the city's market square, a brass band playing, and men carrying pictures of the candidates or large signs bearing such mottos as "No Man Owns the Irish Vote" and "We Are Opposed to Rings and Cliques" were by no means unusual. Pre-election rallies were sometimes introduced by cornet music, and crowds would gather in the streets to hear five or six speakers praise their candidates.

Jim Pendergast took his first active interest in Kansas City politics in 1884. In March of that year, prior to the city election, Pendergast attended the Democratic primary in the West Bottoms' Sixth Ward. The "Bloody Sixth," as the ward was tagged because of the many fights there on election day, held its primaries in the same manner that the other five wards did. "Mob" primaries, as those meetings were called, were merely assemblages of the party's voters who met en masse and voted on delegates to represent them in the party's city convention. Jim Pendergast was one of the eleven delegates elected by the Democrats in the "Bloody Sixth" to represent them in the 1884 Democratic City Convention.

For the next two years, the West Bottoms saloonkeeper was not active in either the primaries or the city convention. Then in 1887 he was selected again to represent the West Bottoms in the city convention. By this time, Pendergast was representing the First Ward. A change in the ward boundaries in 1886 had altered the old "Bloody Sixth" so that it included virtually all of the West Bottoms, and it was renamed the First Ward.

In 1888 the First Ward became more centralized, when the Democratic leaders decided that voters should elect a chairman of the meeting instead of participating in the old "mob" primaries. The chairman would then appoint a committee which would handpick the delegates to the city convention. By rallying a simple majority to the lightly attended primary, a faction leader could get himself or one of his men elected chairman. By controlling the chair, a faction could control the delegates and have a solid block of votes for any of the candidates it might wish to support in the city convention.[4]

This change in the method of selecting delegates was not unique to the First Ward. It in fact had been going on in the Democratic primaries in several other wards since 1885. Just how much influence Jim Pendergast had in making this change is impossible to say, although in 1888 he was selected to be on the committee which chose the delegates and again in 1889.

Pendergast was by no means the commander of the First Ward Democracy at this time. Two First Ward faction leaders, Edward Kelly and John Grady, were competing for leadership. Since the mid-'eighties these two Irishmen had been struggling for control of the primaries, but they usually agreed to a compromise. On two occasions, however, they failed to compromise and competed in the primaries. The struggles resulted in the election of two groups of delegates one time, and a deadlocked primary which was forced to adjourn the other. It was on those two occasions, 1886 and 1890, that the astute Pendergast took no part in the First Ward primaries.

Neither Kelly nor Grady ever managed to direct the Democratic politics of the First Ward. That was to be reserved for Jim Pendergast. All the time that Kelly, the First Ward member of the Democratic City Executive Committee, and Grady, the twice-elected councilman from the First Ward, fought for control, Pendergast refused to take sides. He co-operated with both men. In 1890 he opened the doors of his hotel, Pendergast Hall, to Kelly so that he could hold a campaign meeting for First Ward Democrats. Pendergast had gained the favor of Grady, too, for in March 1892 the latter made known his wish to retire from the council, if Jim Pendergast could replace him.

Pendergast's refusal to take sides in the First Ward faction troubles paid rich dividends. By 1892 he was the undisputed leader of the First Ward Democracy. For the first time in years the *Kansas City Star*, an independent local newspaper, could report that a Democrat had "a walk away for the [alderman] nomination" in the First Ward.[5]

The nominee for the First Ward's seat in the lower house of the city council had more than just party support; he had the support of the citizens in the West Bottoms. A First Ward political rally just prior to the city election demonstrated "Big Jim's" popularity. A local newspaper reported that the meeting on Genesee Street, in the West Bottoms, was attended by

the hard handed men of the First Ward . . . in oily blue jumpers, . . . with packing house mud on their boots, switchmen, freight handlers, engineers. Lots of them, too. There were not many silk hats in the crowd . . . . [6]

One speaker, after complimenting the First Ward Democrats for nominating Pendergast, continued by saying:

there is no kinder hearted or more sympathetic man in Kansas City than Jim Pendergast. He will go down in his pockets after his last cent to help a friend. No man is more easily moved to sympathy or good sense than Jim Pendergast.[7]

When the speech was finished, the laboring-men's applause produced "a prodigious noise" and then Pendergast entered. "Terrific yells" ensued, and the saloonkeeper responded by saying, "I never attempted a speech in all my life, but if you elect me I will do my duty."[8]

The election returns confirmed all reports of Jim Pendergast's popularity. He defeated his Republican opponent by a five-to-one majority. From April 1892 until April 1910 "Alderman Jim" would direct First Ward politics. The West Bottoms would no longer be without consistency in its political behavior, nor would it be split by factional strife. The political situation had changed. Pendergast, according to the *Kansas City Star*, was to be "King of the First."

In April 1892 Jim Pendergast took his seat in the lower house of Kansas

City's Common Council. The Charter of 1889 had created a bicameral legislature for Kansas City, consisting of an upper and lower house with each containing as many members as there were wards. Members of the upper house were elected at large for a period of four years, while members of the lower house were elected by the ward they represented for two years. Neither house wielded more strength than the other, for ordinances of any type could originate in either house, had to pass both houses before they could be sent to the mayor for approval, and required a two-thirds majority of both houses to survive the mayor's veto.[9]

During his initial year in the lower house, the inexperienced alderman did nothing to attract attention. He was ignored by the newspapers and scarcely known outside of the First Ward. But in his own neighborhood most people knew Jim Pendergast. He could not be overlooked when walking down the street. A man who loved to eat, by this time he weighed well over two hundred pounds. Overweight but obviously strong, "Big Jim" became famous for his black Bismarck mustache and his small bow tie.

After a year though, the politician from the West Bottoms became well known. William Rockhill Nelson, the reformist editor of the *Kansas City Star*, focused his attention on Pendergast. Baron Bill, as Nelson's enemies called him, believed that a municipal government should be run as "a business affair."[10] Using his newspaper to support and inaugurate many progressive projects in Kansas City, Nelson was first attracted to Alderman Pendergast because of his position on the appropriation of city funds for a garbage system. Pendergast according to the *Star*, said that "there is nothing that this city needs more than a garbage system," as he pledged his support for a $20,000 garbage fund.[11]

Alderman Jim also received early praise as a friend of progress when he took a bold stand in the lower house against a "wide open [telephone] franchise" which might well have pushed the telephone rates much higher than they were at that time. Even in the face of increased pressure from the Telephone Company to change his position, Pendergast remained adamant and the company was forced to compromise.[12]

The First Ward alderman distinguished himself as a fighter for the working-man as well. He urged the construction of a city park for the poor West Bottomites, and he led a battle to allow the city to go into debt if necessary rather than cut the salaries of the already underpaid firemen.

This issue over the firemen's salaries drew much attention. The mayor and city comptroller had discovered that the fire department had overdrawn its budget for the year. The two officials, therefore, asked the council to cut firemen's salaries by 15 per cent. The mayor and comptroller were Democrats, but they met strong opposition from four aldermen within their own party.

The city hall was located in the North End, and on the night that the salary issue was taken up in the council, a crowd of laborers gathered outdoors. The upper house voted to cut the firemen's salaries. When the news reached the gathering outdoors, a chorus of hooting and yelling began. The crowd challenged the upper house to send the ordinance to the lower house, where four friends of the low-income working-men resided. The ordinance was detained several days, but when it did go to the lower house, the two North End aldermen, Martin Regan of the Sixth Ward, and Andy Foley of the Second, joined forces with Pendergast and his friend John Fitzpatrick from an adjoining neighborhood. The "Big Four" as the *Star* called them, buried the bill so deep that it was never resurrected.[13]

A few months later Pendergast again supported his constituents by working against a proposal to move the only fire station in the West Bottoms to Quality Hill. Again Alderman Jim allied himself with Regan and Foley, and the three men were able to win enough support to block the move.

Pendergast's stand in the council undoubtedly produced a vote or two of confidence for him. The big saloonkeeper, however, did as much work outside the council to increase his following during his first term in office as he did from within. When a dozen men were arrested for working bunco games (betting swindles) at the race track, Alderman Jim put up bond in the police court for several of them. Although running to help a man arrested for working a bunco game would have been looked upon with disdain by the voters on Quality Hill, the laborers in the West Bottoms were more convinced than ever that Jim was their friend.

One did not have to be in trouble to get help from the First Ward Irishman, because every month Pendergast was a bank teller for many of the railroad and packing-house workers in the West Bottoms. Cash was scarce in those days, so Jim kept the safe in his saloon full of paper and silver on payday in order to cash the checks of the working-men. "They spent some of it across the bar," asserted William Reddig, who knew personally some of Alderman Jim's close friends,

> but Jim did not make that a requisite. Men learned that he had an interest in humanity outside of business and that he could be trusted, and they returned the favor by patronizing his saloon and giving him their confidence.[14]

During his first term in the lower house, Pendergast had done much both in and out of the city council to increase his popularity with the First Ward voters. In other quarters though, he had made enemies. William R. Nelson and his *Star* criticized the Irish saloonkeeper on occasion, especially when he fought the efforts to cut firemen's salaries and move the fire station. The *Star* was not alone in criticizing Pendergast and some of his fellow politicans. Kansas City's bosses could sympathize with New York's "Big Tim" Sullivan and Richard Croker, for they had their own counterpart of New York's Reverend Charles Parkhurst to contend with. The Reverend John Sewell, one of Kansas City's Congregational ministers, was an ardent reformer in the style of Parkhurst. Attempting to reform the city government as well as souls, Sewell hoped to purge Kansas City of all "professional politicians . . . who emerge from tending bar in some corner dram shop, [and] begin to rapidly climb the ladder of political influence."[15]

Kansas Citians did not have to look far to find the men to whom Sewell was referring. Only three city politicians who had gained prominence in the past two years were saloonkeepers, and all three, Pendergast, Regan, and Foley, represented the wards of West Bottoms and North End. However, opposition to Jim Pendergast was ineffective in the face of all that he had been doing for his West Bottoms neighbors. When he decided to run for alderman again in the spring of 1894, his popularity, which he had enhanced by his actions in the council, from behind the bar of his saloon, and by the little personal favors that he performed, was confirmed by his re-election.

The significance of Pendergast's re-election in 1894 can only be appreciated when one views the opposition he faced. The strongest opposition, according to the Democratic *Kansas City Times*, was "a new factor" in local politics. It was the American Protective Association. According to the *Times*, the A.P.A. had "but one plank in its platform . . . opposition to Catholics."[16] The A.P.A. was strong in the Middle West at that time and had a sizable influence on Kansas City politics. The A.P.A. members managed to gain partial control of the Republican City Convention in 1894, and they succeeded in getting several of their candidates nominated, including Webster Davis, a candidate for mayor.

The Irish-Catholic Pendergast not only had the A.P.A.-dominated Republicans to face in the election of 1894, he also had a newly formed Independent ticket to fight. It was headed by a Democrat, Frank Cooper, a partner in the livestock firm of Offut, Elmore & Cooper. This nonpartisan ticket had well-known Republicans and Democrats on it, all of whom were calling for a municipal government run on business principles, not political influence. The independent *Kansas City Star* and the hitherto

Democratic *Times* both threw their support to the infant movement. The city's other leading newspaper, the *Journal*, backed the Republican ticket as usual and did not even mention the A.P.A. issue.

The many-sided opposition to the straight Democratic ticket, and especially the anti-Catholic crusade of the A.P.A. Republicans, pushed Jim Pendergast into an alliance with another rising young Catholic politician, Joe Shannon. Having made his political debut about the same time that Pendergast had, Joe Shannon, with the help of his brother Frank, was trying to establish himself in the city's largest ward, the Ninth.[17]

Pendergast, Shannon, and some other regular Democrats put up a ticket with a labor leader, Frank Johnson, at the top. But the wave of support won by the A.P.A. was too strong, and only Pendergast's First Ward gave Johnson a majority of its voters. The Republicans gained twenty-three out of twenty-five city offices, not one of the Independents was elected; and only two Democrats, Pendergast and Regan, were victorious. Actually, Pendergast was barely threatened. He had received 687 votes, and the Republican nominee obtained only 212. The Independent candidate proved to be the weakest of the three, finishing with only 137 votes.

The election demonstrated beyond a doubt that Pendergast was the only Democratic ward leader in the city who could deliver the votes when the chips were down. Every other ward in the city but two, including Regan's Sixth Ward and Shannon's Ninth, gave a majority of its votes to Webster Davis, the A.P.A. Republican. Although Andy Foley's old bailiwick, the Second Ward, did not go to Davis, it fell to the Independent candidate, Frank Cooper. And while Martin Regan had been able to get himself elected in the Sixth, he could not carry the remainder of the Democratic ticket with him. Only Pendergast had produced majorities for himself and the ticket.

There had been some fraud in the city election of 1894, but not in Pendergast's ward. The Shannons, who could not swing the Ninth Ward either legally or illegally, were involved in some crooked voting practices.[18] Investigators never found any evidence of fraud in the First Ward while Pendergast resided there. With illegal voting practices being discovered in many other wards throughout the city during the years that Pendergast was a power in city politics, many people questioned the absence of fraud in the First. Alderman Jim had the answer. "I never needed a crooked vote. All I want is a chance for my friends to get to the polls."[19]

Although the First Ward Boss stole no votes, he did not consider the ordinances prohibiting gambling to be sacred—at least not during his early years as chief of the First Ward Democracy. By 1892, Jim had closed his saloon on St. Louis Avenue in the West Bottoms, but he retained the Pendergast Hotel. He had also opened a saloon in the North End's Second Ward, and another one in the West Bottoms' First Ward. There was gambling upstairs over both of these saloons during the summer of 1894. In August 1894, thirty-eight men were arrested in a big dice game in the North End saloon.[20]

As long as Thomas M. Speers remained the chief of police in Kansas City, gamblers were threatened. As early as April 1895 Marcy K. Brown, a faction leader in Jackson County politics, began pressuring Governor Stone to get rid of Speers. The control of the police was in the hands of the state at this time. The governor appointed a board of police commissioners for the city, and this board had the power to remove and appoint the chief of police and all of the patrolmen. The board also established the salaries of all members of the police force.

In late April 1895 Governor Stone appointed a new board of police commissioners. The new board soon dropped Speers as chief of police and replaced him with L. E. Irwin. Throughout the remainder of the year, the gambling games over both of Pendergast's saloons, which were operated by the notorious gambler Ed Findley, ran wide open without police interference.[21]

This situation caused the *Star* to begin a campaign against Chief Irwin and the "police-protected" games in the Alderman's saloons. There was increased pressure on Irwin from both the *Star* and a local reform organization, the Civic Federation, to close down the illegal games. The chief was forced into some token action. He made several raids on the Pendergast saloons, but the gamblers were usually tipped off by the police beforehand and had time to close the games before the raiding parties arrived.[22]

The way Pendergast had gained police protection for the illegal activities in his saloons is easy to understand. Marcy K. Brown, the influential county politician who persuaded Governor Stone to appoint a new board of police commissioners hostile to Speers, had been defeated in a power struggle the previous summer at the Democratic County Convention. The big fight in the convention had been over the nomination for county prosecuting attorney. Brown and the delegates he controlled voted for Frank G. Johnson. Jim Pendergast, on the other hand, joined forces with the Ninth Ward politician, Joe Shannon. Together, Pendergast and Shannon had enough delegates to defeat Brown's man, and get their own candidate, J. H. Bremmerman, nominated.

Brown, who had seldom found his power in the county so successfully challenged, realized that he must form an alliance with at least one of the rising young bosses from Kansas City. He decided to try Pendergast, and the two men agreed on a compromise. Pendergast was to support

Brown in the next county battle, and Brown was to use his influence to get the police force revamped. Pendergast would help select the new policemen, and Brown promised to use his influence to get the gambling protected in Pendergast's two saloons. Thus, the next spring, less than four weeks after Brown began pressuring Governor Stone to have Chief Speers removed, Jim Pendergast abandoned his alliance with Joe Shannon and supported Brown for re-election to the chairmanship of the Democratic County Committee instead of Shannon's candidate, George Shelley.

Soon, though, Pendergast was unhappy with his new ally because Brown failed to do all that he promised. The rising young ward boss, according to a newspaper reporter, had been promised the right to appoint more of the members to the revamped police force than Brown ultimately allowed.[23] But Pendergast's gambling games were being protected by the police, and any bitterness that existed over patronage was gone by summer. The First Ward alderman and Brown fought side by side in an unsuccessful effort to prevent the election of George Shelley to the chair of the county committee. When Shelley was elected, Pendergast and Brown took their men and stormed out of the meeting. The two bosses refused to recognize the new chairman and they kept the county Democracy split almost until Christmas. The refusal of Brown and Pendergast to support Shannon's candidate paid off. In December, Shelley resigned the chairmanship to which he had been fairly elected. A compromise candidate agreeable to both factions was soon selected.[24]

The alliance with Brown allowed Pendergast to keep the gambling rooms open with only a minimum of police interference. This freedom the big saloonkeeper had not enjoyed before. But the cooperation of the police force brought its problems too. A Kansas City police judge, James Jones, made known his opposition to the gambling in Kansas City. The A.P.A. Republicans nominated Jones for mayor in 1896, and he ran on a platform which pledged to run Ed Findley, the gamekeeper at Pendergast's two saloons, out of Kansas City.

The 1896 election campaign, though based on opposition to gambling, did not discourage Alderman Jim. He ran for re-election anyway. And the vociferous attacks on the police-protected games in his saloons had no apparent effect. The A.P.A.-controlled Republicans again swept the city election, leaving only five lower house posts to the Democrats. Jim Pendergast, however, took one of the five seats for himself, as he trounced his A.P.A. opponent with 632 votes to 372.

It was not at all surprising that "Big Jim" had won again, for even though he was busier than ever before, especially with his first active involvement in county politics, he continued to aid his constituents. The Negroes, for example, who populated a large portion of the First Ward, were undoubtedly impressed when Alderman Jim took the time and effort to put up bail bond for a Negro.[25]

While Pendergast looked out for the special interests of his people in the West Bottoms, he also worked for the general welfare of the city and gained even more prestige. His stand on the gas company franchise illustrated this. In 1895 Kansas Citians were paying $1.60 per 1000 cubic feet of gas to the Philadelphia Gas Company, which held the gas franchise. The company thought it could count on Pendergast's vote when it was time for a franchise renewal. But Pendergast, according to the *Star's* bold headline, "STOOD BY THE CITY AT A CRITICAL MOMENT." With a picture of the big alderman on the front page, the *Star* praised Pendergast for voting against the "trust" and casting the deciding vote in favor of the Dollar Gas Company, which promised to deliver 1000 cubic feet of gas for $1.00.[26] A saving such as this was not only important to hotel-owners like Pendergast, it was important to home-owners all over the city. The reduction was especially important in 1895, because the nation was in the midst of a depression.

During Pendergast's second term in the lower house, he also spoke out for such important issues as lower telephone rates, which were badly needed in Kansas City. On another occasion, he voted for a resolution to appropriate $25,000 to purchase a thirty-three-acre estate for a city park. Although the resolution did not pass the lower house, Pendergast had put himself on record as a supporter of public improvements for Kansas City.[27]

Probably the most significant example of Pendergast's labors during his second term in office concerned the passage of two charter amendments: one for the purchase of a water works plant, and the other for financing the construction of parks and boulevards. Since the 1870's many citizens had been demanding parks and boulevards, as well as a municipally owned water works. These two issues were drawn up in the form of charter amendments and placed before the people for their adoption or rejection in a special election in June 1895. Pendergast gave his full support to the amendments. In fact, he joined a group referred to as "the general committee of friends of the park and water works amendments." After working with the committee in his ward, Alderman Jim told a newspaper reporter that

> nearly every voter in the ward is for the amendments. I think that the amendments will carry by an overwhelming majority. I can find scarcely anyone who is against them. I am in favor of them and have always been so, as my official acts in the city council show.[28]

No one could have known more about what the First Ward would do on election day than the "King of the First." Pendergast had been correct. The amendments were ratified in the First Ward by a six-to-one majority. Hardly anyone had opposed the issues that Jim Pendergast had requested them to support. His ability to bring voters into line in the West Bottoms seemed incredible. The way he had gathered support for the amendments he backed, and the way he had kept the Republican landsides in the past two city elections from touching his ward amazed those who did not understand the source of his popularity. The following description of the Alderman, written by one of his contemporaries, helps one understand why he had the devoted support of his West Bottoms' neighbors:

> He had a big heart, was charitable and liberal. . . . No deserving man, woman or child that appealed to "Jim" Pendergast went away empty handed, and this is saying a great deal, as he was continually giving aid and help to the poor and unfortunate. The extent of his bounty was never known, as he made it an inviolable rule that no publicity should be given to his philanthropy. There never was a winter in the last twenty years that he did not circulate among the poor of the West Bottoms, ascertaining their needs, and after his visit there were no empty larders. Grocers, butchers, bakers and coal men had unlimited orders to see that there was no suffering among the poor of the West Bottoms, and to send the bills to "Jim" Pendergast.[29]

The personal favors that Pendergast performed for his constituents, his actions within the council chamber which benefited many of them, and the police department patronage which aided at least a few, all helped Alderman Jim dominate the First Ward politically. But the big Irishman was not satisfied with being just the leader of the West Bottoms. He wanted to extend his power into the North End.

NOTES

[1]*Political History of Jackson County* (Kansas City: Marshall and Morrison, 1902), p. 183; William Reddig, *Tom's Town, Kansas City and the Pendergast Legend* (New York: Lippincott, 1947), pp. 25, 29.

[2]*Kansas City Star*, July 29, 1905.

[3]United States Department of Interior, *Eleventh Census of the United States: 1890. Vital Statistics*, Vol. IV, Part II (Washington, D.C.: Government Printing Office, 1896) pp. 245-50. Wards 3 and 4 made up most of Quality Hill, and the Census shows that business houses were located there in many places by this time. Wards 8 and 9 were to the east of Quality Hill. Ward 9 was also south. Both wards had many good residences. Ward 8, the Census reported, encompassed the best residential neighborhood in the city.

[4]*Kansas City Times*, March 20, 1888.
[5]*Star*, March 15, 1892.
[6]*Times*, March 26, 1892.
[7]*Ibid.*
[8]*Ibid.*
[9]Kansas City, Missouri, *Charter of 1889* (Kansas City: Lawton, Hanens, and Burnap Stationers, 1889), Articles II, III.
[10]Reddig, *op. cit.*, p. 38.
[11]*Star*, March 15, 1893.
[12]*Ibid.*, October 31, 1893; November 2, 1893.
[13]*Ibid.*, August 24, 29, 1893.
[14]Reddig, *op. cit.*, p. 29.
[15]*Star*, December 11, 1893.
[16]*Times*, January 30, 1894.
[17]Charles P. Blackmore, "Joseph B. Shannon, Political Boss and Twentieth Century 'Jeffersonian' " (unpublished Ph.D. dissertation, Columbia University, 1954) pp. 8, 9, 38.
[18]*Star*, March 14, 1894; April 9, 1894.
[19]Quoted by Reddig, *op. cit.*, pp. 31-2.
[20]*Star*, July 15, 1894.
[22]*Ibid.*, November 8, 1895; January 10, 1896.
[23]*Ibid.*, May 8, 1895.
[24]*Ibid.*, December 9, 14, 1895.
[25]*Ibid.*, February 22, 1896.
[26]*Ibid.*, January 10, 1895.
[27]*Ibid.*, December 27, 1894.
[28]*Ibid.*, May 26, 1895.
[29]*Kansas City Journal*, November 11, 1911.

THE CASE—McALLISTER INVESTIGATING COMMITTEE

The Investigation of "Boss" Frank Hague

Frank Hague probably typifies the urban boss of the early twentieth century. Born in 1876, Hague became at the age of thirty the Democratic boss of Ward 2 (the "horseshoe district") in Jersey City, a slum tenement area bordering on the marshes and facing the rear of the Statue of Liberty. During the depression of 1907, Hague consolidated his grip on horseshoe politics by providing jobs and relief for the unemployed, despite the presence of Jersey City's Irish-Catholic, Republican reform mayor, Mark M. Fagan. Since "reform mayors" dominated the city's politics in the first decade of the twentieth century, Hague frequently posed as a reformer in order to exploit such Wilsonian measures as the direct primary and the commission form of municipal government. Hague was elected to the newly created City Commission

From the *Journal of the Eighty-Fifth Senate of the State of New Jersey* (Trenton, N.J.: McCrellish & Quigley Company, 1929), pp. 1098-1151.

in 1913 as the first commissioner of public safety, and his organization of the police force won him a reputation as a crusader against vice and graft and the support of a number of church groups. In 1917, he was chosen mayor of Jersey City, and two years later, in the famous "applejack campaign" of 1919, he successfully "elected" his first governor, Edward I. Edwards, and emerged as the new leader of New Jersey Democracy. Through his ability to produce substantial pluralities for his candidates in Hudson County, he became a major power in state politics, effectively controlling governors, United States Senators and Representatives, state legislators, and judges. By 1922, Hague had eliminated the Republican party as an effective opposition force in Jersey City.

The only serious threat to Frank Hague's political power in state or local politics before 1940 resulted from the Case-McAllister Committee's investigations of his machine in 1928 and 1929. The immediate impetus for the investigation was Hague's involvement in the Republican primary in May, 1928, when his Hudson County organization encouraged thousands of Democrats to support State Senator Morgan Larson of Middlesex County against his opponent, former Jersey City Judge Robert C. Carey. Larson carried Jersey City, especially the Democratic precincts, and the 1400 Republican votes in Hague's own horseshoe district were eight times the "normal" GOP vote in general elections. Although Hague's fraudulent attempts to control the Republican primary had sparked the investigation, the Case-McAllister Committee went on to make a broad inquiry into machine activities, and into Hague's personal finances, that entailed forty-four public hearings, the examination of 335 witnesses, and some 8,200 pages of testimony.

When Hague refused to answer certain questions concerning the sources of his considerable wealth, the committee cited him for contempt. Hague maintained that the state legislature had usurped the powers of the judiciary by making inquiries designed to reveal a criminal conspiracy, and had violated the "due process" clause of the Fourteenth Amendment. The Court of Errors and Appeals eventually upheld this position, and the machine's control of the local judiciary in Jersey City prevented any further investigation into machine activities. Hague was required to pay $60,000 in back income taxes—a sum actually remitted for the mayor by his temporary ally, Theodore Brandle, czar of Hudson County's building trades union. The revelations of the Case-McAllister Committee did give rise to a bipartisan effort in May, 1929, to wrest control of the city commission from Hague and his organization. Although the fusion ticket severely reduced the machine's normal majorities, Hague and his four commissioners were reelected by an average plurality of nearly 25,000 votes. The Depression and the New Deal quickly revived the machine and its rule was unshaken until the late 1940s.

The committee's investigation, aside from its importance as a challenge to Hague's power in Jersey City, provides students of the urban machine with an unusual look into the operations of city political organizations in the twentieth century. In reading those portions of the committee's report reprinted here, attempt to isolate the principal methods employed by the machine to preserve and entrench its power. In particular, how might the machine have benefited politically from violations of the Sunday closing law and the ordinances against gambling, or from its questionable financial management of the Jersey City Hospital? In other words, was the machine's corruption simply for the purpose of personal financial gain, or did it serve more basic political needs of the organization as a whole? And did corruption in this instance have any conceivable positive benefits for the urban community?

PRIMARY ELECTION

The Committee investigated the primary election held in Jersey City, Hoboken and Bayonne in May, 1928. Many violations of the election law and many irregularities opposed to the intent and spirit of the law, if not its letter, were disclosed.

There were found 116 voters who voted in the Democratic primary in 1927 and in the Republican primary in 1928, and five who voted in the Republican primary in 1927 and in the Democratic primary in 1928. These are clear violations of the election law.

Forty-eight Democratic election officers, functioning as such in the May, 1928, primary election, voted in the Republican primary, with the acquiescence, if not the connivance, of the Republican board members in the districts in which they were serving. Nine voters who had filed applications for appointment as Democratic election officers at the May, 1928 primary, voted in the Republican primary. Twenty-seven Jersey City members of the Hudson County Democratic County Committee voted in the Republican primary. More than one thousand Democrats, who signed Democratic nominating petitions for the May, 1928 primary, in which they declared themselves Democrats, voted in the Republican boxes in that primary. These likewise are clear violations of the election law, inasmuch as these voters were all members of the Democratic party, and were prohibited by the act from voting in the Republican primary.

The evidence showed that approximately 22,000 Democrats voted in the Republican primary. Many of these voters were subpoenaed, all of whom defended their vote on the ground that they had not participated in the primary election of either party in 1927.

The Committee endeavored to ascertain whether this wholesale voting of Democrats in the Republican primary was the result of a conspiracy, but was unable to obtain tangible legal evidence to that effect. Almost without exception the witnesses examined by the Committee were evasive and vague in testifying. For example:

• • •

Arthur J. Foley, a lieutenant of the Hudson County Police, a member of the Hudson County Democratic Committee, voted in the Republican Primary. When asked whether he was a Democrat or a Republican, he testified, "Well, I don't know. At night time I changed my mind, at twelve o'clock. I had some friends I wanted to vote for."

The cases of those who voted in the Democratic Primary in 1927 and in the Republican Primary in 1928, of the election officers who voted in the opposite boxes and of County Committee members who voted in the opposite boxes, were referred to the Attorney-General, then in charge of the Hudson County Prosecutor's office, for appropriate action. To this date no indictments have been found. The Committee is advised that these matters are still before the Grand Jury.

Nothing can be done by way of legislation with reference to such cases. The law is specific and sufficiently broad. It is law enforcement that is needed.

The cases of approximately 22,000 Democrats who did not vote in either primary in 1927 and who voted in the Republican primary in 1928 present a situation which requires Legislative action. Under the construction of the law contended for by those who assert the validity of these votes, it is possible for voters, who are in fact members of the opposite party and who did not participate in the primary of the preceding year, to vote in the primary of the party of which they are not in fact members and if sufficiently numerous, to nominate the candidates of the party to which they are opposed. This is unfair to the primary contestants, contrary to the spirit and intent of the election law, unethical and opens the door to political corruption.

Paragraph 361 of the election law provides that no voter shall be allowed to vote in the ballot box of a political party if the name of such voter appears in the primary poll book of another political party as made up at the next preceding primary election.

Paragraph 362 provides that if a voter is registered and did not vote in the party primary of any other political party at the last preceding primary election, he shall be allowed to vote in the party primary in which he offers to vote.

Paragraph 364 provides that in case a voter desires to vote in the same political party box in which he voted at the next preceding primary election and is challenged, he shall take an oath or affirmation that he is a member of the political party in the ballot box of which he voted at the next preceding primary election; that at the last election for members of the General Assembly at which he voted, he voted for a majority of the candidates of the said party, and that he intends to support the candidates of said party at the ensuing election. If the person so challenged refuses to take the oath or affirmation he is not entitled to vote at the primary election.

The Committee recommends that Paragraphs 361 and 362 be amended so as to provide that no voter shall be allowed to vote in the ballot box of a political party if the name of such voter appears in the primary poll books of another political party as made up at the last two preceding primary elections, and that if a voter is registered and did not vote in the party primary of any other political party at the last two preceding primary elections he shall be allowed to vote in party primary in which he offers to vote.

The Committee further recommends that Paragraph 364 be amended so as to provide that in case the vote of any voter desiring to vote in a primary election is challenged, he shall take an oath or affirmation that he is a member of the political party in the ballot box of which he desires to vote, and that at the last general election for members of the general assembly he voted for a majority of the candidates of the said party nominated for national, state and county offices, and that he intends to support the candidates of that party at the ensuing election, and that if he refuses to take the oath or affirmation, he shall be not entitled to vote at the primary election.

The effect of such an amendment would be that a voter, in order to vote in a certain party primary, would have to show, not only that he did not vote in the party primary of any other political party at the last two preceding primary elections, but that he voted at the last general election for a majority of candidates of the party in the primary of which he desires to participate. In order to change from one party to another, a voter would not only have to refrain from voting in the primary of his original party for two years, but he would have to perform the positive act of voting at a general election for a majority of the candidates of the party of which he desires to become a member.

This would tend to prevent a repetition of frauds which were practiced so extensively in the May, 1928, primary in Hudson County.

The evidence showing that Democratic election officers voted in Republican primary ballot boxes, with the acquiescence or connivance of their Republican colleagues, presents a state of facts even more serious. The purity of any election depends in large measure upon the faithfulness, intelligence and honesty of the election board, particularly in the counting of the votes. When election officers are so blind to the letter of the law and so morally incapable of comprehending its spirit that they violate it and permit it to be violated in this manner, what assurance is there that they are honest in the performance of their most important duty, the counting of the votes? Such conduct destroys faith in the capacity and moral integrity of the election boards involved.

The investigation made by the Committee confirms what is common knowledge, that it ought to be the policy of the election laws to confine the duties of district election boards, as far as possible, to mechanical acts. The boards ought to have a minimum of discretion and judicial or quasi-judicial power.

This Committee recommends that legislation be enacted providing for the use of voting machines. It is not intended here to discuss the arguments for the use of voting machines, such as increased speed in voting, secrecy of the ballot, the elimination of marked and spoiled ballots, immediate and permanent returns, and the prevention of costly recounts, or those contra. This single phase of the problem is emphasized. The evidence before the Committee shows such a lack of comprehension of legal duty and moral obligation on the part of many election boards as to warrant a well-justified fear, if not a belief, that these boards were wholly derelict in the performance of their duty. The use of voting machines would take from the district boards the duty of counting the votes, the one most open to serious wrong doing, and would substitute a mechanical contrivance insuring an honest count.

The Committee further recommends that the offices of members of the district election boards and members of the county committees be forfeited if the holder thereof votes in the current primary election of another party than that with which he is affiliated and that legislation to this effect be enacted.

The Committee further recommends that legislation be enacted providing that no holder of any public office, excepting school teachers, shall be eligible to membership in district boards of election.

PAYROLL PADDING

The Committee spent considerable time in investigating the Jersey City and Hudson County payrolls and examined many witnesses with reference thereto.

Payrolls for Hudson County and for Jersey City, as of May 15, 1928, were introduced into evidence.

The annual payroll for Hudson County amounted to $4,305,644.48, paid to 2,152 employees.

The annual payroll for Jersey City amounted to $8,544,026.70, paid to 3,760 employees, exclusive of the payroll of the Board of Education.

The testimony shows that a considerable part of this money is wasted. Many witnesses were examined whose testimony leads this Committee to conclude that many persons on the payroll perform no service or inadequate service for the compensation which they receive.

An outstanding case was that of Alfred H. Mansfield, an employee of the Hudson County Board of Health, who served as a health inspector at a salary of $4,000 per year. He has worked in that capacity for twenty-five years. He was unable to give the Committee the name and address of the owner of any place that he had ever inspected, and testified that he had never made a complaint or arrest, and that if a man has a job he is "supposed to get the vote out."

. . .

Sheriff Coppinger of Hudson County has under him a staff of thirty employees who receive approximately $122,000 per year. He had utterly no knowledge of the duties supposed to be performed by those subordinates and the salaries which they received. There was no check of any kind designed to make sure that the County received its money's worth in services for this payroll.

. . .

Chauffeurs are paid, in many instances, from $3,000 to $3,500 per year.

It costs Jersey City approximately $83,500 per year for salaries for telephone service, elevator service and the operation of the heating plant in the City Hall, and the cleaning of it. This sum is expended for salaries for the maintenance of the City Hall, exclusive of the repairs—clearly an exorbitant sum.

According to the testimony of Commissioner Potterton, it costs Jersey City $7,300 per acre per annum, for salaries for the maintenance of fourteen parks, containing thirty-seven acres of land, likewise an exorbitant sum.

Hudson County pays approximately $202,000 per year for salaries for the maintenance of its Court House, not including the services of "County mechanics" who repair it. Six of these employees are listed as cuspidor cleaners. That the expenditure of this sum of money for this purpose is a gross waste of public funds needs no argument. The custodian of the Court House, John F. Callahan, was unable to give to the Committee any clear or convincing explanation of the need for the large number of Court House employees, or of their individual duties.

The Superintendent of County Mechanics, James Doody, has seventy men of his payroll who receive approximately $127,000 per year. It is the duty of these men to make repairs on the approximately seventy-five County buildings. A more unbusinesslike system of administration than that presented by Superintendent Doody's testimony could not be imagined. The men are not employed by the Superintendent of the Department. They are employed by the Board of Freeholders without the request of the Superintendent whether they are needed or not and he does the best he can to keep them busy. The system requires no written requisition for work in the various county buildings. No record of the work done is kept by the Superintendent and no report of work done is made to the Board of Freeholders. There is no timekeeper, there are no time cards or clocks, and no record of the time worked by the individual employees or spent in the various operations is kept. The only supervision of the employees of this department, to determine whether the work which they do is necessary and their pay reasonable, or whether they work at all, is that of Superintendent Doody and his assistant, who depend upon personal visits to the seventy-five county buildings and their eyesight to see that their subordinates are usefully employed. The Board of Freeholders has no way of knowing whether the money expended in this department is wisely or necessarily expended.

No attention is paid to seasonal demands. Seasonal employees, such as tree trimmers, park laborers, firemen and heater men are employed the year round. A street laborer is paid $1,700 per year for keeping two blocks of the highway clean. He testified, "If boxes would fall off a truck and block the road, it would be my job to keep the road clear." This is an illustration of the wasteful expenditure of public funds for unnecessary labor.

The Committee recommends that the legislature consider legislation intended to prevent or to render more difficult the waste of public money by what is properly called "payroll padding."

Taxation has become one of the most important public problems. The cost of State, county and municipal government has increased progressively in recent years at an alarming rate. Taxation is becoming an increasingly heavy burden upon the home-owner, the tenant, the farmer, the businessman and upon industry. It is one of the factors that has caused certain kinds of industry to leave this section of the country and which tends to prevent certain other kinds of industry from locating here. It is impossible to discontinue expenditures for public improvements constructed by the State, counties and municipalities. They are necessary to our manner of living and the expeditious conduct of our business affairs. The most effectual method of decreasing State, municipal and county taxation is the introduction of economy and greater efficiency into government. The most vulnerable points in the armor of the high cost of government are the public payroll, pensions and tenure of office.

This Committee recommends that legislation be enacted imposing upon the Civil Service Commission the duty of supervising State payrolls and county and municipal payrolls where the act is operative, and the responsibility of certifying that all employments under its jurisdiction are necessary, that the holder of each position renders a necessary and adequate service, and that the compensation received is reasonable, with severe penalties for any violation of duty in these respects. Such legislation should also aim to eliminate, as far as possible, part-time employment in the public service by the consolidation of existing part-time positions.

CIVIL SERVICE

Shortly after its organization, the Committee subpoenaed the payrolls of the City of Jersey City and of the County of Hudson, and the Civil Service records of the employees of Jersey City and Hudson County, all as of May 15, 1928.

The Jersey City payrolls were furnished by the City Clerk in response to the subpoena. The Hudson County payrolls were produced by the Board of Freeholders. The Civil Service lists of both Jersey City and Hudson County were produced by the Trenton Office of the Civil Service Commission.

•   •   •

It should be noted that the Civil Service law authorizes the employment of temporary employees in an emergency for not more than two months, which may be extended for a further period of not more than two months, making a total period of four months for which employees may be legally temporarily employed.

As to Hudson County

Names on County payroll and not on Civil Service list 104
Names on Civil Service list and not on County payroll..............132
Instances of variance in salary between the County payroll
and the Civil Service list 47
Number of temporary employees on the Civil Service list
over four months... 38
Total for Hudson County..321
Total for Jersey City..963

Total number of discrepancies between the Jersey City and
Hudson County payrolls and the Civil Service lists and
irregularities 1284

Mr. Smith testified that he had been a member of the Commission for about nine years and Chairman for about eight years. He said that the State was divided into zones, and that each member of the Commission was in charge of a zone. He was in charge of the Hudson County Zone, having jurisdiction over Jersey City and Hudson County, with a branch office in the City Hall of Jersey City.

He testified that the original reports of the Commission were kept in Trenton, that duplicate records concerning each zone were kept in each zone office, and that under this system Jersey City's office kept duplicate records and transmitted the originals to the main office of the Commission at Trenton.

It was originally the intention that the branch offices should handle routine matters of local interest, but the practice has developed in such manner that each branch is an independent unit and each Commissioner supreme in his domain. The result of this procedure is a personal Civil Service administration in each zone in accordance with the notions of the Commissioner assigned thereto. There is no warrant in the law for this system of administration and the Commission must accept responsibility for this perversion of the law.

Mr. Smith was questioned concerning the discrepancies and irregularities enumerated in the items first above set forth, his explanation was that the Trenton records were not up to date. He said that all data concerning Civil Service employees in the Hudson County zone were reported to the Trenton office by the Jersey City office and that the Trenton office did not keep up its records accurately and completely.

It appeared that the system of keeping records was very lax and that it was possible for the Jersey City office to violate the Civil Service

Act or to permit it to be violated by the City or County administration, without the Trenton office having any record of such violations.

Several violations of the Civil Service law were shown to exist and were brought to Mr. Smith's attention. Among these were cases of persons in public employ in Jersey City and Hudson County who had never taken a Civil Service examination, as required by the statute; persons who were temporarily in the public employ longer than four months without having taken an examination; persons assigned to perform duties other than those properly pertaining to the position to which they were originally appointed; and the promotion of an employee without taking an examination.

Several employees were found in the City Clerk's office of Jersey City who were paid for every day in the year for keeping ballot boxes in repair. Their names did not appear on the Civil Service records. Their payrolls were not submitted to the Civil Service commission for certification. They were employed and paid in violation of law. The significance of this appears when we understand that Mr. Parsells, Chief Clerk of the Hudson County Zone office, was similarly employed by the city contrary to the Civil Service law, as will be reported presently.

More than forty persons were employed in the Water Department of Jersey City of whose employment there was no record either in the Jersey City office or in the Trenton office.

Mr. Smith testified that no check or comparison of the records of the Trenton office and the various zone offices had been made during the period of his service on the Commission.

He said that after the organization of this Committee a check and comparison had been made of the records of all of the zone offices with the Trenton office, which showed more errors and irregularities existing in the other zone offices than were found in the records of the Jersey City office.

An itemized list of all the irregularities found to exist in the Jersey City lists was submitted to the Civil Service Commission by the Committee. After an examination of it, the Commission submitted to the Committee a statement explaining the discrepancies and irregularities. The gist of the explanation was that a check and comparison of the Trenton records and the Hudson zone records had been made and that the two sets of records had been brought into unity. The fact remains that on May 15, 1928, the condition of the records of the two offices was as above set forth.

On March 21, 1929, the Commission submitted to the Committee a list of discrepancies between the Hudson County payroll and the Trenton office list, disclosed by its own examination. The variances and discrepancies enumerated in this list number 251, some of a minor nature, but substantially of the same kind as those appearing in the City list. In its letter submitting this list the Civil Service Commission made the following statement:

> As a matter of fact, while the Trenton office records are looked upon as the official records, under the plan of administration of the Commission the local office records must be recognized as the final and controlling records since payrolls are submitted to and checked in the local office, an opportunity is had to continually check the records against the payroll as submitted.

The vice of this plan appears in the operation of the Hudson County Zone office. It is possible for the Commissioner in charge of the Zone office, or his assistant, to violate the Civil Service law without the Trenton office having any notice or knowledge of it. Not only is it possible, but in fact, it was done.

It further appeared that Mr. Smith had been frequently appointed a condemnation commissioner in Hudson County and that he had received from $8,000 to $10,000 in fees.

Mr. Elmer S. Parsells, Chief Clerk of the Jersey City office, was questioned with reference to the functioning of the Jersey City office. Mr. Parsells had charge of the routine work of the office under the supervision of Mr. Smith.

It was shown that Mr. Parsells had been employed by the City of Jersey City and had been paid "on claim" for a period of at least two years, a salary of $150 a month. "On claim" means that he submitted a verified bill for his services each month which was approved for payment by resolution of the Board of Commissioners of Jersey City, and that his name did not appear on the regular Jersey City payroll or on the Civil Service list.

That he was, in fact, being paid as a Jersey City employee, in addition to his compensation as an employee of the State Civil Service Commission, was discovered by the Committee accidentally. Mr. Parsells at first denied that he was employed by the City, but being confronted with the evidence in the possession of the Committee, he admitted the fact.

When asked what service he rendered the city, he said he served as clerk to the police and fire reserves. He testified that the work which he did for the City was outside of his hours as clerk in the Civil Service department. His testimony describing the services rendered to the City was very vague. His memory was faulty and his answers were evasive. Whether in fact he rendered service to the City or not, his employment was a direct violation of the Civil Service law. He had taken no examination and his name did not appear on the City payroll, which it was the duty of the Civil Service Commissioner to certify.

Mr. Smith, being recalled to the stand, testified that he knew that Mr. Parsells occupied this position and admitted that in so doing he was violating the Civil Service law, and that his two positions were incompatible.

Whether there was any connection of cause and effect between the secret and unlawful employment of Mr. Parsells by the City, and the discrepancies and irregularities brought out by the testimony, is a matter of deduction. It is a fact that the Civil Service law was being inefficiently administered in Jersey City and in Hudson County and that Mr. Parsells, responsible for the routine of the Hudson County zone office, was himself violating the Civil Service law for his own profit with the connivance of Jersey City officials.

The evidence showed a lack of cooperation and coordination between the Trenton office and the various zone offices and that there was no adequate supervision or control of the various zone offices by the Board of Civil Service Commissioners, as a whole.

The Commission has published no report since 1923 containing complete or satisfactory data as to the numbers of employees and the amounts of the payrolls in the municipalities and counties where the law applies. Statistical data of this kind are important and if maintained from year to year they would furnish valuable information to public officials and to the public about the increase in the number of public employees and the growing cost of city and county administration. In rendering its report, such figures as to the growth of the State service are given. No figures of value as to the municipalities and counties are published.

It is stated in subsequent reports that data for the cities and counties are unavailable and this is significant. The place to get this kind of information is from the payrolls or the records in the zone offices. If this information is not available, it should be. Here too the zone system has broken down.

The annual reports of the Commission frequently refer to the classification of positions in the city and county services. The Civil Service law provides that such classification of positions shall be made for each county and city service and that uniform salary schedules shall be prepared and submitted to the various city and county authorities. It cannot be determined from the annual reports of the Commission for what cities and for what counties such a classification of salary schedules has been worked out and presented. The Committee is informed that no such classification and salary schedule scheme has been prepared for either Hudson County or Jersey City. The rules of the Commission show that there is authority for a different and what appears to be a useless plan of grading positions according to the salary which happens to be paid. The law makes it the duty of the Commission to provide a classification and to suggest salary schedules for all the cities and counties in which the law applies. This duty, imposed upon the Commission by law, has not been performed in Hudson County or in Jersey City.

The Civil Service law was originally adopted in 1908. Since then it has been amended and supplemented scores of times with resulting confusion. The law as it now stands provides one system of administration for the State service and another substantially different for the city and county service. As pointed out under the title, "PAYROLL PADDING," there is nothing in the law that gives authority to the Commission to disapprove the creation of a new position, or a hundred new positions for that matter in any department, or division of the Government even though there is the clearest kind of evidence that the position or positions are not required to carry on necessary public business.

The Civil Service law should be rewritten and codified.

Responsibility for administration should be centered in the chief executive officer of the Commission. His authority and responsibility should be similar to that of the Commissioner of Education, and the activities of the Commission should be limited to matters of policy and appeals from removal and investigations.

The Committee recommends that legislation be enacted prohibiting the practice heretofore existing by which each zone office is virtually an independent unit and requiring that the Board function as an administrative body through the concerted action of all of its members directing, controlling and supervising the operations of the zone offices; providing that the Civil Service Commission be limited to the determination of matters of policy, to the hearing of appeals, and to conducting investigations and rendering decisions thereon; providing that the chief executive officer of the Commission be given the authority and charged with the responsibility of administering the Civil Service law in accordance with policies established by the Commission, and that he be placed in charge of the technical and professional administrative work in both the Trenton office and in such zone offices as may be maintained, and that the Civil Service law be rewritten, so that it be one comprehensive document.

BUS FRANCHISE FEES

Testimony was taken with reference to the failure of bus operators to report correctly their gross receipts, as required by Section 3 of the Kates Act, as amended by Chapter 144 of the laws of 1926, particularly operators on the Bergen Avenue line and the Central Avenue line in Jersey City.

The testimony showed that the operators on these lines habitually under-reported their gross receipts.

An audit of the records of these two lines was made for the Committee by J. Emory Mills, of Mills & Company, Public Accountants and Auditors of 42 Broadway, New York City. The records for the four weeks ending September 29, 1928, were available and disclosed that the gross receipts for that period were under-reported. Some prior records had been destroyed, but enough remained to show that the gross receipts of the operators of these two lines were grossly under-reported for the four years beginning January 1, 1925.

The gross receipts of the Bergen Avenue line for the four weeks ending September 29, 1928, amounted to $40,399.91, of which only $25,706.27 was reported.

On the Central Avenue line for the same period the gross receipts amounted to $28,366.41, of which only $20,180.20 was reported.

From available records and information for the first eight months of 1928, it appeared that the gross receipts of the Bergen Avenue line were at least $331,218.29, of which only $155,632.60 was reported, a loss to the City in taxes of $8,789.19. The average gross receipts for the first eight months of 1928 were at least $40,000 a month. Applying this monthly average for the period between January 1, 1925, and ending September 1, 1928, the underpayment of taxes on this line amounted to $46,963.76.

From available records and information it appeared that the gross receipts for the Central Avenue line for the first eight months of 1928, amounted to at least $233,784.14, of which only $123,645.38 was reported. The monthly average of gross receipts for this period on this line was at least $29,000. Assuming this amount as the average monthly receipts for the period beginning January 1, 1925, and ending September 1, 1928, the underpayment of taxes for this line amounts to at least $32,218.40.

The evidence shows that the bus operators on these two lines made no effort to report accurately their gross receipts as required by the statute. Officials of the lines admitted that the gross receipts reports were mere estimates. In many cases the operators of different buses reported identical gross receipts for the same month. For instance, the operators of twelve different buses on the Bergen Avenue line reported gross receipts for the month of April, 1928, of $420.40 for each bus. In each case the affidavits attached to the report were taken by Charles A. Tattem, a clerk in the Jersey City Jitney Bureau. Many instances of this kind were found. It is so incredible that so many buses could give gross receipts of identical amounts that the possibility of coincidence is eliminated. The only inference that can be drawn is that there existed a conspiracy to defraud the City.

• • •

The City employed a staff of twelve inspectors and starters whose duty it was to inspect the buses for cleanliness and safety. No effort was made by the City to check the number of passengers carried or the receipts, as is done by private corporations. There was a complete lack of effort to safeguard the interests of the City, the officials in charge wilfully shutting their eyes to prima facie evidence of false reporting of gross receipts, sufficient to arouse in the mind of any reasonable and honest man strong suspicion of wrongdoing—certainly sufficient to put any honest public employee upon inquiry. The inspectors could have checked the collections, in addition to their other duties. Had this been done the interests of the City would have been protected without additional cost.

• • •

CAMPAIGN CONTRIBUTIONS

The testimony shows that in Hudson County, Jersey City and Hoboken, a pro rata part of the salaries of public employees, not holding appointive offices, the terms of which are fixed by law, is systematically collected for campaign purposes. The Committee was unable to ascertain the ultimate depository of this fund from which it is finally disbursed. Retired police officers testified they contributed to this fund a portion of salary increases which they received, pursuant to legislative enactment, and also made regular, periodic contributions to campaign funds. Several employees testified to the payment of three per cent of their annual salary.

Having in mind the amount of the Hudson County and Jersey City payroll, more than $13,000,000 per annum, it is at once apparent how inimical it is to the public interest that so huge a fund should be collected each year and disbursed by officials who render no accounting and are subject to no audit. This system is a violation of Section 406 of the Election Law, which reads as follows:

No holder of any public office or position not filled by election by voters shall contribute to the nomination or the election of any person to public office or position; provided that this prohibition shall not apply to any person holding an appointive office or position, the term of which is fixed by law. No person shall invite, demand or accept payment or contributions from such persons for campaign purposes.

The Committee makes no recommendation of further legislation under this title because the statute law above cited applies.

. . .

MOVING PICTURE THEATRE COLLECTIONS

The moving picture theatres in Hoboken and Jersey City pay large amounts in connection with the non-enforcement of Sunday closing laws.

Samuel Tammen testified that he collected $5,400 per year from eight theatres in Hoboken, as the agent of John Delaney, inspector of licenses in Hoboken, and paid the sum collected to him.

In Jersey City, Joseph E. Bernstein was the collector. He collected between $50,000 and $60,000 per year.

Frederick H. Mertens, a theatre owner, testified that he attended a meeting of theatre owners at Joseph E. Bernstein's office in January, 1924. Up to that time the Sunday closing law had been enforced. Bernstein informed the owners present that if they wanted to be open on Sundays it would cost money, and read a list of the amount that each owner would be required to pay. The payments began under this plan and immediately thereafter and ever since Sunday opening has been permitted.

Bernstein's bank accounts were examined from which it was learned that he collected between $50,000 and $60,000 per year, for the period beginning January, 1924, and ending September, 1928.

The bank records however, did not show the disposition of this fund.

This Committee tried diligently to learn how Bernstein distributed these funds. His financial records were subpoenaed. He produced two suit cases full, in response to the subpoena, omitting, however, the check books of the special accounts in which the movie collections were deposited. He testified that those check books were lost and that he could not find them.

He said that $30,000 was paid each year, in cash, to Max Steuer, a New York lawyer, for legal services, $10,000 per year in cash to Roger Boyle, Chief of the Jersey City Fire Department, as a contribution to the Christmas Fund, which is collected each year by the Jersey City Fire Department, and was unable to account in any way for the remaining amount collected by him, more than $10,000 per year.

There was also evidence that Roger Boyle had collected a large sum, $12,500, from the Academy of Music, a moving picture theatre in Jersey City.

James A. Butler, a Jersey City attorney, testified that he had been informed by the officers of the company operating the theatre that this money had been paid at the rate of $325 a week by checks which were still in existence. The Committee subpoenaed the financial records of the operating company. Jack Finkelstein, secretary of the company, responded to the subpoena and testified that all of the financial records of the company during the period in question had been destroyed.

In several cases it was testified by the operators of moving picture theatres that their records had been lost, destroyed or stolen. This condition very much hampered the work of the committee.

The committee also took testimony with reference to the Christmas Fund collected by the Fire Department of Jersey City each year, to which Bernstein's payments were made. This fund was in charge of Roger Boyle. So far as the Committee has been able to learn, this fund is collected in cash and no record is kept of its disbursement, no audit of it is made and no account is rendered to anyone. Roger Boyle has been out of the State of New Jersey since September, 1928, about the time that the Committee's investigation into these matters began. He left Jersey City on sick leave. The Committee has been unable to learn where he has received medical treatment and, if so, from whom, or whether he has been treated in any hospital or sanitarium. Mayor Hague testified that he saw him in Miami in February, 1929.

Max Steuer, the New York lawyer to whom Bernstein made his payment, although requested to do so, has failed to appear before the Committee for examination with reference to the sum of $120,000 alleged by Bernstein to have been paid to him. If there is any documentary evidence of these payments in Steuer's possession, it would tend to support Bernstein's story. His failure to appear, therefore, impeaches Bernstein's credibility.

The loss of Bernstein's records—if they are indeed lost, the destruction of the Academy of Music records, if they were in fact destroyed, the disappearance of Roger Boyle coincidentally with the beginning of this inquiry and his continued absence from the state without letting the Committee know where he has been or what he has been doing, the lack of any adequate accounting of the funds ostensibly collected for charity and disbursed by Roger Boyle; the failure of Max Steuer to appear before the Committee to testify as to what he did in return for the $120,000 alleged to have been paid to him, and what disposition he made of the money; and the payments by Bernstein to Boyle and Steuer in cash money, lead irresistibly to the conclusion that there lies back of these incriminating facts an unlawful conspiracy, and that records are "lost" and witnesses stay out of the jurisdiction because the production of the records and the appearance of the witnesses would incriminate someone.

· · ·

The Committee recommends at this time, however, that legislation be enacted making it unlawful for public officials, or employees, in their official capacities to collect and distribute funds for charitable purposes.

Such a practice helps to build up a partisan political machine under the control of the party in power—in the case under discussion, the Committee believes that it has been used to that end—and therefore is contrary to the public interest. Charitable work of this kind might better be left to non-political organizations, religious, fraternal, and social, of which there are many eager and willing to act.

• • •

BOULEVARD BRIDGE

The Journal Square improvement in Jersey City was made at a total cost of $3,162,021.42, the construction work cost $1,643,574.87, of which Stillman, Delehanty, Ferris Company, the principal contractor received $1,409,392.76.

The president of the Stillman, Delehanty, Ferris Company was John J. Ferris, President of the Board of Education of Jersey City, he having been appointed a member of the Board by Mayor Frank Hague, and William R. Delehanty was the treasurer. Mr. Ferris died while the work was in progress.

There was submitted in evidence three pocket diaries which had been kept by John J. Ferris, and a memorandum writing in lead pencil, of which the following is a copy:

Boulevard Bridge.

Hague & Freeholders	200,000.
O'Marra	10,000.
Mitchell	50,000.
Cohen—Changed by H. & Cohen 3/13/24 to 15,000 from 25,000	25,000.
Radigan	5,000.
	290,000.

Elbridge W. Stein, a handwriting expert, testified that the writer of the diaries was the writer of the memorandum, from which the Committee concluded that John J. Ferris was the writer of the memorandum.

• • •

Counsel for the Committee testified that in his official capacity, representing the Committee he interviewed Mr. Lynch on September 13, 1928, and that Mr. Lynch told him that it was the practice of Stillman, Delehanty,

Ferris Company to create a cash fund by means of a fictitious payroll; that there appeared on the payroll the names of persons who were not in fact employees; that payroll envelopes containing wages appearing on the books of the company to have been earned by these fictitious employees were made up in regular course; that the money purporting to be the wages of these fictitious employees was not delivered, the persons named on the envelopes not being in existence, and was disposed of in some way of which Mr. Lynch had no knowledge.

The Committee endeavored to learn whether there was any connection between this fictitious payroll and the memorandum above referred to. Lynch issued newspaper statements from his refuge in New York City, denying the statements attributed to him by counsel of the Committee, but notwithstanding a written request to do so, he failed to appear for examination.

Frank Hague was examined as to his connection with the transaction, his name appearing on the Ferris memorandum. He showed that after the introduction into evidence of the Ferris memorandum he sent to Mr. Stein for his expert opinion a letter bearing a forged signature, John J. Ferrigno, and a part of an authentic signature made by John J. Ferris, to wit, "John J. Ferri." Mr. Stein was asked whether, in his opinion, the writer of the forged signature "John J. Ferrigno" also was the writer of the standard "John J. Ferri." Mr. Stein gave it as his opinion that the same person wrote both signatures, in which he was mistaken if Mr. Hague's statement of the fact is correct. Mr. Hague asserted that the memorandum was the fabrication of the former Chairman of this Committee and its counsel, and denounced them as frauds.

. . .

JERSEY CITY HOSPITAL

Jersey City maintains a municipal hospital at an annual expense of approximately $1,000,000, with a total revenue of approximately $50,000. Jersey City gives free medical and hospital service of approximately $950,000 per year.

The hospital is a well conducted institution.

There is virtually no effort made to ascertain whether patients at the hospital are able to pay for the service which they receive. There is no investigation of their ability to pay. An investigation made by the Committee shows that a considerable proportion of the patients treated at the hospital are able to pay for their care and treatment.

In effect, the expense of treating these patients is paid for by other taxpayers.

The Committee makes no recommendation under this title. The policy of treating patients financially able to pay at the expense of other taxpayers is one which should be left to the governing body of the city.

GAMBLING

The Committee investigated race track gambling conditions in Jersey City, and found that Jersey City occupies an important place in that business. The evidence disclosed the existence of several pool rooms with elaborate telephonic equipment. One pool room conducted by Samuel A. Mateer, is the center of a system by which information is relayed to various other points in Jersey City and Hoboken. Mateer left New Jersey and has remained outside the jurisdiction during the progress of this investigation. Other places were found to be connected by wire with various cities throughout the country, in the neighborhood of important race tracks.

The Committee was not interested in race track gambling *per se*, which is purely a police problem. The Committee endeavored to ascertain whether this system is politically protected, and if so, to what extent and by what means it is arranged. Beyond the inference that pool rooms with elaborate telephonic connections with nearby points and distant cities cannot carry on extensive business without the acquiescence or connivance of the police authorities, the investigation of the Committee on this point was fruitless.

MAYOR HAGUE

The Committee conducted an exhaustive investigation in an effort to ascertain whether Frank Hague, Mayor of Jersey City and the leader of the political organization which controls Jersey City and Hudson County, profited personally as a result of the extravagance, inefficiency and political and governmental practices hereinbefore referred to.

Mr. Hague has been a member of the City Commission since 1913 and has been Mayor since 1917. His highest salary has been $8,000 per annum. He testified that he has had no other gainful occupation.

The testimony showed that it has been Mr. Hague's custom to carry on his business dealings in cash through dummies, avoiding check books, banks and usual business practices in his larger transactions.

In 1918 or 1919 he acquired for $12,000 a part of the property on which was afterwards built the apartment house, in which he resides in Jersey City. The consideration was paid by John Milton's check. Mr. Hague reimbursed Mr. Milton in cash.

In 1921, Mr. Hague bought the remainder of the land upon which Duncan Hall stands for $51,000. The consideration was paid by John Milton's check and Mr. Hague reimbursed him in cash.

The Duncan company was organized and built the Duncan Hall apartments on this tract. Mr. Hague received $65,000 in stock of the Duncan Company for this land and in further consideration thereof, has since occupied, rent free, an apartment, the rental value of which is $7,000 per year.

On May 3, 1921, Mr. Hague acquired a property at Deal, New Jersey, for which he paid $18,000. The title was taken in John Milton's name, the purchase price was paid by John Milton's check and Mr. Hague reimbursed Mr. Milton in cash.

On July 18, 1921, Mr. Hague bought one hundred and fifty shares of stock in the First National Bank of Jersey City from Edward I. Edwards for $37,500, which he paid in cash money.

On July 21, 1922, Mr. Hague acquired one hundred shares of stock of the Trust Company of New Jersey, by subscribing to rights originally in the name of a deceased stockholder for which he paid $34,500.

On June 16, 1923, he purchased a property at Deal, New Jersey, in the name of John J. McMahon, as a dummy, for $30,000. The purchase price was paid by John Milton's check and Mr. Hague reimbursed him in cash.

In 1924, Mr. Hague was assessed $12,000 as a stockholder in the Duncan Company. The assessment was paid by John Milton's check. Mr. Hague reimbursed him in cash.

In 1926, Mr. Hague acquired property on Gifford Avenue, Jersey City, at a cost of $27,500. The title was taken in the name of Thomas McNulty, as a dummy, and the purchase money was paid by John Milton's check. Mr. Hague afterwards reimbursed him in cash.

On June 9, 1926, Mr. Hague acquired thirty-four shares of Trust Company of New Jersey stock for which he paid $8,464.

On October 11, 1926, Mr. Hague purchased property at Deal, New Jersey, in John Milton's name as a dummy. The purchase price was $65,000. Mr. Milton paid it with his check. Mr. Hague afterwards reimbursed him in cash.

In 1927, Mr. Hague improved the property at Deal, New Jersey, just referred to, and paid to the contractors $59,520.50. These payments were made by John Milton's checks as the work progressed. Mr. Hague reimbursed him in cash. Mr. Hague personally paid one of the contractors $600 in cash for some extra work.

In 1927, Mr. Hague acquired thirty-four shares of Trust Company of New Jersey stock for which he paid $10,150 and later in the same year thirty-four shares of stock in the same bank for which he paid $13,676. In June, 1928, he purchased one hundred and thirty-five shares of the same bank stock for which he paid $13,500.

These transactions total $392,910.50. Omitting the first item, the transactions for the seven years, 1921 to 1928, amount to $380,910.50.

It also appeared that the taxes on the Deal property were paid in part in cash and in part by Mr. Milton's check, for which he was reimbursed in cash.

He rented one of his Deal properties to Michael Scatourchio, holder of the garbage and refuse collection contract in Jersey City, who paid his rent, $2,000 per annum, in cash.

The Committee interrogated Mr. Hague and asked him whether the facts just related, which had been testified to by other witnesses, were true, and if true, where he got the money, why he acquired property through dummies, why he used cash money instead of checks, why he avoided banks, why he failed to keep financial records and similar questions. He refused to answer these questions on the ground that they related to his private affairs and that the Legislature had no constitutional right to interrogate him as to those matters.

It is the Committee's view that, inasmuch as Mr. Hague has been a public office holder through the years covered by this investigation with no other gainful occupation and has been Mayor of Jersey City and leader of the political party in power in Hudson County, it is properly a matter of public interest whether Mr. Hague amassed his wealth by means of the practices and conditions set forth in this report.

The Committee recommends that appropriate action be taken by the Legislature to test the validity of these questions and if found to be valid, to compel Mr. Hague to answer them.

II The Dynamics of Urban Reform

Few subjects in American history have inspired more interpretive controversy than the origins, activities, and consequences of "reform" during the periods known as the "Gilded Age" and the "Progressive Era." The literal weight of words and pages on this single topic would, in fact, almost equal the bulk of recent scholarly literature on the Civil War. It would thus be impossible to attempt a comprehensive review of "reform" at this point, and unfair to present any one or two interpretations as definitive, since historians disagree so widely on many of the principal issues.[1] The purpose of these brief introductory remarks, therefore, is to acquaint the reader in a general way with some of the major theories of "reform" in the years from 1880 to 1920, especially as they relate to urban politics.

Reform can, perhaps, be initially viewed as any change or demand for change in existing social, economic, and political conditions with a view toward the improvement of those conditions. Beyond this vague and more or less all-encompassing definition, however, variety and profusion rather than unity or consistency have characterized the American quest for change. Reformers during the years from 1880 to 1920 supported different goals, ideals, and methods, drew upon varied bases of support, and agreed upon no one ideology or platform. Furthermore, reformers as a whole were not grouped under a permanent leadership, organized into a single political party, or effectively united in any single disciplined organization. Consequently, "reform" was in reality a heterogeneous, evolutionary process that reflected the hodge podge of ideas and often contradictory elements which composed it. Some recent historians, impressed by this diversity, have begun to balk at the use of such terms as *progressive* and *movement*—even the term *reformer* itself—as implying a degree of unity and consistency that did not exist. Indeed, if there is any single notion that has emerged from the recent literature on the subject, it is that substantial change was achieved only by coalitions of various political and socioeconomic groups, coalitions which varied widely in composition and duration depending on the specific situation, and from city to city and region to region.

Reform in the Gilded Age (roughly the last three decades of the nineteenth century) has usually been discussed in terms of middle- and upper-class elite groups, whose members sought to exert control over society because they feared a loss of social deference and power, or because they felt a sense of responsibility to lead the confused masses and preserve traditional values in the face of new social and economic circumstances. Among the principal concerns of these reformers were economy, honesty, and efficiency in government, the introduction of civil service, and the preservation of the gold standard. Their failure to significantly change the social, economic, and political system has been attributed to their limited objectives, their unwillingness to work with other groups in society (especially the working classes), and their inability to come to grips with the wrenching social and economic forces of the Industrial Revolution.

The failure of the Gilded Age reformers to alleviate the problems of urban, industrial America provided an impetus, however, for other, more successful, reform efforts in the Progressive Era (generally, the years from 1900 to 1916). Unlike the Populists, whose agrarian crusades constituted the most dramatic reform surge of the late nineteenth century, the progressives were depicted by many historians as largely urban, middle-class, old-stock, Protestant, relatively youthful and well-educated. Arising from the movements for municipal reform in the 1890s, these reformers were apparently motivated by a desire to preserve and reaffirm older values, to remove the inequities of corporate monopoly, and to purify the democratic process by eliminating governmental graft and corruption. Some historians have argued that progressive reform was grounded in middle-class values, aspirations, and fears, and was the product of anxiety over the decline in social status that many middle-class Americans—caught between the growth of individual and corporate wealth on the one hand, and the rising expectations and restiveness of the lower classes on the other—experienced in the urban, industrial society that began to take shape in the years after 1880. Other scholars, however, have called attention to the participation of working- and lower-class elements, immigrants, political machines, businessmen, and corporate titans in the movement for change, suggesting that progressivism was a movement of considerable class and ethnic diversity. The middle-class background of progressive reformers has been challenged as a significant differentiating factor on the grounds that it was by no means unique to the reformers. And a few historians have even put forth the notion that progressivism was in some areas primarily rural, rather than urban, in its origins.

Clearly, the interpretive synthesis for which all historians ultimately yearn has been particularly elusive in the case of American reform in an era that appears now, more than ever, as Peter G. Filene wrote, ''to be characterized by shifting coalitions around different issues, with the specific nature of these coalitions varying on federal, state and local levels, from region to region, and from the first to the second decade of the century."[2] The challenge to historians at present seems to be not so much the construction of a new synthesis—though this is obviously important—as it is the development of precise distinctions between the myriad reform schemes, ideals, and personalities that appeared in the years between 1870 and 1920. The only major conclusions which seem fairly evident at this point are that reformers of all types were responding in various ways to the changing socioeconomic reality of American society—urbanization, industrialization, immigration, and technological innovation—and that the changes they wrought in basic American practices and institutions were less radical and fundamental than we had previously believed. The reader should be particularly alert, however, to the possibility that genuine and lasting change was possible only when supported by coalitions of varied groups welded together by self-interest or policy. Those "reform" movements in many American cities that were composed of upper- and middle-class elements and were solely motivated by a desire to do away with the political machine were able to achieve power for short periods of time, only to give way inevitably to the more organized party structures they had temporarily displaced. If new coalitions, rather than class conflict, made progressive reform possible and in many respects successful, what does this suggest with respect to the role of the urban political boss or, for that matter, the role of the social worker or the businessman?

The following selections are not intended to be representative of the multitude of historical views of urban reform, but rather to provide the reader with some sense of the relationship between progressivism and the city, and between the attitudes and social theories of many reformers and their attempts to apply these theories to the urban situation.

NOTES

[1]The bibliography of American reform in the late nineteenth and early twentieth centuries is massive. For a listing of the major secondary works on the subject, the reader is referred to the "Suggestions for Further Reading" at the end of this volume.

[2]Peter G. Filene, "An Obituary for 'The Progressive Movement'," *American Quarterly*, 22 (Spring, 1970), 20–34.

ROY LUBOVE

The Twentieth Century City: The Progressive as Municipal Reformer

Roy Lubove is professor of history at Temple University. His article, originally published in 1959, tends to group a wide variety of reformers under the single rubric "Progressive." In most cases the "Progressives" that Professor Lubove refers to are those reformers usually identified by historians as belonging to the "social justice wing" of the movement, the settlement workers, academicians, and local reformers most concerned with the existence of urban poverty and ignorance and most opposed to the consequences of economic privilege. Did these men and women look upon the city as a threat or a challenge? What, according to Professor Lubove, was the "new urban ethic" that many of these reformers advocated? What might their search for "a new instrument of control" suggest concerning their motivations, and how might it explain their urban activities in the early twentieth century? Finally, how did they conceive of their own role in the process of urban social and economic change?

John Adams once warned that "none but an idiot or madman ever built a government upon a disinterested principle." The Progressives were neither idiots nor madmen, certainly, but they did expect to build an "organic city" based upon a disinterested principle. Historians have not always recognized the importance of the organic concept as a factor in Progressive thought. Speaking of Progressivism in Memphis, William D. Miller has written:

> The movement in Memphis—and this was true of progressivism generally—had been largely a reorganization of externals, a pragmatic social patching. In keeping with its pragmatic character, it possessed no unifying philosophy. Progressivism never bothered much with defining the basic values out of which the reform movement developed, and it is this fact that accounts for its lack of penetration and its inconsistencies.[1]

The assertion that Memphis Progressivism lacked a "unifying philosophy" may be correct, but this does not justify the generalization that Progressives elsewhere ignored the quest for "basic values." On the contrary, Progressivism was often distinguished by its vision of the city as an organism which, if properly directed, would enable men to attain the good life.

Reprinted by permission from *Mid-America*, 41 (October, 1959), 195-209.

I

Lincoln Steffens, whose influential book *The Shame of the Cities* was published in 1904, did not suddenly reveal to Americans that civic virtue was absent from New York, Philadelphia, St. Louis and other cities. He simply documented what they had known for many years—that the people ruled in name only, while the political machine ruled in fact. *Apres-moi, le déluge*, Steffens might have cried after *The Shame of the Cities*. In countless magazine articles and books, his successors muckraked the American city, searching for evidence of "invisible government."

The reformers discovered, much to their horror, that the worst enemy of reform was the "respectable businessman":

> Now, the typical American citizen [Steffens had written] is the businessman. The typical businessman is a bad citizen; he is busy. If he is a 'big businessman' and very busy, he does not neglect, he is busy with politics, oh, very busy and very businesslike. I found him buying boodlers in St. Louis, defending grafters in Minneapolis, originating corruption in Pittsburgh, sharing with bosses in Philadelphia, deploring reform in Chicago, and beating good govern-ment with corruption funds in New York. He is a self-righteous fraud, this big businessman. He is the chief source of corruption, and it were a boon if he would neglect politics.[2]

The big businessman opposed reform because good government might prove incompatible with "good" business. He needed special privileges, such as a fifty-year street car franchise or a monopoly over the city's construction projects. The "boss," who controlled the political machine, could provide such bonanzas at terms more favorable to the privilege-seeker than to the city. Fred Howe's indictment of Boss Cox is a typical Progres-sive broadside describing the alliance between politics and privilege:

> Today, Boss Cox rules the servile city of Cincinnati as a medieval baron did his serfs. He rose to this eminence by binding together and to himself the rich and powerful members of the community, for whom he secured and protects the franchises of the street-railway, gas and electric lighting companies. They in turn, became his friends and protectors, and through him, and for him, controlled the press and organized public opinion.[3]

Privilege governed the American city in the name of the people. What could be done? The Progressives rejected the Mugwump solution for corrupt politics. It was not enough to "turn the rascals out" and elect "good" men in their place. The Progressives knew that spasms of civic virtue since the 1870's had indeed "turned the rascals out" in different cities. Unfortunately, the "rascals" did not stay out long, nor could the reformers accomplish much while in office. The Progressives, however, who denounced "invisible government" in the name of the people, could hardly conclude that the people did not want good government. They concluded, instead, that the people wanted it but could not get it.[4] The people must be taught how to become free.

The Shame of the Cities symbolized for a generation of reformers the corrupt alliance between politics and privilege. Progressives, deeply conscious of the poverty and the class divisions which belied the American dream of a classless, prosperous society, had a second symbol in Jacob Riis's *How the Other Half Lives*. Riis described the life of the urban poor and warned his contemporaries of a coming day of judgement:

> The sea of a mighty population, held in galling fetters, heaves uneasily in the tenements. Once already our city, to which have come the duties and responsibilities of metropolitan greatness before it was able to fairly measure its task, has felt the swell of its resistless flood. If it rise once more, no human power may avail to check it. The gap between the classes in which it surges, unseen, unsuspected by the thoughtless, is widening day by day.[5]

The Progressives warned their generation that the problem of urban poverty must be solved. If not, blood would wash the streets of the city. The poor were sure to rise one day in their righteous wrath and destroy their exploiters. "We are standing at the turning of the ways," Walter Rauschenbusch proclaimed:

> We are actors in a great historical drama. It rests upon us to decide if a new era is to dawn in the transformation of the world into the kingdom of God, or if Western civilization is to descend to the graveyard of dead civilizations and God will have to try once more.[6]

It is not surprising, given such apocalyptic visions, that Progressive urban reformers rejected the traditional American response to poverty. Poverty was too extensive to be ignored in the expectation that "progress" would automatically dispose of the problem. Similarly, urban poverty had become too ubiquitous for private charity to handle. Americans of the Progressive period had finally caught up to Henry George. They realized that poverty was not an occasional and temporary by-product of industrial capitalism. In order to achieve social justice they insisted that it was necessary for the community to regulate industrial activity.

The Progressives argued that the war against poverty was immeasurably complicated by the close relationship between poverty and immigration.

Economic reform and "Americanization" of the immigrant were insepa-rable. Immigrants, particularly newcomers from southern and eastern Europe, had to become Americanized before they could begin to lift their economic status. Conversely, something had to be done about their poverty before they could be successfully Americanized.

Poverty and immigration, political corruption and privilege—these were the evils which Progressives thought were bringing ruin upon the American city. In order to meet the challenge of the city, Progressive urban reformers were forced to reject much of the nineteenth century liberal tradition. In place of this tradition, with its emphasis on property rights, individualism and economic *laissez-faire*, many Progressives substituted a new urban ethic which I shall define as the concept of the organic city.

II

Despite the prevalent political corruption and social injustice, the Progres-sives responded optimistically to "the challenge of the city." In the words of Richard Ely:

> . . . if we look back upon past history, and ask ourselves whence the sources of the highest achievements in the way of culture and civilization, we shall find much to give us hope in the prospect of the domination of the city in the twentieth century. . . . The city is destined to become a well-ordered household, a work of art, and a religious institution in the truest sense of the word 'religious.'

Josiah Strong agreed that America's rapid urban expansion marked the beginning of a new era:

> The sudden expansion of the city marks a profound change in civiliza-tion, the results of which will grow more and more obvious; and nowhere probably will this change be so significant as in our own country, where the twentieth century city will be decisive of national destiny.

The ultimate significance of the twentieth century city, as Fred Howe suggested, was that "never before has society been able to better its own conditions so easily through the agency of government." "The ready responsiveness of democracy," Howe claimed, "under the close associa-tion which the city involves, forecasts a movement for the improvement of human society more hopeful than anything the world has known."[7]

Jeffersonians, Jacksonians and Populists had all looked upon the city with suspicion, if not hatred. For Bryan the city was an evil and unnatural excresence—simply a place where the grass would grow in the absence of vigorous farm and village life. "Virtue," Jefferson had earlier warned, would exist in America only "so long as agriculture is our principal object." "When we get piled upon one another in large cities as in Europe," Jefferson admonished, "we shall become corrupt as in Europe, and go to eating one another as they do there."[8]

The Progressives, on the contrary, were the first group in the American liberal tradition to embrace the city lovingly. They accepted the city as the potential "torch-bearer of civilization, the priestess of culture, the herald of democracy."[9] "The problem of the city," the Progressives insisted, was "the problem of civilization."[10] If the disruptive forces of urban life such as poverty and class division could be eradicated, twentieth century man could achieve a civilization superior to any in the past.

Why was the rise of the city so profound a crisis in American life? Why were the Progressives so certain of chaos and catastrophe if we failed to meet the challenge of the city? In large measure the answer lies in the fact that the Progressives straddled two worlds. One was in the process of disintegration. The other had not yet emerged in the form which they desired. The Progressives would insure a safe and orderly transition from the old order to the new—from rural, agrarian America to urban, industrial America:

> One of the keys to the American mind at the end of the old century and the beginning of the new [Richard Hofstadter has written] was that American cities were filling up in very considerable part with small town or rural people. . . . To the rural migrant, raised in the respectable quietude and the high-toned moral imperatives of evangelical Protestantism, the city seemed not merely a new social form or way of life but a strange threat to civilization itself.[11]

Our choice, the Progressives argued, lay between further disintegration and ultimate chaos, or the creation of a socially integrated and physically beautiful city.

In defining a new urban ethic compatible with their vision of the role of the city, the Progressives were forced to re-examine traditional theories concerning the relationship between the individual and society. Nineteenth century liberalism had relied upon the hand of Providence to insure social order. Americans had often assumed that unrestricted pursuit of economic self-interest would result in optimum individual happiness and social harmony. The promise of American life was automatic. Communal regulation of the divine mechanism would upset the guaranteed equilibrium.

The Progressives, however, had lost faith in the liberal creed. They challenged the assumption that "progress" was a necessary accompaniment to the unregulated pursuit of private profit. Confronted by what they thought was the disintegration of the American way of life, they could hardly embrace the doctrine of automatic equilibrium. The divine mechanism was not only upset, it was shattered. A new instrument of control was needed to replace beneficent Providence. This could only be the community.

Rejecting liberal individualism, the Progressives forged an ethic more appropriate to an industrial-urban society. They first attempted to define the nature of the city which for them was both the hope and possible nemesis of democracy. Basic to an understanding of the nature of city life, the Progressives argued, is the fact of "specialization." The city lived by the division of labor. Men developed special skills and used them to satisfy the needs of other men. No one, in urban life, was self-sufficient. The Progressives often contrasted the relatively self sufficient and independent life of the farmer against the highly specialized and dependent existence of the city dweller. Because of the inter-dependent character of city life, mutual aid and cooperation were imperative. "The very nature of city life," Delos Wilcox wrote, "compels manifold cooperations." "The individual cannot 'go it alone'; he cannot do as he pleases; he must conform his acts in an ever increasing degree to the will and welfare of the community in which he lives." [12] Fred Howe, surveying *The Modern City and Its Problems*, concluded that:

> The city can only live by cooperation; by cooperation in a million unseen ways. Without cooperation for a single day a great city would stand still. Without cooperation for a week it would be brought to the verge of starvation and be decimated by disease.
>
> The city has destroyed individualism. It is constantly narrowing its field. And in all probability, cooperation, either voluntary or compulsory, will continue to appropriate an increasing share of the activities of society. [13]

The modern industrial city, built upon a foundation of specialization and cooperation, could survive only by carefully regulating the economic activities of the individual. The amassing of population and industry in the city meant that a single individual held magnified potentialities for good and evil. The slum landlord, for example, who refused to meet minimum health standards in his tenements, caused untold misery. Under such circumstances, the Progressives concluded that "we must combine more and more and compete less and less; life is not possible to us on any other terms." [14]

The Progressives sanctioned communal control over the property and profits of the individual, not only because men were inter-dependent, but also because the city fostered irresponsibility. Men were remote from one another; they did not always calculate the consequences of their actions. When a man bought a coat made in a sweatshop, he unwittingly supported a barbaric system of economic exploitation. The food manufacturer who adulterated his product felt no guilt because he did not see the consequences of his handiwork. The widows and orphans who owned stock in a corporation were interested only in dividends. They did not concern themselves with the possibility that their dividends were created through the exploitation of other widows and orphans.

Adherents of the liberal creed had regarded government as a necessary evil at best, fit only for the role of policeman. The Progressives swung to the opposite extreme and embraced government as a positive good. They emphasized the beneficent possibilities of government to a degree unprecedented in American history. Government was the community's major instrument of control. It would protect the community against individual or group exploitation. It would actively promote the interests of all the people.

Many Progressives enthusiastically favored municipal ownership of public utilities. They justified municipal ownership on the grounds that a conflict of interest existed between the community and monopolistic capitalism. The directors of a street railway, for example, were interested in profits, not service. The right of the people to cheap and safe transportation was subordinated, under private ownership, to the right of the stockholders to maximum profits. Furthermore, private ownership of public utilities was the offspring of privilege. In order to operate a sewerage or gas plant, a special franchise had to be acquired from the city council. The efforts of businessmen to win these franchises and keep them secure from regulation was regarded by Progressives as the root of corruption in municipal government. Thus the struggle for municipal ownership was closely connected to the broader Progressive campaign against monopolistic capitalism based on privilege and political corruption.

Many of the municipal reformers, such as Tom Johnson and Fred Howe, were single-taxers. The single-taxers agreed that private owership of utilities created a conflict of interest between the public and stockholders. They agreed that municipal ownership was necessary in order to clean up municipal government. The single-taxer also insisted, however, that the community had a right to the "unearned increment" which private monopoly gobbled up. The "unearned increment," springing from the mere growth of the community, ought to return to its source; it should enrich the community rather than a few private individuals.

The revolt against liberalism, the revised theory of the individual's relationship to society and government which I have been discussing, is the intellectual basis for the Progressive ideal of the organic city. Every community, of course, is organic in the sense that all the parts are related in some fashion. Few communities, however, are organic in the sense that all the parts work together to achieve a common goal, as the organs of the human body cooperate to maintain life. The latter concept of organic, which implies purposive cooperation and not merely random relationship, was what the Progressives had in mind. In the organic city, men would define common goals and cooperate to realize them. Individual and group activity would be judged in relation to their contribution to the common good. "But always the people remain," Brand Whitlock once wrote, "pressing onward in a great stream up the slopes, and always somehow toward the light. For the great dream beckons, leads them on, the dream of social harmony always prefigured in human thought as the city."[15]

In the organic city, the community was to be consciously and deliberately "organized for the higher and more comprehensive purpose of promoting the convenience, the comfort, the safety, the happiness, the welfare, of the whole people."[16] America had blindly stumbled into urban life. This urban civilization held great promise for good if controlled and directed. It threatened destruction if left to itself. In short, the organic community was the essence of the new urban ethic. Government, transformed from "an agency of property" into an "agency of humanity," would translate the desire for an organic city into action:

> The life of the individual must be brought into organic and vital touch with the life of the community. The citizen must think of the city as far more than a protector of person and property. In his mind, the city must be associated with a large group of services upon the efficiency of which the maintenance of his standard of life depends.
>
> All this involves a wide extension of municipal functions: the creation of a new city environment.[17]

The organic city, devoted to the service of all the people, would restore the social harmony once guaranteed by the invisible hand of Providence.

III

The American Institute of Social Service published, in 1906, the results of a survey concerning the church affiliations of social reformers. Questionnaires were sent to 1,012 individuals. Of this number, 401 were connected with charity work, 339 with settlements, 272 were connected with various national reform organizations. Eight hundred and seventy-eight of the 1012 reported on religious affiliation. Significantly, only fifteen per cent of these were non-Protestant.[18] In order to understand more fully the Progressive vision of the organic city, it is necessary to examine in detail the religious ethos which inspired it.

Fred Howe, in his *Confessions*, tried to explain the moral impulse which guided the conscience of his generation. "Physical escape from the embraces of evangelical religion," Howe wrote, "did not mean moral escape."

> From that religion my reason was never emancipated. By it I was conformed to my generation and made to share its moral standards and ideals. It was with difficulty, that realism got lodgment in my mind; early assumptions as to virtue and vice, goodness and evil remained in my mind long after I had tried to discard them. This is, I think, the most characteristic influence of my generation.[19]

Although the agrarian, Protestant world of the Progressives was dissolving, it is important to understand that the Progressives did not reject the agrarian, Protestant values. Their object was to adapt those values to urban life—to insure the safe transition of these values from one environment to another.

Progressive municipal reformers complained that an exaggerated "materialism" had betrayed Americans into neglecting their highest responsibilities and endangering their secular souls. They had worshipped Mammon and had forgotten their obligations to their fellow men. A necessary prelude to the creation of the organic city was a *renaissance* of moral instinct. Men's latent moral idealism would effect an inner transformation, a transvaluation of values. The spirit of service and sacrifice would replace the will-to-power and the will-to-profits. The fundamental brotherhood of man would be revealed as men subordinated superficial differences and proved their essential unity by cooperating to substitute order for chaos in the city. In the words of Josiah Strong:

> Society is beginning to arrive at self consciousness; that is, it is beginning to recognize itself as an organism whose life is one and whose interests are one. . . .
> There are two laws fundamental to every living organism, which must be perfectly obeyed before society can be perfected; one is the law of service, the other that of sacrifice.[20]

There was a third law still more important—the law of love. The law of love "vitalizes the other two." "To him who loves," Strong announced, "service is its own reward, and sacrifice is privilege."[21]

In striving to create a "union of all the people, seeking in conscious ways the betterment of human conditions,"[22] the Progressives exemplified the Protestant "moral athlete." Teach men the truth about politics, poverty and other urban evils, the Progressives preached. Once the truth was known and conscience aroused, then man's instinctive moral idealism would rouse his will to action. By sheer force of will, he could generate the internal reformation so basic to the creation of the organic city.

The Progressives did not believe that social disorder and misunderstanding developed from limitations in man's nature. Conflict and chaos could not be ascribed to "inherent defects" in man. Indeed, social disequilibrium was a departure from the "wisdom of God's plan." "Is there not truth," Howe asked, "in the suggestion that society itself is responsible for the wreckage which industry has cast upon our shores? Are not poverty and the attendant evils of ignorance, disease, vice, and crime the children of our own flesh and blood."[23] If there was tumult in the city, then we alone were the "architects of our own misfortunes." We had worshipped Mammon, and thus sanctified a sordid commercialism oblivious of human rights and needs. It was not surprising that our cities grew unplanned and impervious to the comfort and happiness of the people. The philosophy of entrepreneurial "individualism" had protected the "rights" of the tenement landlord, but not those of his poverty stricken tenants. "Individualism" insured to the directors of a street railway the right to exploit their employees and the public, while the city looked on helplessly. We had, in short, permitted an irresponsible commercial ethos to govern our activity and shape the institutions which now exploited us. By force of will, we could alter both the ethos and the institutions.

The Progressive organic city, characterized by the spirit of service, sacrifice and love, was nothing less than God's Kingdom-on-Earth. Just as antebellum Protestant reformers had called for the eradication of evil in order to hasten the millennium, so also the Progressives preached a millennial gospel. The evils which the Progressives faced were often different, but the apocalyptic spirit was the same. Urban reform, like abolition, was a great moral drama. In Act I the participants must become conscious of their personal guilt for the evils which surrounded them. In Act II this sense of guilt must merge with a conviction of personal responsibility for the eradication of evil. Act III would witness the transvaluation of values—consumation and salvation.

IV

Protestant moral idealism is a most important explanation for the millennial aura which envelops the organic city. Also very significant in explaining the aspirations of municipal reformers was the influence of the European municipality. Most Progressive municipal reformers were conscious of the efforts of European, and especially German and English cities to meet the problems created by rapid population growth and industrialization.

Progressive reformers like Fred Howe and Albert Shaw were greatly impressed by the European municipality. They were inspired by what they thought was the spectacle of cities dedicated to the "service of humanity." Albert Shaw's description of the German city is typical:

> The practical management of German cities proceeds in harmony with the German conception of the municipality as a social organism. . . . It is enough for us to understand that in Germany the community, organized centrally and officially, is a far more positive factor in the life of the family or the individual than in America. The German municipal government is not a thing apart, but is vitally identified with every concern of the municipality; and the municipality is the aggregation of human beings and human interests included within the territorial boundaries that fix the community's area and jurisdiction. There are, in the German conception of city government, no limits whatever to municipal functions. It is the business of the municipality to promote in every feasible way its own welfare and the welfare of its citizens.[24]

Shaw was correct in saying that the German city was a "far more positive factor" in the individual's life than in America. More debatable was his assumption that such interference developed primarily out of a tender concern for the happiness of all the people. Given their desire for order and harmony in place of ruthless economic individualism, I suspect that the Progressives confused German administrative control with the organic city. In fact, Progressive studies of the European city reveal more about the Progressives than about the European city. For this very reason, however, such works are valuable to the student of Progressive municipal reform.

The Progressives assumed that the European city illustrated the organic city in action, not only because it was ostensibly an "agency of humanity," but also because it relied so much on administrative expertise and science. Fred Howe admiringly reported that:

> The German city is a cross section of the nation. It is Germany at her best. Here, as in the army, in the navy, and the civil service, one finds the most highly organized efficiency and honesty. . . . The higher municipal offices are filled with men prepared for the

profession of administration by education, long experience and achievement.[25]

Clearly, if Protestant idealism was the heart and nervous system of the organic city, then science was its brain. Talent and intelligence would rule, they were the instruments by which the municipality would serve the people. Howe revealed:

> I cared about beauty and order in cities—cities that chose for their rulers university men, trained as I was being trained. Possibly because I was disorderly myself, I wanted order. And I hated waste. That I had been taught to esteem a cardinal sin, and American cities, I was told, were wasteful because they were ruled by politicians, whose only interest was in jobs.[26]

Sometimes, as with E. A. Ross, this Progressive faith in expertise emerged as an anti-democratic élitism:

> Politically, democracy means the sovereignty, not of the average man—who is a rather narrow, shortsighted, muddle-headed creature—but of a matured public opinion, a very different thing. 'One man, one vote,' does not make Sambo equal to Socrates in the state, for the balloting but registers a public opinion. In the forming of this opinion the sage has a million times the weight of the field hand. With modern facilities for influencing mind, democracy, at its best, substitutes the direction of the recognized moral and intellectual élite for the rule of the strong, the rich, or the privileged. . . .
> Let the people harken a little less to commercial magnates and a little more to geologists, economists, physicians, teachers and social workers.[27]

There are two important explanations for the Progressive infatuation with the expert. First, only trained intelligence could successfully cope with the complexity of an urban-industrial civilization. Science alone could transform the idealism of the new urban ethic into reality. The day of the well-rounded Jacksonian democrat was over. He was an anachronism, in government and elsewhere. The future belonged to the specialist.

In the second place, the expert was "disinterested." Remote from the mart of commerce, and the stench of the all-mighty dollar, he was devoted to his work alone. He would not promote only his interests or those of his class, but the general interest. The expert, in his selfless dedication to his work and to the commonweal, was a key figure in the organic city. The Progressive believed that this reign of "disinterested" talent typified the European city. As Shaw explained:

The conditions and circumstances that surround the lives of the masses of people in modern cities can be so adjusted to their needs as to result in the highest development of the race, in body, in mind, and in moral character. The so-called problems of the modern city are but the various phases of the one main question, How can environment be most perfectly adapted to the welfare of urban populations. And science can meet and answer every one of these problems. [This reliance upon the services of the expert] would seem to rest so palpably at the bottom of all that is encouraging and inspiring in the recent progress of municipal life in Europe that a discussion from any more restricted point of view would be well-nigh useless.[28]

The European city, supposedly devoted to the service of all the people and drawing upon the skill of the expert, offered visible proof to the Progressives that their millennial hopes were not in vain.

In summary, then, the Progressive period witnessed the growth of a new urban ethic which interpreted the city as an organism and which redefined the relationship between the individual and society. The Progressives demanded politics which were moral and disinterested, and politicians who were "social engineers." They demanded a moral consensus which stressed the spirit of service, sacrifice and love. Once such a consensus was achieved, the city would become an "agency of humanity" instead of the nemesis of democracy. In the organic city men would transcend class and ethnic differences. They would perceive and fulfill all human needs—biological, cultural, social, economic. Progressive municipal reform failed, not so much because it lacked a philosophy, but because it wove a reform program around the fragile possibility that men could transcend their "superficial" differences and cooperate in the building of the organic city, the city devoted to the deliberate "culture of life."

NOTES

[1]William D. Miller, *Memphis During the Progressive Era, 1900-1917*, Madison, 1957, 190-191.

[2]Lincoln Steffens, *The Shame of the Cities*, Sagamore Press: New York, 1957, 3.

[3]Frederic C. Howe, *The City, The Hope of Democracy*, New York, 1905, 80.

[4]For municipal reform in the 1890's see William H. Tolman, *Municipal Reform Movements in the United States*, New York, 1895.

[5]Jacob A. Riis, *How the Other Half Lives: Studies Among the Tenements of New York*, Sagamore Press: New York, 1957, 226.

[6]Walter Rauschenbusch, *Christianity and the Social Crisis*, New York, 1909, 210.

[7]Richard Ely, *The Coming City*, New York, 1902, 71-72; Josiah Strong, *The Twentieth Century City*, New York, 1898, 32; Howe, *The City*, 301.

[8]Saul K. Padover (ed.), *The Complete Jefferson*, New York, 1943, 123.
[9]Delos F. Wilcox, "The Inadequacy of Present City Government," in Edward A. Fitzpatrick (ed.) *Experts in City Government*, New York, 1919, 33.
[10]In the words of Delos F. Wilcox: ". . . if democracy fails here [in the city], the story of America will be a closed chapter in the annals of freedom." *The American City, A Problem in Democracy*, New York, 1904, 416.
[11]Richard Hofstadter, *The Age of Reform: From Bryan to F. D. R.*, New York, 1955, 175. Fred Howe, Jane Addams and Richard Ely, to name just three of the most prominent Progressives, emerge from the rural-Protestant background. Most important, all three are highly conscious of the fact.
[12]Delos F. Wilcox, *Great Cities in America: Their Problems and Their Government*, New York, 1910, 12; also Charles Zueblin: "The characteristic note of the new era is social. Individual effort is sanctioned because it promotes social welfare." "The New Civic Spirit," The *Chautauquan*, 38 (1903-04), 56.
[13]Frederic C. Howe, *The Modern City and Its Problems*, New York, 1915, 4.
[14]Washington Gladden, *Social Facts and Forces*, New York, 1897, 165.
[15]Brand Whitlock, *Forty Years of It*, New York, 1914, 374.
[16]Gladden, *Social Facts*, 163.
[17]L. S. Rowe, *Problems of City Government*, New York, 1908, 93, 94.
[18]W. D. P. Bliss, "The Church and Social Reform Workers," *Outlook*, 82 (1906), 122-125.
[19]Frederic C. Howe, *The Confessions of a Reformer*, New York, 1925, 16-17.
[20]Josiah Strong, *The Twentieth Century*, 117, 123.
[21]*Ibid.*, 127; Progressive literature is replete with appeals for service, sacrifice and love. I will quote just a few such appeals in order to capture the spirit of Progressive municipal reform:
1. Delos Wilcox: "The real character of our national mission is inconsistent with mere self seeking. Freedom, democracy, equality of rights, all speak of brotherhood and cooperation and prophesy that human nature, so cruel and selfish in its ancient and primitive manifestations, is being changed to something benevolent and social." *The American City: A Problem in Democracy*, 3.
2. Brand Whitlock: "He [Mayor Jones of Toledo] saw that the law on which the Golden Rule is founded, the law of moral action and reaction, is the one most generally ignored. Its principle he felt to be always at work, so that men lived by it whether they wished to or not, whether they knew it or not. According to his law hate breeds hate and love produces love in return; and all force begets resistance, and the result is the general disorder and anarchy in which we live so much of the time." *Forty Years of It*, 149.
3. Richard Ely: "And this development of human powers in the individual is not to be entirely for self, but it is to be for the sake of their beneficent use in the service of one's fellows in a Christian civilization. It is for self and for others; it is the realization of the ethical aim expressed in that command which contains the secret of all true progress, "Thou shalt love thy neighbor as thyself. . . ." "It is in this duty to love and serve our fellows that I find the most convincing proof of the divinity of Christ." *Ground Under Our Feet: An Autobiography*, New York, 1938, 67, 74.
4. Washington Gladden: "This battle for good government in our cities will not be won without a great deal of heroic, costly, consecrated service. It is because you and I have been so busy with our mills and our mines and our merchandise, with our selfish schemes and our trivial enjoyments and our narrow professionalism . . . and have left our one main business of ruling the city in the fear of God to those who feared not God nor regarded man, that such a great hour of darkness rests now upon our cities. *Social Facts and Forces*, 190.
5. Frank Parsons: "There is no quarrel between true individualism and the cooperative philosophy. The savage individualist of the primeval forest has of course no use for

government or cooperation of any sort. But the developed individualist of a highly civilized society is naturally cooperative to a large degree in his conduct and thought, no matter what sort of nonsense he may talk. Primitive individualism expressed itself in absolute independence; ennobled individualism just as naturally expresses itself in cooperation and mutual help; and the noblest individualism would necessarily express itself in complete mutualism or universal cooperation." *The City for the People*, Philadelphia, 1899, 237.
[22]Howe, *Hope of Democracy*, 312.
[23]Frederic C. Howe, *Privilege and Democracy in America*, New York, 1910, x.
[24]Albert Shaw, *Municipal Government in Continental Europe*, New York, 1895, 323.
[25]Frederic C. Howe, *Socialized Germany*, New York, 1915, 265.
[26]Howe, *Confessions*, 6.
[27]Edward A. Ross, *Changing America*, New York, 1912, 4-5, 106.
[28]Albert Shaw, *Municipal Government in Great Britain*, New York, 1898, 3, 4.

JACOB A. RIIS
Reform by Humane Touch

Jacob A. Riis, born in Ribe, Denmark in 1849, did perhaps more than anyone else to draw attention to the horrors and injustices of the urban slum in late nineteenth-century America. Twenty years after his arrival in the United States, Riis published *How the Other Half Lives: Studies Among the Tenements of New York* (1890), the result of his personal observations in the city as a reporter for the *New York Tribune*. Riis's book was a detailed presentation of human struggle in a degrading environment, and a plea for the destruction of the slum and its replacement with the principles of Christian love and morality.

In 1894 he wholeheartedly supported the fusion "reform ticket" headed by William L. Strong. The reformers succeeded in overcoming the Tammany Hall Democrats at the polls, and in 1895 the new mayor brought in a young Republican politician, Theodore Roosevelt, as police commissioner, and George E. Waring, a sanitary engineering expert, to head the city's street cleaning department. Riis, a close friend of both men, was especially interested in the construction of parks and playgrounds in the tenement districts. The new administration did not last long, however, and was roundly defeated in the next election by the forces of Richard Croker, partly because Roosevelt had insisted on enforcing the Sunday closing law for saloons. Though Roosevelt was elected Governor of New York in 1898, political power still seemed by the turn of the century to rest in the hands of men

From Jacob A. Riis, *A Ten Years' War: An Account of the Battle with the Slum In New York* (Boston and New York: The Houghton Mifflin Company; 1900), later reprinted as *Battle With the Slums* (New York: The Macmillan Company).

like Thomas Collier Platt, undisputed leader of the state Republican machine, and the notorious Mr. Croker.

Riis was no doctrinaire revolutionary; he essentially sought to achieve in the crowded cities the values and close personal relationships he had known in his small-town Danish boyhood. For him the solutions to urban ills were moral and personal. "When we have learned to smile and weep with the poor," he remarked, "we shall have mastered our problem. Then the slum will have lost its grip and the boss his job." In *A Ten Years' War* (1900) a portion of which is reprinted below, Riis recounted his "battle with the slum" over the course of the preceding decade and presented his major assessments of society and urban politics. What were his concepts of morality, duty, and "civic righteousness"? How does Riis view the role of the political boss? Even more important, to what extent were his perceptions of the city and its lower classes accurate, and were his reform goals and ideals practicable in the urban milieu of the late nineteenth and early twentieth centuries?

I have sketched in outline the gains achieved in the metropolis since its conscience awoke. Now, in closing this account, I am reminded of the story of an old Irishman who died here a couple of years ago. Patrick Mullen was an honest blacksmith. He made guns for a living. He made them so well that one with his name on it was worth a good deal more than the market price of guns. Other makers went to him with offers of money for the use of his stamp; but they never went twice. When sometimes a gun of very superior make was brought to him to finish, he would stamp it P. Mullen, never Patrick Mullen. Only to that which he himself had wrought did he give his honest name without reserve. When he died, judges and bishops and other great men crowded to his modest home by the East River, and wrote letters to the newspapers telling how proud they had been to call him friend. Yet he was, and remained to the end, plain Patrick Mullen, blacksmith and gunmaker.

In his life he supplied the answer to the sigh of dreamers in all days: when will the millennium come? It will come when every man is a Patrick Mullen at his own trade; not merely a P. Mullen, but a Patrick Mullen. The millennium of municipal politics, when there shall be no slum to fight, will come when every citizen does his whole duty as a citizen; not before. As long as he "despises politics," and deputizes another to do it for him, whether that other wears the stamp of a Croker or of a Platt—it matters little which—we shall have the slum, and be put periodically to the trouble and the shame of draining it in the public sight. A citizen's duty is one thing that cannot be farmed out safely;

and the slum is not limited by the rookeries of Mulberry or Ludlow streets. It has long roots that feed on the selfishness and dullness of Fifth Avenue quite as greedily as on the squalor of the Sixth Ward. The two are not nearly so far apart as they look.

I am not saying this because it is anything new, but because we have just had an illustration of its truth in municipal politics. Waring and Roosevelt were the Patrick Mullens of the reform administration which Tammany has now replaced with her insolent platform, "To hell with reform." It was not an ideal administration, but it can be said of it, at least, that it was up to the times it served. It made compromises with spoils politics, and they were wretched failures. It took Waring and Roosevelt on the other plan, on which they insisted, of divorcing politics from the public business, and they let in more light than even my small parks over on the East Side. For they showed us where we stood and what was the matter with us. We believed in Waring when he demonstrated the success of his plan for cleaning the streets: not before. When Roosevelt announced his program of enforcing the excise law because it *was* law, a howl arose that would have frightened a less resolute man from his purpose. But he went right on doing the duty he was sworn to do. And when, at the end of three months of clamor and abuse, we saw the spectacle of the saloonkeepers formally resolving to help the police instead of hindering them; of the prison ward in Bellevue Hospital standing empty for three days at a time, an astonishing and unprecedented thing, which the warden could only attribute to the "prompt closing of the saloons at one A.M."; and of the police force recovering its lost self-respect, we had found out more and greater things than whether the excise law was a good or a bad law. We understood what Roosevelt meant when he insisted upon the "primary virtues" of honesty and courage in the conduct of public business. For the want of them in us, half the laws that touched our daily lives had become dead letters or vehicles of blackmail and oppression. It was worth something to have that lesson taught us in that way; to find out that simple, straightforward, honest dealing as between man and man is after all effective in politics as in gunmaking. Perhaps we have not mastered the lesson yet. But we have not discharged the teacher, either.

Courage, indeed! There were times during that stormy spell when it seemed as if we had grown wholly and hopelessly flabby as a people. All the outcry against the program of order did not come from the lawless and the disorderly, by any means. Ordinarily decent, conservative citizens joined in counseling moderation and virtual compromise with the law-breakers—it was nothing else—to "avoid trouble." The old love of fair play had been whittled down by the jackknife of all-pervading expediency to an anemic desire to "hold the scales even"; that is a favorite modern device of the devil for paralyzing action in men. You cannot hold the scales even in a moral issue. It inevitably results in the triumph of evil, which asks nothing better than the even chance to which it is not entitled. When the trouble in the Police Board had reached a point where it seemed impossible not to understand that Roosevelt and his side were fighting a cold and treacherous conspiracy against the cause of good government, we had the spectacle of a Christian Endeavor Society inviting the man who had hatched the plot, the bitter and relentless enemy whom the Mayor had summoned to resign, and afterward did his best to remove as a fatal obstacle to reform—inviting this man to come before it and speak of Christian citizenship! It was a sight to make the bosses hug themselves with glee. For Christian citizenship is their nightmare, and nothing is so cheering to them as evidence that those who profess it have no sense.

. . .

. . . There has been a good deal of talk lately about the saloon as a social necessity. About all there is to that is that the saloon is there, and the necessity too. Man is a social animal, whether he lives in a tenement or in a palace. But the palace has resources, the tenement has not. It is a good place to get away from at all times. The saloon is cheery and bright, and never far away. The man craving human companionship finds it there. He finds, too, in the saloonkeeper one who understands his wants much better than the reformer who talks civil service in the meetings. "Civil service" to him and his kind means yet a contrivance for keeping them out of a job. The saloonkeeper knows the boss, if he is not himself the boss or his lieutenant, and can steer him to the man who will spend all day at the City Hall, if need be, to get a job for a friend, and all night pulling wires to keep him in it, if trouble is brewing. Mr. Beecher used to say, when pleading for bright hymn tunes, that he didn't want the devil to have the monopoly of all the good music in the world. The saloon has had the monopoly up to date of all the cheer in the tenements. If its owner has made it pan out to his own advantage and the boss's, we at least have no just cause of complaint. We let him have the field all to himself.

As to this boss, of whom we hear so much, what manner of man is he? That depends on how you look at him. I have one in mind, a district boss, whom you would accept instantly as a type, if I were to mention his name, which I shall not do for a reason which I fear will shock you: he and I are friends. In his private capacity I have real regard for him. As a politician and a boss I have none at all. I am aware that this is taking low ground in a discussion of this kind, but perhaps the reader will better understand the relations of his "district" to him, if I let him into mine. There is no political bond between us, of either district or party; just the reverse. It is purely personal. He was once a police justice—at that time he kept a saloon—and I never knew one with more common sense, which happens to be the one quality especially needed in that office. Up to the point where politics came in I could depend upon him entirely. At that point he let me know bluntly that he was in the habit of running his district to suit himself. The way he did it brought him under the just accusation of being guilty of every kind of rascality known to politics. When next our paths would cross each other, it would very likely be on some errand of mercy, to which his feet were always swift. I recall the distress of a dear and gentle lady at whose dinner table I once took his part. She could not believe that there was any good in him; what he did must be done for effect. Some time after that she wrote asking me to look after an East Side family that was in great trouble. It was during the severe cold spell of last winter, and there was need of haste. I went over at once; but although I had lost no time, I found my friend the boss ahead of me. It was a real pleasure to me to be able to report to my correspondent that he had seen to their comfort, and to add that it was unpolitical charity altogether. The family was that of a Jewish widow with a lot of little children. He is a Roman Catholic. There were no men, consequently no voters, in the house, which was far outside of his district, too; and as for effect, he was rather shamefaced at my catching him at it. I do not believe that a soul has ever heard of the case from him to this day.

My friend is a Tammany boss. During that same cold spell a politician of the other camp came into my office and gave me a hundred dollars to spend as I saw fit among the poor. His district was miles uptown, and he was most unwilling to disclose his identity, stipulating in the end that no one but I should know where the money came from. He was not seeking notoriety. The plight of the suffering had appealed to him, and he wanted to help where he could, that was all.

Now, I have not the least desire to glorify the boss in this. He is not glorious to me. He is simply human. Often enough he is a coarse and brutal fellow, in his morals as in his politics. Again, he may have some very engaging personal traits that bind his friends to him with the closest of ties. The poor man sees the friend, the charity, the power that is able and ready to help him in need; is it any wonder that he overlooks the source of this power, this plenty—that he forgets the robbery in the robber who is "good to the poor"? Anyhow, if anybody got robbed, it was "the rich." With the present ethical standards of the slum, it is easy to construct even a scheme of social justice out of it that is very comforting all round, even to the boss himself, though he is in need of no sympathy or excuse. "Politics," he will tell me in his philosophic moods, "is a game for profit. The city foots the bills." Patriotism means to him working for the ticket that shall bring more profit. "I regard," he says, lighting his cigar "a repeater as a shade off a murderer, but you are obliged to admit that in my trade he is a necessary evil." I am not obliged to anything of the kind, but I can understand his way of looking at it. He simply has no political conscience. He has gratitude, loyalty to a friend—that is part of his stock in trade—fighting blood, plenty of it, all the good qualities of the savage; nothing more. And a savage he is, politically, with no soul above the dross. He would not rob a neighbor for the world; but he will steal from the city—though he does not call it by that name—without a tremor, and count it a good mark. When I tell him that, he waves his hand toward Wall Street as representative of the business community, and toward the office of his neighbor, the padrone, as representative of the railroads, and says with a laugh, "Don't they all do it?"

The boss believes in himself. It is one of his strong points. And he has experience to back him. In the fall of 1894 we shook off boss rule in New York, and set up housekeeping for ourselves. We kept it up three years, and then went back to the old style. I should judge that we did it because we were tired of too much virtue. Perhaps we were not built to hold such a lot at once. Besides, it is much easier to be ruled than to rule. That fall, after the election, when I was concerned about what would become of my small parks, of the Health Department in which we took such just pride, and of a dozen other things, I received one unvarying reply to my anxious question, or rather two. If it was the Health Department, I was told: "Go to Platt. He is the only man who can do it. He is a sensible man, and will see that it is protected." If small parks, it was: "Go to Croker. He will not allow the work to be stopped." A playgrounds bill was to be presented in the legislature, and everybody advised: "Go to Platt. He won't have any objection: it is popular." And so on. My advisers were not politicians. They were businessmen but recently honestly interested in reform. . . .

I had voted on the day of the Greater New York election—the Tammany election, as we learned to call it afterward—in my home out in the Borough of Queens, and went over to the depot to catch the train for the city. On the platform were half a dozen of my neighbors, all businessmen, all "friends of reform." Some of them were just down from breakfast. One I remembered as introducing a resolution, in a meeting we had held, about the discourtesy of local politicians. He looked surprised when reminded that it was election day. "Why, is it today?" he said. "They didn't send any carriage," said another regretfully. "I don't see what's the use," said the third; "the roads are just as bad as when we began talking about it." (We had been trying to mend them.) The fourth yawned and said: "I don't care. I have my business to attend to." And they took the train, which meant that they lost their votes. The Tammany captain was busy hauling his voters by the cartload to the polling place. Over there stood a reform candidate who had been defeated in the primary, and puffed out his chest. "The politicians are afraid of me," he said. They slapped him on the back, as they went by, and told him that he was a devil of a fellow.

So Tammany came back. The Health Department is wrecked. The police force is worse than before Roosevelt took hold of it, and we are back in the mud out of which we pulled ourselves with such an effort. And we are swearing at it. But I am afraid we are swearing at the wrong fellow. The real Tammany is not the conscienceless rascal that plunders our treasury and fattens on our substance. That one is a a mere counterfeit. It is the voter who waits for a carriage to take him to the polls, the man who "doesn't see what's the use"; the businessman who says "business is business," and has no time to waste on voting; the citizen who "will wait to see how the cat jumps, because he doesn't want to throw his vote away"; the cowardly American who "doesn't want to antagonize" anybody; the fool who "washes his hands of politics." These are the real Tammany, the men after the boss's own heart. For every one whose vote he buys, there are two of these who give him theirs for nothing. We shall get rid of him when these withdraw their support, when they become citizens of the Patrick Mullen stamp, as faithful at the polling place as he was at the forge; not before.

The true work of reform is at the top, not at the bottom. The man in the slum votes according to his light, and the boss holds the candle. But the boss is in no real sense a leader. He follows instead, always as far behind the moral sentiment of the community as he thinks is safe. He has heard it said that a community will not be any better than its citizens, and that it will be just as good as they are, and he applies the saying to himself. He is no worse a boss than the town deserves. I can conceive of his taking credit to himself as some kind of a moral instrument by which the virtue of the community may be graded, though that is most unlikely. He does not bother himself with the morals of anything.

But right here is his Achilles heel. The man has no conscience. He cannot tell the signs of it in others. It always comes upon him unawares. Reform to him simply means the "outs" fighting to get in. The real thing he will always underestimate. Such a man is not the power he seems. He is formidable only in proportion to the amount of shaking it takes to rouse the community's conscience.

The boss is like the measles, a distemper of a self-governing people's infancy. When we shall have come of age politically, he will have no terrors for us. Meanwhile, being charged with the business of governing, which we left to him because we were too busy making money, he follows the track laid out for him, and makes the business pan out all that is in it. He fights when we want to discharge him. Of course he does. No man likes to give up a good job. He will fight or bargain, as he sees his way clear. He will give us small parks, play piers, new schools, anything we ask, to keep his place while trying to find out "the price" of this conscience which he does not understand. Even to the half of his kingdom he will give, to be "in" on the new deal. He has done it before, and there is no reason that he can see why it should not be done again. And he will appeal to the people whom he is plundering to trust him because they know him.

Odd as it sounds, this is where he has his real hold. I have shown why this is so. To the poor people of his district the boss is a real friend in need. He is one of them. He does not want to reform them; far from it. No doubt it is very ungrateful of them, but the poor people have no desire to be reformed. They do not think they need to be. They consider their moral standards quite as high as those of the rich, and resent being told that they are mistaken. The reformer comes to them from another world to tell them these things, and goes his way. The boss lives among them. He helped John to a job on the pipes in their hard winter, and got Mike on the force. They know him as a good neighbor, and trust him to their harm. He drags their standard ever farther down. The question for those who are trying to help them is how to make them transfer their allegiance, and trust their real friends instead.

It ought not to be a difficult question to answer. Any teacher could do it. He knows, if he knows anything, that the way to get and keep the children's confidence is to trust them, and let them know that they are trusted. They will almost always come up to the demand thus made upon them. Preaching to them does little good; preaching at them still less. Men, whether rich or poor, are much like children. The good in them is just as good as it is said to be, and the bad, considering their enlarged opportunities for mischief, not so much worse than it is called.

A vigorous optimist, a stout belief in one's fellow man, is better equipment in a campaign for civic virtue than stacks of tracts and arguments, economic and moral, are. There is good bottom, even in the slum, for that kind of an anchor to get a grip on. . . .

It comes down in the end to a question of common sense and common honesty. For how many failures of reform effort is insincerity not to blame! Last spring I attended a meeting at Albany that had been called by the governor to discuss the better enforcement of the labor laws. We talked the situation over, and Mr. Roosevelt received from those present their ready promise to aid him in every way in making effective the laws that represented so much toil and sacrifice, yet had until then been in too many instances barren of results. Some time after, a workingman told me with scorn how, on our coming home, one of our party had stopped in at the factory inspector's office to urge him to "let up" on a friend, a cigar manufacturer, who was violating a law for which the labor organizations had fought long years as absolutely necessary to secure human conditions in the trade. How much stock might he and his fellows be supposed to take in a movement that had such champions? "You scratch my back and I'll scratch yours," is a kind of politics in which the reformer is no match for the boss. The boss will win on that line every time. A saving sense of humor might have avoided that and many other pitfalls. I am seriously of the opinion that a professional humorist ought to be attached to every reform movement to keep it from making itself ridiculous by either too great solemnity or too much conceit. As it is, the enemy sometimes employs him with effect. Failing the adoption of that plan, I would recommend a decree of banishment against photographers, press-clippings men, and the rest of the congratulatory staff. Why should the fact that a citizen has done a citizen's duty deserve to be celebrated in print and picture as if something extraordinary had happened? The smoke of battle had not cleared away after the victory of reform, in the fall of 1894, before the citizens' committee and all the little subcommittees rushed pell-mell to the photographer's to get themselves on record as the men who did it. The spectacle might have inspired in the humorist the advice to get two sets made, while they were about it—one to serve by and by as an exhibit of the men who didn't; and, as the event proved, he would have been right.

But it is easy to find fault, and on that tack we get no farther. Those men did a great work, and they did it well. The mileposts they set up on the road to better things will guide another generation to the goal, however the present may go astray. Good schools, better homes, and a chance for the boy are arguments that are not lost upon the people.

They wear well. It may be that, like Moses and his followers, we of the present day shall see the promised land only from afar and with the eye of faith, because of our sins; that to a younger and sturdier tomorrow it shall be given to blaze the path of civic righteousness that was our dream. I like to think that it is so, and that that is the meaning of the coming of men like Roosevelt and Waring at this time with their simple appeal to the reason of honest men. Unless I greatly err in reading the signs of the times, it is indeed so, and the day of the boss and of the slum is drawing to an end. Our faith has felt the new impulse; rather, I should say, it has given it. The social movements, and that which we call politics, are but a reflection of what the people honestly believe, a chart of their aims and aspirations. Charity in our day no longer means alms, but justice. The social settlements are substituting vital touch for the machine charity that reaped a crop of hate and beggary. They are passenger bridges, it has been truly said, not mere "shoots" for the delivery of coal and groceries; bridges upon which men go over, not down, from the mansion to the tenement. We have learned that we cannot pass off checks for human sympathy in settlement of our brotherhood arrears. The church, which once stood by indifferent, or worse, is hastening to enter the life of the people. In the memory of men yet living, one church, moving uptown away from the crowd, left its old Mulberry Street home to be converted into tenements that justly earned the name of "dens of death" in the Health Department's records, while another became the foulest lodginghouse in an unclean city. It was a church corporation which in those bad days owned the worst underground dive downtown, and turned a deaf ear to all remonstrances. The church was "angling for souls." But souls in this world live in bodies endowed with reason. The results of that kind of fishing were empty pews and cold hearts, and the conscience-stricken cry that went up, "What shall we do to lay hold of this great multitude that has slipped from us?"

Ten years have passed, and today we see the churches of every denomination uniting in a systematic canvass of the city to get at the facts of the people's life of which they had ceased to be a part, pleading for parks, playgrounds, kindergartens, libraries, clubs, and better homes.There is a new and hearty sound to the word "brother" that is full of hope. The cry has been answered. The gap in the social body, between rich and poor, is no longer widening. We are certainly coming closer together. Ten years ago, when the King's Daughters lighted a Christmas tree in Gotham Court, the children ran screaming from Santa Claus as from a "bogey man." Last Christmas the boys in the Hebrew Institute's schools nearly broke the bank laying in supplies to do him honor. I do not mean that the Jews are deserting to join the Christian church. They are doing that which is better—they are embracing its spirit; and they and we are the better for it. God knows we waited long enough; and how close we were to each other all the while without knowing it! Last Christmas a clergyman, who lives out of town and has a houseful of children, asked me if I could not find for them a poor family in the city with children of about the same ages, whom they might visit and befriend. He worked every day in the office of a foreign mission in Fifth Avenue, and knew little of the life that moved about him in the city. I picked out a Hungarian widow in an East Side tenement, whose brave struggle to keep her little flock together had enlisted my sympathy and strong admiration. She was a cleaner in an office building; not until all the arrangements had been made did it occur to me to ask where. Then it turned out that she was scrubbing floors in the missionary society's house, right at my friend's door. They had passed each other every day, each in need of the other, and each as far from the other as if oceans separated them instead of a doorstep four inches wide.

ALLEN F. DAVIS
Settlement Workers in Politics, 1890-1914

Of all the various attempts to secure social justice in the city after 1890, none was perhaps as interesting or significant as the Settlement House Movement. Five years after the founding of the first social settlement in London in 1884, the College Settlement House was established in New York City and Hull House began its operations in Chicago. The settlement house was intended as the center of social and cultural activity in the urban neighborhood, offering a wide variety of educational and social services for the benefit of those who most needed assistance in their adjustment to the patterns of city life. The idea caught on rapidly among college students, clergymen, social scientists, and a number of others interested in social reform. Their commitment to reform was evidenced by their "permanent" residence in the urban neighborhood and by their attempts to become functioning members of the communities they sought to serve.

Between 1891 and 1910 the number of social settlements grew from 6 to more than 400, and the bulk of these were concentrated in the larger

Reprinted with permission from The Review of Politics, 26 (October, 1964), 505-517.

cities of the Northeast and Midwest. Settlement workers did not attempt, like missionaries, to proselytize on behalf of a particular religion, and unlike most philanthropists, they were not simply interested in distributing food and clothing to the poor; their principal efforts were directed toward substantial social and economic change in the urban community. Social and economic change involved politics, of course, and it was not long before settlement workers were engaged, as Allen F. Davis records in the following selection, in efforts to redress the grievances of their neighbors, efforts which often included attacks on the traditional political machines that usually relied heavily on the lower-class immigrant wards of the core city. In some cases, when local bosses were weak or ineffective, settlement workers were successful. More often they were only able to achieve at best a sort of working compromise with the machine. Their efforts in ward politics soon led them into involvement at the state and national levels, and they provided much of the membership and direction for the more radical wing of American social reform and the Progressive party of 1912.

In most respects the Settlement House Movement failed to alter fundamentally the character of the urban slum, though it should be noted that the revivification of the urban neighborhood through the services of a "community center" remains a principal goal and device of social activists today. The limitations and strengths of the movement are perhaps best revealed in the selection by Jane Addams which appears later in this section. Regardless of their successes and failures, however, settlement workers were in the forefront of urban social reform in the years after 1890, and their political activities tell us a great deal about themselves, the political machines they so often confronted, and the industrial metropolis.

Settlement workers during the Progressive era were probably more committed to political action than any other group of welfare workers before or since. Charity organization workers also cooperated on occasion in political reform projects, but Robert Hunter, the itinerant radical, settlement worker, and charity expert was probably right in 1902, even if he exaggerated, when he decided that the settlement worker and the charity worker had basically different temperaments. The charity worker was hesitant to get involved with reform, Hunter decided; he had a philosophy of "don't, don't" and was constantly troubled by the fear that his relief would destroy independence. The settlement worker, on the other hand, was more often the victim of unbounded enthusiasm than of moral questioning. "He is constantly doing, urging; he is constantly pressing forward, occasionally tilting at wind mills, at times making mistakes, often perhaps doing injury, but filled with enthusiasm, warmth and purpose, without much question."[1]

Settlement workers were usually activists. The pioneer settlement workers in the United States had enthusiasm and purpose as well as a few doubts, but they had no political theory in mind when they established their outposts in the slums. Indeed they had little interest in politics. Influenced largely by the British settlement and university extension movements, young men and women like Stanton Coit, Jane Robbins, Robert Woods, Ellen Gates Starr, and Jane Addams set out to solve the problems of industrial America by living in an urban working-class district. They sought to re-create a feeling of neighborhood in the sprawling, crowded city. They wanted to share their lives and their learning with those less fortunate, but beyond that they were not sure. They were reformers, but not political reformers in the beginning.[2]

The early settlement workers, however, soon discovered that they had invaded a political world. When Jane Robbins, Jean Fine, and the other well-dressed, young Smith College graduates began the New York College Settlement on the lower East Side in 1889 their first visitor was a local policeman who thought they were opening another house of prostitution. He stopped by to let them know that he would not disturb them as long as they made a regular monthly contribution to his income. The young settlement workers may have been shocked, but at least they learned that they could not reform the neighborhood without clashing with the existing political structure.[3]

Nearly every activity begun by the settlement workers was interpreted in political terms by the men and women in the neighborhood. Even the picture and art exhibitions that they fancied were bringing meaning and beauty into the drab lives of the workingmen seemed to one New York politician, "a cleverly disguised trick on the part of the eminent mugwumps in the University Settlement Society to get a grip on the district in the ante-election months." When the settlement workers moved from picture exhibitions and classes in Dante to attempts to improve the living and working conditions in their neighborhood they became even more aware of the political structure and of political realities. Jane Addams and the other residents of Hull House started a campaign to clean up the streets of the nineteenth ward soon after they moved to the area. At first they thought that it was a lack of knowledge about the spread of disease, and a dearth of pride in the neighborhood among the citizens, that caused the filthy streets. Jane Addams began a campaign of education, but then an investigation by Edward Burchard, the first male resident of Hull House, revealed that Johnny Powers, the shrewd and powerful ward boss, used the position of garbage collector as a political plum. One of his henchmen collected the money, but little of the garbage. Jane Addams' attempt to promote cleaner streets caused her to submit a bid for the collection of garbage in the ward, resulted in the mayor appointing her a garbage inspector, and led her eventually into two unsuccessful attempts to unseat Powers from his position as alderman from the nineteenth ward. In this instance of Jane Addams the settlement idea led inevitably to political action.[4]

Other settlement workers discovered as they tried to "re-create a feeling of neighborhood" in the industrial city that the precinct and the ward already provided one form of neighborhood organization. But not all settlement workers could agree with Jane Addams that they had "no right to meddle in all aspects of a community's life and ignore politics." Mary K. Simkhovitch of Greenwich House in New York argued that political parties did not express, in any vital way, the real interest of the citizens of the neighborhood, and that the settlement therefore ought to remain aloof from partisan politics. Robert Woods, the tall and taciturn head resident of South End House in Boston, agreed basically with Mrs. Simkhovitch. He argued that the settlement lost more than it gained by a partisan stand in local politics. He maintained that it was better to cooperate with the ward boss than to try to defeat him. Of course, the situation in Boston's ninth ward was somewhat unusual; James Donovan, the affable Irish boss, in part because he was badly in need of allies, seemed willing to cooperate with the settlement workers in making the ward a better place in which to live. Despite their statements, however, both Woods and Mrs. Simkhovitch on occasion took part in reform campaigns when evidently they felt the public's interest was being expressed by a political organization.[5]

More successful than Hull House, South End House, or Greenwich House in influencing the politics in their ward was Chicago Commons founded in 1894 by Graham Taylor. After preliminary and unsuccessful attempts to cooperate with the boss in the ward the settlement men's club managed to defeat him, and then for nearly two decades the settlement effectively controlled elections for alderman in the ward. Instead of running an independent candidate the settlement concentrated on getting good candidates nominated from the major parties. The settlement workers controlled enough votes so that their endorsement was tantamount to election. The Commons had the advantage of being located in a ward where the local political boss had little real power. But Taylor alone could not have made his settlement into a successful political machine. He was aided by a group of young, politically oriented social workers who, unlike the settlement pioneers, consciously sought to make the settlement a base for political reform in the ward and the city. Such men as Allen T. Burns, who came to the settlement after graduate work at the University of Chicago, and Raymond Robins, who wandered into Chicago Commons in 1901 after he had been a coal miner, a fruit grower, a lawyer, and minister, became experts at managing political campaigns. They made surveys, filed reports, checked for voting frauds, organized political rallies and torch parades, distributed posters and handbills. Most important they became acquainted with the people and the politicians in the ward and the city. For Burns and Robins Chicago Commons and the seventeenth ward provided practical lessons in political reform that they utilized for years after they left the settlement.[6]

Chicago had no monopoly on politically active settlement workers. James B. Reynolds, an ordained Congregational minister gave up his work for the Y.M.C.A. in 1893 to become head resident of University Settlement in New York. As early as 1896 he urged a group of social workers to "Go into politics." "Be earnest, be practical, be active," he advised: "political reform is the great moral opportunity of our day." To Henry Moskowitz politics was more than a moral opportunity; it was a way of life. Unlike most of the settlement workers Moskowitz, a Rumanian Jew, had grown up in a tenement on the lower East Side. He was inspired by classes at Neighborhood Guild and eventually became a settlement worker himself at Madison House. He battled the boss in the ward, fought for better city government, and dreamed of the day when there would be a settlement in every neighborhood in the city to counteract the influence of the political machines. Like Raymond Robins, James B. Reynolds, and Graham Taylor, he believed the settlement could become the antidote to boss rule in ward politics, and the base for political reform in the city.[7]

The politically minded settlement workers, whether they took an active part in local politics or not, learned a great deal about the nature of politics in the downtown wards of the great industrial cities. Many of them, especially Robert Woods and Jane Addams, contributed to a better understanding of city politics through their writings. They discovered, for example, that often the political machine depended upon an elaborate structure of boys' gangs, that duplicated in miniature the political organization of the city. It was from these gangs that the ward heelers as well as the bosses got their leadership experience. The political boss often remained in power, they learned, through a combination of ruthlessness and genuine neighborliness. There was an element of truth in Johnny Powers' bald statement; "The trouble with Miss Addams," he announced on one occasion, "is that she is jealous of my charitable work in the ward.'' He was a friendly visitor all right; he gave away turkeys at Christmas time, provided free passes on the railroad, bailed men out of jail, and got the unemployed jobs. There was no charge, no forms to fill out (as there always were at the charity organization society). The only thing expected in return was a vote cast in the proper way on election day. Despite the obvious corruption of the boss, no matter how he robbed the ward, he was known for his philanthropy rather than for his dishonesty. The settlement workers, however, learned from the politicans. Although they soon discovered they could not compete in handing out favors, they could emulate the politician's real concern for the problems of his constituents. They could be a little less critical of the present situation, talk less about their elaborate plans for the future, and concentrate, as the bosses did on making their reforms "concrete and human."[8]

In part because of their vantage point in a working-class neighborhood and their close observation of local politics, settlement workers often put less emphasis than some reformers on the revision of a charter or the defeat of a corrupt politician. They could appreciate the usefulness of the boss even as they were in despair at his lack of civic pride. Jane Addams decided it was not worthwhile to oppose Powers after he had twice defeated her candidate. Most settlement workers soon realized that, even if it were possible to defeat the local boss, it was impossible to accomplish much in one ward. For this reason they were often active, though somewhat cautious, participants in a variety of municipal reform campaigns, especially in Boston, New York, and Chicago.[9]

Settlement workers seldom ran for political office in the city, rather they served as campaign managers, advisors on policy, statistics gatherers, and "brain trusters" for reform administrations. In Boston in the 1890's Mayor Josiah Quincy often depended on the advice and aid of Robert Woods in attempting to provide the city with public bathhouses, gymnasia, and playgrounds. In Boston as in other cities, the settlements contributed to municipal reform by demonstrating the need for action, by initiating kindergartens, playgrounds and bathhouses, and then convincing the municipal authorities that it was the city's responsibility to take them over and expand their usefulness. In the first decade of the twentieth century Boston settlement workers played important roles in the nearly futile campaigns of the Good Government Association to bring honesty and reform into the city government. In the reform campaign of 1909-10 four young men closely associated with South End House virtually ran the unsuccessful campaign of James J. Storrow. One served as his campaign manager, another as his assistant campaign manager, a third as his personal secretary and a fourth as the secretary of the Good Government Association. In the long run the settlements' most important contribution to better city government may have been through their education of a generation of young men in the tactics of municipal reform and the training of a group of experts in city administration.[10]

In New York, James B. Reynolds was a prominent member of the Citizens Union and he was in part responsible for drafting Seth Low, the President of Columbia University and a member of the University Settlement Council, to run for mayor in 1901. Reynolds worked behind the scenes to manage Low's campaign and enlisted the support of his settlement friends, especially Lillian Wald of Henry Street Settlement, Henry Moskowitz of Madison House, and Elizabeth Williams of College Settlement, in the campaign. When Low was elected, Reynolds became his personal secretary and closest advisor. For two years the settlement workers, having a direct line to the mayor, used it to promote better housing laws, more playgrounds, and a city-supported system of visiting nurses in the public schools. Lillian Wald and the others at Henry Street Settlement were primarily responsible for the latter innovation. They had been troubled for some time by the number of children prevented from going to school because they had eczema, hookworm, or some other disease. Doctors had been inspecting the students in the city for several years, but no one made any attempt to treat the ill children. Low's reform administration only complicated a difficult situation for it made the inspection more rigorous but did nothing to treat the rejects. Because she knew Mayor Low and many other officials in his administration Lillian Wald was able to suggest a solution. She offered to supply visiting nurses who could work with the doctors and treat the sick children. Before she began, however, she made the city officials promise that, if the experiment proved successful, they would maintain it with city funds. After only one month the Board of Estimate appropriated the money to hire school nurses and soon the experiment was being copied in other cities. Lillian Wald and other settlement workers often accomplished much because they were respected and listened to by at least some of the politicians who occupied positions of power in city hall and the state capital.[11]

Sometimes the settlement worker's entry into the arena of municipal politics was concerned with opposition to a proposed measure rather than with a positive suggestion for reform. This was the case in 1905 when the settlements on the lower East Side banded together to defeat a proposed elevated loop that would have connected the Brooklyn and Williamsburg bridges. The settlement workers feared that the loop would cause needless blight and more congestion in one of the most crowded areas in the city.

They favored a subway and suggested making Delancy Street into a boulevard. Lillian Wald, Florence Kelley, Charles Stover, with help from housing reformer, Lawrence Veiller, led the campaign that helped to defeat the measure. Stover, who had spent a lifetime fighting for more playgrounds in New York, called the first meeting and enlisted the support of many organizations on the lower East Side. Sometimes the settlement workers had a difficult time convincing their immigrant neighbors of the need for opposing a ward boss or for supporting a reform bill, but this time it was easy to win their cooperation. The settlement workers organized mass meetings, sent out letters to influential people, persuaded newspapermen to present their point of view, and bombarded the city council with letters and petitions. Henry Street, College and University settlements handled most of the clerical work, gathered most of the names for the petitions and helped arouse their members and supporters to protest the measure. They had a lot of help during the campaign. One source of aid they never suspected. Only after the measure was defeated did they learn that an unknown businessman, who feared the elevated loop would ruin his business, had spent $50,000 to oppose the measure. Whether it was bribe money or the aroused social conscience of the lower East Side that caused the defeat of the elevated loop the campaign illustrates how settlement workers could organize neighborhood opinion and bring that opinion to bear on public officials.[12]

In Chicago, Graham Taylor, Raymond Robins, and an energetic group of young settlement workers, who became experts at ferreting out the records of candidates, worked closely with the Municipal Voters' League and had some success in electing honest and well-qualified aldermen to the city council. Early in the twentieth century Hull House, which Henry Demarest Lloyd liked to call the best club in Chicago, served as the headquarters for a well-organized, but futile, attempt to promote the municipal ownership of street railways. The settlement at its best became a clearinghouse for reform, and a meeting place for reformers.[13]

Settlement workers played important roles in several kinds of municipal reform campaigns. Many would have agreed with Jane Robbins; when asked why she was so interested in politics, she replied: "I never go into a tenement without longing for a better city government."[14] Most settlement workers, however, soon learned that to improve the tenements and the working and living conditions in the city it was necessary to go beyond city hall to the state capital and even to Washington. Much more important, in the long run, than the settlement workers' attempts to defeat the ward boss or elect a reform mayor was their influence on state and national reform legislation.

Robert Bremner notes the important role that social workers played in communicating to the public the great need for reform. This of course they did, but they also played a large part in the practical task of getting bills passed at Springfield, Albany, or Washington. Arthur Schlesinger, Jr., describes the "subtle and persistent saintliness of the social workers." "Theirs," he says, "was the implacability of gentleness."[15] But behind the gentleness many settlement workers were tough-minded realists who understood the way the American political system operated. It is true, of course, that they were also idealists who sometimes came perilously close to believing that, if they gathered enough statistics and found out enough information about the social evils in America, the solution would follow naturally. Yet a large number of settlement workers became experts not only at collecting statistics, but also at using them to influence public opinion and elected officials. They had learned their politics in the precinct and the ward, not from a textbook, and their experience served them well in Springfield and Washington.

The passage of a series of amendments to the child labor law in 1897 in Illinois may serve as a case in point. The amendments were drafted by Florence Kelley who, more than anyone else, led the crusade against child labor. There was little publicity or fanfare in the beginning. Florence Kelley remarked to Henry Demarest Lloyd: "We want to get them out of committee before the editorial column raises its voice in defense of the infant newsboys and the toddling 'cash' who will both come under its provisions." Persuasion was more important than publicity in the beginning. Jane Addams led a contingent of social workers, labor leaders, and enlightened businessmen to the state capital to testify before the Senate committee on Labor, to display impressive statistics, and tell human stories about the results of child labor. Alzina Stevens, a Hull House resident and also a member of a labor union, got workingmen and women to write to the members of the Senate committee. George Hooker, a settlement worker and ordained minister, got the support of various members of the clergy in Chicago. When the amendments were reported out of committee the settlement workers made sure they got the proper publicity in the newspapers. They also prepared pamphlets and scrapbooks filled with clippings demonstrating the need for better child labor laws and sent them to every member of the state legislature. The amendments passed; they did not end the problem of child labor by any means, but their passage illustrates the way settlement workers operated realistically in state politics.[16]

In New York a committee of settlement workers led by Robert Hunter organized in 1902 to protest against the incredible conditions of labor among children in the city. Florence Kelley, now in New York as general secretary of the National Consumers' League and a resident of Henry Street Settlement, along with young men and women like William English Walling, Ernest Poole, and Lillian Wald, took on the task of collecting information, arousing public opinion, and lobbying for better laws at Albany. J. G. Phelps Stokes, a wealthy, young Yale graduate and resident of University Settlement, used the staff in his father's uptown office to turn out propaganda in favor of more effective child labor laws. The New York child labor committee played an important part in the passage of a better child labor bill for New York in 1903; it also became the nucleus of the National Child Labor Committee.[17]

Just as the child labor reformers in New York began to realize in the first decade of the twentieth century that reform to be effective would have to be organized on the national level, so settlement workers in several cities began to devote more and more time to national organizations and national legislation. In addition to the National Child Labor Committee they helped to organize the National Women's Trade Union League, the National Association for the Advancement of Colored People, a national investigation of women and children in industry, and a national Industrial Relations Commission.[18] Men like William English Walling, Henry Moskowitz, and Paul Kellogg became experts at bringing the right people together and getting a program of reform organized. They worked behind the scenes and so have never received the attention from historians that they deserve. They used much the same tactics on the national level that they had perfected in the ward, the city, and the state. They gathered statistics, collected information, and then used their knowledge and influence to exert pressure on elected officials.

In 1906 when James Reynolds was in Washington lobbying for the passage of a bill that would provide for federal inspection of meat packing plants he wrote to Jane Addams asking her to "secure a strong expression of public sentiment in Chicago favoring passage of the Beveridge Amendment." Sometimes public sentiment could be effective, but often more direct tactics were needed. The next year Mary McDowell was in Washington lobbying for a bill to provide a federal investigation of women and children in industry. She wrote to Anita McCormick Blaine, the daughter of Cyrus McCormick, asking her to get letters from "conservative employers who have good conditions and are willing to have this significant subject of women in industry freed from confusion." Again in 1912 when Allen T. Burns and Graham Taylor, Jr. were coordinating a social work campaign for the passage of a bill in Congress, providing for an Industrial Relations Commission, they asked the settlement workers to get pointed letters addressed to members of the Congressional Committee from labor leaders and businessmen as well as from social workers and university professors.[19]

Despite the realistic political tactics on the local, state and national level most settlement workers were disturbed by the slow and halting nature of their attempts to humanize the industrial city. Reform administrations were rarely re-elected, and reform bills were often bypassed or ignored. They talked sometimes of the need of a great cause to unite all local efforts. In 1912 when Roosevelt bolted the Republican convention a group of social workers led by Paul Kellogg and Henry Moskowitz were ready with a platform of industrial minimums. When the Progressive Party adopted their platform, they convinced themselves that this was the great cause for which they had been waiting. Primarily because of the Progressive platform Jane Addams, Raymond Robins, Henry Moskowitz, and many other young social workers flocked to the new party and threw themselves into the political campaign. They contributed to the religious enthusiasm; they also helped in the realistic task of organizing a new party.[20] Edward T. Devine of the New York Charity Organization Society could warn that it was "the first political duty of social workers to be persistently and aggressively non-partisan, to maintain such relations with men of social good will in all parties as will insure their cooperation in specific measures for the promoting of the common good." But Jane Addams felt differently. "When the ideas and measures we have long been advocating become part of a political campaign . . . would we not be the victims of a curious self-consciousness if we failed to follow them there?" she asked.[21] To Jane Addams the settlement idea led inevitably to political action even on the national level, and there were a large number of settlement workers who agreed with her.

Of course the Progressive campaign of 1912 seemed in some ways more like a crusade than like politics and the collapse of the Progressive Party and the outbreak of World War I altered, if it did not end, the political interests of the settlement workers. After 1914 there was a little less optimism, a little less confidence that evils could be righted by gathering statistics. It was perhaps more important that, after 1914 settlement workers and other reformers became more interested in international affairs and a little less concerned with domestic reform and politics. In the twenties it was not so easy for settlement workers to have confidence in reform, and a new kind of social worker emerged who seemed to be more concerned with professional status than with political action. Something of the settlement workers' interest in political reform, something of their realistic tactics remained, of course, in the twenties and thirties, and something of that tradition survives even today, but it was in the Progressive Era that settlement workers were most concerned with political action—it was a concern that developed from their experience.²² They could not always agree among themselves, but if they took the settlement idea seriously, they became involved one way or another in politics, first in the ward, then in the city, the state, and the nation.

NOTES

¹Robert Hunter, "The Relation Between Social Settlements and Charity Organizations," *Journal of Political Economy*, XI (1902), 75-88, *Proceedings of the National Conference of Charity and Correction*, 1902, pp. 302-14.

²Robert Woods, "The University Settlement Idea," *Philanthropy and Social Progress* (New York, 1893), pp. 57-97, Cannon Barnett, *Practicable Socialism* (London, 1915); Jane Addams, "The Objective Value of the Social Settlement," *Philanthropy and Social Progress*, pp. 27-56.

³Helen Rand Thayer, "Blazing the Settlement Trail," *Smith Alumnae Quarterly* (April, 1911), 130-37; Jane Robbins, "The First Year At The College Settlement," *Survey*, XXVII (February 24, 1912), 1802.

⁴A. C. Bernheim, "Results of Picture Exhibition on Lower East Side," *Forum*, XIX (July, 1895), 612. See also Allen F. Davis, "Jane Addams vs. The Ward Boss," *Journal of the Illinois State Historical Society*, LIII (Autumn, 1960), 247-65.

⁵"Are Social Settlers Debarred from Political Work?" handwritten Ms., n.d. Mary K. Simkhovitch MSS., Radcliffe Women's Archives, Cambridge, Mass.; Robert Woods, "Settlement Houses and City Politics," *Municipal Affairs*, IV (June, 1900), 396-97.

⁶Minutes of the Seventeenth Ward Council of the Civic Federation, 1895-97. Graham Taylor MSS., Newberry Library, Chicago; see also Allen F. Davis, "Raymond Robins: The Settlement Worker as Municipal Reformer," *Social Service Review*, XXXIII (June, 1959), 131-41.

⁷James B. Reynolds, "The Settlement and Municipal Reform," *Proceedings of the National Conference*, 1896, pp. 140-42; J. Salwyn Schapiro, "Henry Msokowitz: A Social Reformer in Politics," *Outlook*, CII (October 26, 1912), 446-49; Moskowitz, "A Settlement Followup," *Survey*, XXV (December 10, 1910), 439-40.

⁸See especially Addams, "Ethical Survivals in Municipal Corruption," *International Journal of Ethics*, VIII (April, 1898), 273-91; Woods, "The Roots of Political Power," *City Wilderness: A Settlement Study* (Boston, 1898), 114-47 (probably written by William Clark); "Traffic in Citizenship," *Americans in Process* (Boston, 1902), pp. 147-49.

⁹Interview with Jane Addams, *Chicago Tribune*, Feb. 19, 1900; Addams, "Ethical Survivals," 273-91.

¹⁰Eleanor Woods, *Robert A. Woods* (Boston, 1929), pp. 119-23; George E. Hooker, "Mayor Quincy of Boston," *Review of Reviews*, XIX (May, 1899), 575-78; *Southend House Report*, 1910, p. 6.

¹¹"Reformatory Influence of Social Service Upon City Politics," *Commons*, VI (March, 1902), 3-4. Lillian Wald, *House on Henry Street* (New York, 1915), pp. 46-53. Wald to Dr. Abbott E. Kitteredge, October 29, 1903; Wald MSS., New York Public Library.

¹²James H. Hamilton, "The Winning of the Boulevard," *University Settlement Studies Quarterly*, II (December, 1906), 24-26; Lillian Wald, "The East Side in Danger," *Commons*, X (April, 1905), 222.

¹³Edwin Burritt Smith, "Council Reform in Chicago,": Work of the Municipal Voters' League, *Municipal Affairs*, IV (June, 1900), 347-62; John Commons to Henry Demarest

Lloyd, July 27, 1903; George Hooker to Lloyd, July 5, 13, 1903; Lloyd to Edward Bemis, July 30, 1903, Henry Demarest Lloyd MSS., Wisconsin State Historical Society, Madison.

[14]Jane Robbins, "The Settlement and the Immigrant," *College Settlement Association Quarterly*, I (June, 1916), 7.

[15]Robert Bremner, *From the Depths: The Discovery of Poverty in the United States* (New York, 1956), pp. 201-203. Arthur Schlesinger, Jr., *The Crisis of the Old Order* (Boston, 1957), p. 25.

[16]The quotation is from Florence Kelley to Lloyd, March 2, 1895, Lloyd MSS., and actually refers to the campaign of that year for child labor laws in Illinois. The campaign was not successful and was renewed with similar tactics two years later. Jane Addams to Lloyd, March 16, 1897.

[17]Helen Marot, "The Child Labor Movement in New York," *Commons*, VIII (April, 1903), 5-6; Interview J. G. Phelps Stokes, January 22, 1959.

[18]Alice Henry, "Women and the Labor Movement," (New York, 1930), 109; Mary McDowell, "The Need of a National Investigation," *Charities and the Commons,* XVII (January 5, 1907), 634-36; William English Walling, "The Founding of the NAACP," *The Crisis*, XXXVI (July, 1929), 226; "Movement Under Way For an Industrial Commission," *Survey*, XXVII (March 2, 1912), 1821-22.

[19]Reynolds to Jane Addams, June 7, 1906, Addams MSS. Peace Collection, Swarthmore College, Swarthmore, Penn. McDowell to Mrs. Emmons Blaine, February 9, 1907, Blaine MSS. McCormick Collection, Wisconsin State Historical Society, Madison. Graham Taylor to Graham R. Taylor, March 10, 1912, Taylor MSS.

[20]Jane Addams, "The Steps By Which I Became A Progressive," syndicated article, 1912, Addams MSS.; Paul Kellogg, "The Industrial Platform," *Survey*, XXVIII (August 24, 1912), 668-70, "Jane Addams Tells Why," *New York Evening Post*, August 8, 1912, clipping, Addams MSS.; Henry Moskowitz to Lillian Wald, August 2, 1912, Wald MSS. See Allen F. Davis, "The Social Workers and The Progressive Party, 1910-1916," *American Historical Review*, April, 1964.

[21]Edward T. Devine, "Politics and Social Work," *Survey*, XXIX (October 5, 1912), 9; Jane Addams, "Pragmatism in Politics," *Survey*, XXIX (October 5, 1912), 12.

[22]See John Haynes Holmes, "War and the Social Movement," *Survey*, XXXII (September 26, 1914), 629-30; Edward T. Devine, "Civilization's Peril," *Survey*, XXXIII (February 6, 1915), 518-19. Paul Kellogg, "To the Unfinished Work," *Survey*, XLII (July 5, 1919), 513-14. See also Clarke A. Chambers, "Creative Effort in an Age of Normalcy," *The Social Welfare Forum* (1961), pp. 252-71.

JANE ADDAMS
Political Reform

Jane Addams probably ranks as the most famous social worker in American history. Born in a small town in northern Illinois in 1860, she attended nearby Rockford Seminary and graduated in 1881. After a brief enrollment in medical school and several excursions to Europe, she decided in 1888 to establish a settlement house in a large American city. The following year

From Chapter 7 of Jane Addams, *Democracy and Social Ethics,* ed. Anne Firor Scott (Cambridge: The Belknap Press of Harvard University Press, 1964), pp. 221–238, 240–261, 262–273. (Originally published by The Macmillan Company in 1902.)

the doors of Hull House opened on South Halsted Street in Chicago, in the midst of the polyglot immigrant community of the Nineteenth Ward. The house grew rapidly in the number of its facilities and services, and the stature of Jane Addams among American reformers also increased. Often regarded as the principal spokesman for the entire Settlement House Movement, she became involved in a wide range of reform causes from garbage collection to public schools, from child labor to factory working conditions. She served on literally hundreds of committees and spread the message of her work through the publication of *Twenty Years at Hull House* in 1910, *The Second Twenty Years at Hull House* in 1930, and a number of other books and articles. In 1931 she received the Nobel Peace Prize. At the time of her death in 1935 Jane Addams was justifiably regarded as one of the most significant and respected figures in the pursuit of social justice in America.

In the course of her years at Hull House she inevitably became embroiled in local politics, an experience she later recalled as having been both terribly frustrating and highly educational, for it was in the political arena that so many of the realities of the city emerged, and it was in the local community that the settlement house sought to make its most lasting contribution. Alderman John Powers was one of the major forces in Chicago government, and the virtually undisputed leader of the 50,000 people of some twenty different nationalities who resided in the Nineteenth Ward. The residents of Hull House were understandably upset by Powers' boodling (he excelled in the sale of utility franchises) and by his failure to provide for the long-range needs of his constituents. They attempted to blunt the alderman's authority in 1895, when they succeeded in electing a member of the Hull House Men's Club to the Common Council, and in two full-scale assaults on Powers himself in 1896 and 1898. In the first instance the Hull House candidate was quickly enticed into the Powers camp, and in 1896 and 1898 the incumbent alderman handily won reelection.

In the final chapter of *Democracy and Social Ethics*, first published in 1902, Jane Addams attempted an analysis of "Political Reform," based largely on her experiences in local urban politics in the 1890s. In the portions of this chapter which follow, Jane Addams is revealed as a sensitive observer of politics in the city. Crucial to her activities were various conceptions—which she largely shared with many other middle- and upper-class reformers—of the city, the lower-class immigrant population of the Nineteenth Ward, and the political boss. What were these conceptions, and how were they related to her definition of democracy? What suggestions did she have for other reformers about the means of achieving enduring political success, and how do these compare with those offered by Jacob Riis?

Throughout this volume we have assumed that much of our ethical malad-justment in social affairs arises from the fact that we are acting upon a code of ethics adapted to individual relationships, but not to the larger social relationships to which it is bunglingly applied. In addition, however, to the consequent strain and difficulty, there is often an honest lack of perception as to what the situation demands.

Nowhere is this more obvious than in our political life as it manifests itself in certain quarters of every great city. It is most difficult to hold to our political democracy and to make it in any sense a social expression and not a mere governmental contrivance, unless we take pains to keep on common ground in our human experiences. Otherwise there is in various parts of the community an inevitable difference of ethical standards which becomes responsible for much misunderstanding.

It is difficult both to interpret sympathetically the motives and ideals of those who have acquired rules of conduct in experience widely different from our own, and also to take enough care in guarding the gains already made, and in valuing highly enough the imperfect good so painfully acquired and, at the best, so mixed with evil. This wide difference in daily experience exhibits itself in two distinct attitudes toward politics. The well-to-do men of the community think of politics as something off by itself; they may conscientiously recognize political duty as part of good citizenship, but political effort is not the expression of their moral or social life. As a result of this detachment, ''reform movements,'' started by business men and the better element, are almost wholly occupied in the correction of political machinery and with a concern for the better method of adminis-tration, rather than with the ultimate purpose of securing the welfare of the people. They fix their attention so exclusively on methods that they fail to consider the final aims of city government. This accounts for the growing tendency to put more and more responsibility upon executive officers and appointed commissions at the expense of curtailing the power of the direct representatives of the voters. Reform movements tend to become negative and to lose their educational value for the mass of the people. The reformers take the rôle of the opposition. They give themselves largely to criticisms of the present state of affairs, to writing and talking of what the future must be and of certain results which should be obtained. In trying to better matters, however, they have in mind only political achievements which they detach in a curious way from the rest of life, and they speak and write of the purification of politics as of a thing set apart from daily life.

On the other hand, the real leaders of the people are part of the entire life of the community which they control, and so far as they are representative at all, are giving a social expression to democracy. They are often politically corrupt, but in spite of this they are proceeding upon a sounder theory. Although they would be totally unable to give it abstract expression, they are really acting upon a formulation made by a shrewd English observer; namely, that, "after the enfranchisement of the masses, social ideals enter into political programmes, and they enter not as something which at best can be indirectly promoted by government, but as something which it is the chief business of government to advance directly."

Men living near to the masses of voters, and knowing them intimately, recognize this and act upon it; they minister directly to life and to social needs. They realize that the people as a whole are clamoring for social results, and they hold their power because they respond to that demand. They are corrupt and often do their work badly; but they at least avoid the mistake of a certain type of business men who are frightened by democracy, and have lost their faith in the people. The two standards are similar to those seen at a popular exhibition of pictures where the cultivated people care most for the technique of a given painting, the moving mass for a subject that shall be domestic and human.

This difference may be illustrated by the writer's experience in a certain ward of Chicago, during three campaigns, when efforts were made to dislodge an alderman* who had represented the ward for many years. In this ward there are gathered together fifty thousand people, representing a score of nationalities; the newly emigrated Latin, Teuton, Celt, Greek and Slav who live there have little in common save the basic experiences which come to men in all countries and under all conditions. In order to make fifty thousand people, so heterogeneous in nationality, religion, and customs, agree upon any demand, it must be founded upon universal experiences which are perforce individual and not social.

An instinctive recognition of this on the part of the alderman makes it possible to understand the individualistic basis of his political success, but it remains extremely difficult to ascertain the reasons for the extreme leniency of judgment concerning the political corruption of which he is constantly guilty.

This leniency is only to be explained on the ground that his constituents greatly admire individual virtues, and that they are at the same time unable to perceive social outrages which the alderman may be committing. They thus free the alderman from blame because his corruption is social, and they honestly admire him as a great man and hero, because his individual acts are on the whole kindly and generous.

*She is referring here, of course, to Alderman John Powers of the Nineteenth Ward. [Editor's note.]

In certain stages of moral evolution, a man is incapable of action unless the results will benefit himself or some one of his acquaintances, and it is a long step in moral progress to set the good of the many before the interest of the few, and to be concerned for the welfare of a community without hope of an individual return. How far the selfish politician befools his constituents into believing that their interests are identical with his own; how far he presumes upon their inability to distinguish between the individual and social virtues, an inability which he himself shares with them, and how far he dazzles them by the sense of his greatness, and a conviction that they participate therein, it is difficult to determine.

Morality certainly develops far earlier in the form of moral fact than in the form of moral ideas, and it is obvious that ideas only operate upon the popular mind through will and character, and must be dramatized before they reach the mass of men, even as the biography of the saints have been after all "the main guide to the stumbling feet of thousands of Christians to whom the Credo has been but mysterious words."

Ethics as well as political opinions may be discussed and disseminated among the sophisticated by lectures and printed pages, but to the common people they can only come through example—through a personality which seizes the popular imagination. The advantage of an unsophisticated neighborhood is, that the inhabitants do not keep their ideas as treasures—they are untouched by the notion of accumulating them, as they might knowledge or money, and they frankly act upon those they have. The personal example promptly rouses to emulation. In a neighborhood where political standards are plastic and undeveloped, and where there has been little previous experience in self-government, the office-holder himself sets the standard, and the ideas that cluster around him exercise a specific and permanent influence upon the political morality of his constituents.

Nothing is more certain than that the quality which a heterogeneous population, living in one of the less sophisticated wards, most admires is the quality of simple goodness; that the man who attracts them is the one whom they believe to be a good man. We all know that children long "to be good" with an intensity which they give to no other ambition. We can all remember that the earliest strivings of our childhood were in this direction, and that we venerated grown people because they had attained perfection.

Primitive people, such as the South Italian peasants, are still in this stage. They want to be good, and deep down in their hearts they admire nothing so much as the good man. Abstract virtues are too difficult for their untrained minds to apprehend, and many of them are still simple enough to believe that power and wealth come only to good people.

The successful candidate, then, must be a good man according to the morality of his constituents. He must not attempt to hold up too high a standard, nor must he attempt to reform or change their standards. His safety lies in doing on a large scale the good deeds which his constituents are able to do only on a small scale. If he believes what they believe and does what they are all cherishing a secret ambition to do, he will dazzle them by his success and win their confidence. There is a certain wisdom in this course. There is a common sense in the mass of men which cannot be neglected with impunity, just as there is sure to be an eccentricity in the differing and reforming individual which it is perhaps well to challenge.

The constant kindness of the poor to each other was pointed out in a previous chapter, and that they unfailingly respond to the need and distresses of their poorer neighbors even when in danger of bankruptcy themselves. The kindness which a poor man shows his distressed neighbor is doubtless heightened by the consciousness that he himself may be in distress next week; he therefore stands by his friend when he gets too drunk to take care of himself, when he loses his wife or child, when he is evicted for non-payment of rent, when he is arrested for a petty crime. It seems to such a man entirely fitting that his alderman should do the same thing on a larger scale—that he should help a constituent out of trouble, merely because he is in trouble, irrespective of the justice involved.

The alderman therefore bails out his constituents when they are arrested, or says a good word to the police justice when they appear before him for trial, uses his pull with the magistrate when they are likely to be fined for a civil misdemeanor, or sees what he can do to "fix up matters" with the state's attorney when the charge is really a serious one, and in doing this he follows the ethics held and practised by his constituents. All this conveys the impression to the simple-minded that law is not enforced, if the lawbreaker have a powerful friend. One may instance the alderman's action in standing by an Italian padrone of the ward when he was indicted for violating the civil service regulations. The commissioners had sent out notices to certain Italian day-laborers who were upon the eligible list that they were to report for work at a given day and hour. One of the padrones intercepted these notifications and sold them to the men for five dollars apiece, making also the usual bargain for a share of their wages. The padrone's entire arrangement followed the custom which had prevailed for years before the establishment of civil service laws. Ten of the laborers swore out warrants against the padrone, who was convicted and fined seventy-five dollars. This sum was promptly paid by the alderman, and the padrone, assured that he would be protected from any further trouble, returned uninjured to the colony. The simple Italians were much bewildered by this show of a power stronger than that of the civil service, which they had trusted as they did the one in Italy. The first violation of its authority was made, and various sinister acts have followed, until no Italian who is digging a sewer or sweeping a street for the city feels quite secure in holding his job unless he is backed by the friendship of the alderman. According to the civil service law, a laborer has no right to a trial; many are discharged by the foreman, and find that they can be reinstated only upon the aldermanic recommendation. He thus practically holds his old power over the laborers working for the city. The popular mind is convinced that an honest administration of civil service is impossible, and that it is but one more instrument in the hands of the powerful.

It will be difficult to establish genuine civil service among these men, who learn only by experience, since their experiences have been of such a nature that their unanimous vote would certainly be that "civil service" is "no good."

As many of his constituents in this case are impressed with the fact that the aldermanic power is superior to that of government, so instances of actual lawbreaking might easily be cited. A young man may enter a saloon long after midnight, the legal closing hour, and seat himself at a gambling table, perfectly secure from interruption or arrest, because the place belongs to an alderman; but in order to secure this immunity the policeman on the beat must pretend not to see into the windows each time that he passes, and he knows, and the young man knows that he knows, that nothing would embarrass "Headquarters" more than to have an arrest made on those premises. A certain contempt for the whole machinery of law and order is thus easily fostered.

Because of simple friendliness the alderman is expected to pay rent for the hard-pressed tenant when no rent is forthcoming, to find "jobs" when work is hard to get, to procure and divide among his constituents all the places which he can seize from the city hall. The alderman of the ward we are considering at one time could make the proud boast that he had twenty-six hundred people in his ward upon the public pay-roll. This, of course, included day laborers, but each one felt under distinct obligations to him for getting a position. When we reflect that this is one-third of the entire vote of the ward, we realize that it is very important to vote for the right man, since there is, at the least, one chance out of three for securing work.

If we recollect further that the franchise-seeking companies pay respectful heed to the applicants backed by the alderman, the question of voting for the successful man becomes as much an industrial one as a political one. An Italian laborer wants a "job" more than anything else, and quite simply votes for the man who promises him one. It is not so different from his relation to the padrone, and, indeed, the two strengthen each other.

The alderman may himself be quite sincere in his acts of kindness, for an office seeker may begin with the simple desire to alleviate suffering, and this may gradually change into the desire to put his constituents under obligations to him; but the action of such an individual becomes a demoralizing element in the community when kindly impulse is made a cloak for the satisfaction of personal ambition, and when the plastic morals of his constituents gradually conform to his own undeveloped standards.

The alderman gives presents at weddings and christenings. He seizes these days of family festivities for making friends. It is easiest to reach them in the holiday mood of expansive good-will, but on their side it seems natural and kindly that he should do it. The alderman procures passes from the railroads when his constituents wish to visit friends or attend the funerals of distant relatives; he buys tickets galore for benefit entertainments given for a widow or a consumptive in peculiar distress; he contributes to prizes which are awarded to the handsomest lady or the most popular man. At a church bazaar, for instance, the alderman finds the stage all set for his dramatic performance. When others are spending pennies, he is spending dollars. When anxious relatives are canvassing to secure votes for the two most beautiful children who are being voted upon, he recklessly buys votes from both sides, and laughingly declines to say which one he likes best, buying off the young lady who is persistently determined to find out, with five dollars for the flower bazaar, the posies, of course, to be sent to the sick of the parish. The moral atmosphere of a bazaar suits him exactly. He murmurs many times, "Never mind, the money all goes to the poor; it is all straight enough if the church gets it, the poor won't ask too many questions." The oftener he can put such sentiments into the minds of his constituents, the better he is pleased. Nothing so rapidly prepares them to take his view of money getting and money spending. We see again the process disregarded, because the end itself is considered so praiseworthy.

There is something archaic in a community of simple people in their attitude toward death and burial. There is nothing so easy to collect money for as a funeral, and one involuntarily remembers that the early religious tithes were paid to ward off death and ghosts. At times one encounters almost the Greek feeling in regard to burial. If the alderman seizes upon times of festivities for expressions of his good-will, much more does he seize upon periods of sorrow. At a funeral he has the double advantage of ministering to a genuine craving for comfort and solace, and at the same time of assisting a bereaved constituent to express that curious feeling of remorse, which is ever an accompaniment of quick sorrow, that desire to "make up" for past delinquencies, to show the world how much he loved the person who has just died, which is as natural as it is universal.

· · ·

Indeed, what headway can the notion of civic purity, of honesty of administration make against this big manifestation of human friendliness, this stalking survival of village kindness? The notions of the civic reformer are negative and impotent before it. Such an alderman will keep a standing account with an undertaker, and telephone every week, and sometimes more than once, the kind of funeral he wishes provided for a bereaved constituent, until the sum may roll up into "hundreds a year." He understands what the people want, and ministers just as truly to a great human need as the musician or the artist. An attempt to substitute what we might call a later standard was made at one time when a delicate little child was deserted in the Hull-House nursery. An investigation showed that it had been born ten days previously in the Cook County hospital, but no trace could be found of the unfortunate mother. The little child lived for several weeks, and then, in spite of every care, died. It was decided to have it buried by the county authorities, and the wagon was to arrive at eleven o'clock; about nine o'clock in the morning the rumor of this awful deed reached the neighbors. A half dozen of them came, in a very excited state of mind, to protest. They took up a collection out of their poverty with which to defray a funeral. The residents of Hull-House were then comparatively new in the neighborhood and did not realize that they were really shocking a genuine moral sentiment of the community. In their crudeness they instanced the care and tenderness which had been expended upon the little creature while it was alive; that it had had every attention from a skilled physician and a trained nurse, and even intimated that the excited members of the group had not taken part in this, and that it now lay with the nursery to decide that it should be buried as it had been born, at the county's expense. It is doubtful if Hull-House has ever done anything which injured it so deeply in the minds of some of its neighbors. It was only forgiven by the most indulgent on the ground that the residents were spinsters, and could not know a mother's heart. No one born and reared in the community could possibly have made a mistake like that. No one who had studied the ethical standards with any care could have bungled so completely.

We are constantly underestimating the amount of sentiment among simple people. The songs which are most popular among them are those of a reminiscent old age, in which the ripened soul calmly recounts and regrets the sins of his youth, songs in which the wayward daughter is forgiven by her loving parents, in which the lovers are magnanimous and faithful through all vicissitudes. The tendency is to condone and forgive, and not hold too rigidly to a standard. In the theatres it is the magnanimous man, the kindly reckless villian who is always applauded. So shrewd an observer as Samuel Johnson once remarked that it was surprising to find how much more kindness than justice society contained.

On the same basis the alderman manages several saloons, one down town within easy access of the city hall, where he can catch the more important of his friends. Here again he has seized upon an old tradition and primitive custom, the good fellowship which has long been best expressed when men drink together. The saloons offer a common meeting ground, with stimulus enough to free the wits and tongues of the men who meet there.

He distributes each Christmas many tons of turkeys not only to voters, but to families who are represented by no vote. By a judicious management some families get three or four turkeys apiece; but what of that, the alderman has none of the nagging rules of the charitable societies, nor does he declare that because a man wants two turkeys for Christmas, he is a scoundrel who shall never be allowed to eat turkey again. As he does not distribute his Christmas favors from any hardly acquired philanthropic motive, there is no disposition to apply the carefully evolved rules of the charitable societies to his beneficiaries. Of course, there are those who suspect that the benevolence rests upon self-seeking motives, and feel themselves quite freed from any sense of gratitude; others go further and glory in the fact that they can thus "soak the alderman." An example of this is the young man who fills his pockets with a handful of cigars, giving a sly wink at the others. But this freedom from any sense of obligation is often the first step downward to the position where he is willing to sell his vote to both parties, and then scratch his ticket as he pleases. The writer recalls a conversation with a man in which he complained quite openly, and with no sense of shame, that his vote had "sold for only two dollars this year," and that he was "awfully disappointed." The writer happened to know that his income during the nine months previous had been but twenty-eight dollars, and that he was in debt thirty-two dollars, and she could well imagine the eagerness with which he had counted upon this source of revenue. After some years the selling of votes becomes a commonplace, and but little attempt is made upon the part of the buyer or seller to conceal the fact, if the transaction runs smoothly.

A certain lodging-house keeper at one time sold the votes of his entire house to a political party and was "well paid for it too"; but being of a grasping turn, he also sold the house for the same election to the rival party. Such an outrage could not be borne. The man was treated to a modern version of tar and feathers, and as a result of being held under a street hydrant in November, contracted pneumonia which resulted in his death. No official investigation took place, since the doctor's certificate of pneumonia was sufficient for legal burial, and public sentiment sustained the action. In various conversations which the writer had concerning the entire transaction, she discovered great indignation concerning his duplicity and treachery, but none whatever for his original offence of selling out the votes of his house.

A club will be started for the express purpose of gaining a reputation for political power which may later be sold out. The president and executive committee of such a club, who will naturally receive the funds, promise to divide with "the boys" who swell the size of the membership. A reform movement is at first filled with recruits who are active and loud in their assertions of the number of votes they can "deliver." The reformers are delighted with this display of zeal, and only gradually find out that many of the recruits are there for the express purpose of being bought by the other side; that they are most active in order to seem valuable, and thus raise the price of their allegiance when they are ready to sell. Reformers seeing them drop away one by one, talk of desertion from the ranks of reform, and of the power of money over well-meaning men, who are too weak to withstand temptation; but in reality the men are not deserters because they have never actually been enrolled in the ranks. The money they take is neither a bribe nor the price of their loyalty, it is simply the consummation of a long-cherished plan and a well-earned reward. They came into the new movement for the purpose of being bought out of it, and have successfully accomplished that purpose.

Hull-House assisted in carrying on two unsuccessful campaigns against the same alderman. In the two years following the end of the first one, nearly every man who had been prominent in it had received an office from the reëlected alderman. A printer had been appointed to a clerkship in the city hall; a driver received a large salary for services in the police barns; the candidate himself, a bricklayer, held a position in the city construction department. At the beginning of the next campaign, the greatest difficulty was experienced in finding a candidate, and each one proposed, demanded time to consider the proposition. During this period he invariably became the recipient of the alderman's bounty. The first one, who was foreman of a large factory, was reported to have been bought off by the promise that the city institutions would use the product of his firm. The second one, a keeper of a grocery and family saloon, with large popularity, was promised the aldermanic nomination on the regular ticket at the expiration of the term of office held by the alderman's colleague, and it may be well to state in passing that he was thus nominated and successfully elected. The third proposed candidate received a place for his son in the office of the city attorney.

Not only are offices in his gift, but all smaller favors as well. Any requests to the council, or special licenses, must be presented by the alderman of the ward in which the person desiring the favor resides. There is thus constant opportunity for the alderman to put his constituents under obligations to him, to make it difficult for a constituent to withstand him, or for one with large interests to enter into political action at all. From the Italian peddler who wants a license to peddle fruit in the street, to the large manufacturing company who desires to tunnel an alley for the sake of conveying pipes from one building to another, everybody is under obligations to his alderman, and is constantly made to feel it. In short, these very regulations for presenting requests to the council have been made, by the aldermen themselves, for the express purpose of increasing the dependence of their constituents, and thereby augmenting aldermanic power and prestige.

The alderman has also a very singular hold upon the property owners of his ward. The paving, both of the streets and sidewalks throughout his district, is disgraceful; and in the election speeches the reform side holds him responsible for this condition, and promises better paving under another régime. But the paving could not be made better without a special assessment upon the property owners of the vicinity, and paying more taxes is exactly what his constituents do not want to do. In reality, ''getting them off,'' or at the worst postponing the time of the improvement, is one of the genuine favors which he performs. A movement to have the paving done from a general fund would doubtless be opposed by the property owners in other parts of the city who have already paid for the asphalt bordering their own possessions, but they have no conception of the struggle and possible bankruptcy which repaving may mean to the small property owner, nor how his chief concern may be to elect an alderman who cares more for the feelings and pocket-books of his constituents than he does for the repute and cleanliness of his city.

The alderman exhibited great wisdom in procuring from certain of his down-town friends the sum of three thousand dollars with which to uniform and equip a boys' temperance brigade which had been formed in one of the ward churches a few months before his campaign. Is it strange that the good leader, whose heart was filled with innocent pride as he looked upon these promising young scions of virtue, should decline to enter into a reform campaign? Of what use to suggest that uniforms and bayonets for the purpose of promoting temperance, bought with money contributed by a man who was proprietor of a saloon and a gambling house, might perhaps confuse the ethics of the young soldiers? Why take the pains to urge that it was vain to lecture and march abstract virtues into them, so long as the "champion boodler" of the town was the man whom the boys recognized as a loyal and kindhearted friend, the public-spirited citizen, whom their fathers enthusiastically voted for, and their mothers called "the friend of the poor." As long as the actual and tangible success is thus embodied, marching whether in kindergartens or brigades, talking whether in clubs or classes, does little to change the code of ethics.

The question of where does the money come from which is spent so successfully, does of course occur to many minds. The more primitive people accept the truthful statement of its sources without any shock to their moral sense. To their simple minds he gets it "from the rich" and, so long as he again gives it out to the poor as a true Robin Hood, with open hand, they have no objections to offer. Their ethics are quite honestly those of the merry-making foresters. The next less primitive people of the vicinage are quite willing to admit that he leads the "gang" in the city council, and sells out the city franchises; that he makes deals with the franchise-seeking companies; that he guarantees to steer dubious measures through the council, for which he demands liberal pay; that he is, in short, a successful "boodler." When, however, there is intellect enough to get this point of view, there is also enough to make the contention that this is universally done, that all the aldermen do it more or less successfully, but that the alderman of this particular ward is unique in being so generous; that such a state of affairs is to be deplored, of course; but that that is the way business is run, and we are fortunate when a kind-hearted man who is close to the people gets a large share of the spoils; that he serves franchised companies who employ men in the building and construction of their enterprises, and that they are bound in return to give work to his constituents. It is again the justification of stealing from the rich to give to the poor. Even when they are intelligent enough to complete the circle, and to see that the money comes, not from the pockets of the companies' agents, but from the street-car fares of people like themselves, it almost seems as if they would rather pay two cents more each time they ride than to give up the consciousness that they have a big, warm-hearted friend at court who will stand by them in an emergency. The sense of just dealing comes apparently much later than the desire for protection and indulgence. On the whole, the gifts and favors are taken quite simply as an evidence of genuine loving-kindness. The alderman is really elected because he is a good friend and neighbor. He is corrupt, of course, but he is not elected because he is corrupt, but rather in spite of it. His standard suits his constituents. He exemplifies and exaggerates the popular type of a good man. He has attained what his constituents secretly long for.

At one end of the ward there is a street of good houses, familiarly called "Con Row." The term is perhaps quite unjustly used, but it is nevertheless universally applied, because many of these houses are occupied by professional office holders. This row is supposed to form a happy hunting-ground of the successful politician, where he can live in prosperity, and still maintain his vote and influence in the ward. It would be difficult to justly estimate the influence which this group of successful, prominent men, including the alderman who lives there, have had upon the ideals of the youth in the vicinity. The path which leads to riches and success, to civic prominence and honor, is the path of political corruption. We might compare this to the path laid out by Benjamin Franklin, who also secured all of these things, but told young men that they could be obtained only by strenuous effort and frugal living, by the cultivation of the mind, and the holding fast to righteousness; or, again, we might compare it to the ideals which were held up to the American youth fifty years ago, lower, to be sure, than the revolutionary ideal, but still fine and aspiring toward honorable dealing and careful living. They were told that the career of the self-made man was open to every American boy, if he worked hard and saved his money, improved his mind, and followed a steady ambition. The writer remembers that when she was ten years old, the village schoolmaster told his little flock, without any mitigating clauses, that Jay Gould had laid the foundation of his colossal fortune by always saving bits of string, and that, as a result, every child in the village assiduously collected party-colored balls of twine. A bright Chicago boy might well draw the inference that the path of the corrupt politician not only leads to civic honors, but to the glories of benevolence and philanthropy. This lowering of standards, this setting of an ideal, is perhaps the worst of the situation, for, as we said in the first chapter, we determine ideals by our daily actions and decisions not only for ourselves, but largely for each other.

We are all involved in this political corruption, and as members of the community stand indicted. This is the penalty of a democracy,—that we are bound to move forward or retrograde together. None of us can stand aside; our feet are mired in the same soil, and our lungs breathe the same air.

That the alderman has much to do with setting the standard of life and desirable prosperity may be illustrated by the following incident: During one of the campaigns a clever cartoonist drew a poster representing the successful alderman in portraiture drinking champagne at a table loaded with pretentious dishes and surrounded by other revellers. In contradistinction was his opponent, a bricklayer, who sat upon a half-finished wall, eating a meagre dinner from a workingman's dinner-pail, and the passer-by was asked which type of representative he preferred, the presumption being that at least in a workingman's district the bricklayer would come out ahead. To the chagrin of the reformers, however, it was gradually discovered that, in the popular mind, a man who laid bricks and wore overalls was not nearly so desirable for an alderman as the man who drank champagne and wore a diamond in his shirt front. The district wished its representative "to stand up with the best of them," and certainly some of the constituents would have been ashamed to have been represented by a bricklayer. It is part of that general desire to appear well, the optimistic and thoroughly American belief, that even if a man is working with his hands to-day, he and his children will quite likely be in a better position in the swift coming to-morrow, and there is no need of being too closely associated with common working people. There is an honest absence of class consciousness, and a naïve belief that the kind of occupation quite largely determines social position. This is doubtless exaggerated in a neighborhood of foreign people by the fact that as each nationality becomes more adapted to American conditions, the scale of its occupation rises. Fifty years ago in America "a Dutchman" was used as a term of reproach, meaning a man whose language was not understood, and who performed menial tasks, digging sewers and building railroad embankments. Later the Irish did the same work in the community, but as quickly as possible handed it on to the Italians, to whom the name "dago" is said to cling as a result of the digging which the Irishman resigned to him. The Italian himself is at last waking up to this fact. In a political speech recently made by an Italian padrone, he bitterly reproached the alderman for giving the four-dollars-a-day "jobs" of sitting in an office to Irishmen and the-dollar-and-a-half-a-day "jobs" of sweeping the streets to the Italians. This general struggle to rise in life, to be at least politically represented by one of the best, as to occupation and social status, has also its negative side. We must remember that the imitative impulse plays an important part in life, and that the loss of social estimation, keenly felt by all of us, is perhaps most dreaded by the humblest, among whom freedom of individual conduct, the power to give only just weight to the opinion of neighbors, is but feebly developed. A form of constraint, gentle, but powerful, is afforded by the simple desire to do what others do, in order to share with them the approval of the community. Of course, the larger the number of people among whom an habitual mode of conduct obtains, the greater the constraint it puts upon the individual will. Thus it is that the political corruption of the city presses most heavily where it can be least resisted, and is most likely to be imitated.

According to the same law, the positive evils of corrupt government are bound to fall heaviest upon the poorest and least capable. When the water of Chicago is foul, the prosperous buy water bottled at distant springs; the poor have no alternative but the typhoid fever which comes from using the city's supply. When the garbage contracts are not enforced, the well-to-do pay for private service; the poor suffer the discomfort and illness which are inevitable from a foul atmosphere. The prosperous business man has a certain choice as to whether he will treat with the "boss" politician or preserve his independence on a smaller income; but to an Italian day laborer it is a choice between obeying the commands of a political "boss" or practical starvation. Again, a more intelligent man may philosophize a little upon the present state of corruption, and reflect that it is but a phase of our commercialism, from which we are bound to emerge; at any rate, he may give himself the solace of literature and ideals in other directions, but the more ignorant man who lives only in the narrow present has no such resource; slowly the conviction enters his mind that politics is a matter of favors and positions, that self-government means pleasing the "boss" and standing in with the "gang." This slowly acquired knowledge he hands on to his family. . . .

. . .

During the campaign, when it was found hard to secure enough local speakers of the moral tone which was desired, orators were imported from other parts of the town, from the so-called "better element." Suddenly it was rumored on all sides that, while the money and speakers for the reform candidate were coming from the swells, the money which was backing the corrupt alderman also came from a swell source; that the president of a street-car combination, for whom he performed constant offices in the city council, was ready to back him to the extent of fifty thousand dollars; that this president, too, was a good man, and sat in high places; that he had recently given a large sum of money to an educational institution and was therefore as philanthropic, not to say good and upright, as any man in town; that the corrupt alderman had the sanction of the highest authorities, and that the lecturers who were talking against corruption, and the selling and buying of franchises, were only the cranks, and not the solid business men who had developed and built up Chicago.

All parts of the community are bound together in ethical development. If the so-called more enlightened members accept corporate gifts from the man who buys up the council, and the so-called less enlightened members accept individual gifts from the man who sells out the council, we surely must take our punishment together. There is the difference, of course, that in the first case we act collectively, and in the second case individually; but is the punishment which follows the first any lighter or less far-reaching in its consequences than the more obvious one which follows the second?

Have our morals been so captured by commercialism, to use Mr. Chapman's generalization, that we do not see a moral dereliction when business or educational interests are served thereby, although we are still shocked when the saloon interest is thus served?

The street-car company which declares that it is impossible to do business without managing the city council, is on exactly the same moral level with the man who cannot retain political power unless he has a saloon, a large acquaintance with the semi-criminal class, and questionable money with which to debauch his constituents. Both sets of men assume that the only appeal possible is along the line of self-interest. They frankly acknowledge money getting as their own motive power, and they believe in the cupidity of all the men whom they encounter. No attempt in either case is made to put forward the claims of the public, or to find a moral basis for action. As the corrupt politician assumes that public morality is impossible, so many business men become convinced that to pay tribute to the corrupt aldermen is on the whole cheaper than to have taxes too high; that it is better to pay exorbitant rates for franchises, than to be made unwilling partners in transportation experiments. Such men come to regard political reformers as a sort of monomaniac, who are not reasonable enough to see the necessity of the present arrangement which has slowly been evolved and developed, and upon which business is safely conducted.

A reformer who really knew the people and their great human needs, who believed that it was the business of government to serve them, and who further recognized the educative power of a sense of responsibility, would possess a clew by which he might analyze the situation. He would find out what needs, which the alderman supplies, are legitimate ones which the city itself could undertake, in counter-distinction to those which pander to the lower instincts of the constituency. A mother who eats her Christmas turkey in a reverent spirit of thankfulness to the alderman who gave it to her, might be gradually brought to a genuine sense of appreciation and gratitude to the city which supplies her little children with a Kindergarten, or, to the Board of Health which properly placarded a case of scarlet-fever next door and spared her sleepless nights and wearing anxiety, as well as the money paid with such difficulty to the doctor and the druggist. The man who in his emotional gratitude almost kneels before his political friend who gets his boy out of jail, might be made to see the kindness and good sense of the city authorities who provided the boy with a playground and reading room, where he might spend his hours of idleness and restlessness, and through which his temptations to petty crime might be averted. A man who is grateful to the alderman who sees that his gambling and racing are not interfered with, might learn to feel loyal and responsible to the city which supplied him with a gymnasium and swimming tank where manly and well-conducted sports are possible. The voter who is eager to serve the alderman at all times, because the tenure of his job is dependent upon aldermanic favor, might find great relief and pleasure in working for the city in which his place was secured by a well-administered civil service law.

After all, what the corrupt alderman demands from his followers and largely depends upon is a sense of loyalty, a standing-by the man who is good to you, who understands you, and who gets you out of trouble. All the social life of the voter from the time he was a little boy and played "craps" with his "own push," and not with some other "push," has been founded on this sense of loyalty and of standing in with his friends. Now that he is a man, he likes the sense of being inside a political organization, of being trusted with political gossip, of belonging to a set of fellows who understand things, and whose interests are being cared for by a strong friend in the city council itself. All this is perfectly legitimate, and all in the line of the development of a strong civic loyalty, if it were merely socialized and enlarged. Such a voter has already proceeded in the forward direction in so far as he has lost the sense of isolation, and has abandoned the conviction that city government does not touch his individual affairs. Even Mill* claims that the social feelings of man,

*The British philosopher and reformer John Stuart Mill (1806–1873). [Editors' note.]

his desire to be at unity with his fellow-creatures, are the natural basis for morality, and he defines a man of high moral culture as one who thinks of himself, not as an isolated individual, but as a part in a social organism.

Upon this foundation it ought not to be difficult to build a structure of civic virtue. It is only necessary to make it clear to the voter that his individual needs are common needs, that is, public needs, and that they can only be legitimately supplied for him when they are supplied for all. If we believe that the individual struggle for life may widen into a struggle for the lives of all, surely the demand of an individual for decency and comfort, for a chance to work and obtain the fulness of life may be widened until it gradually embraces all the members of the community, and rises into a sense of the common weal.

In order, however, to give him a sense of conviction that his individual needs must be merged into the needs of the many, and are only important as they are thus merged, the appeal cannot be made along the line of self-interest. The demand should be universalized; in this process it would also become clarified, and the basis of our political organization become perforce social and ethical.

Would it be dangerous to conclude that the corrupt politician himself, because he is democratic in method, is on a more ethical line of social development than the reformer, who believes that the people must be made over by "good citizens" and governed by "experts"? The former at least are engaged in that great moral effort of getting the mass to express itself, and of adding this mass energy and wisdom to the community as a whole.

The wide divergence of experience makes it difficult for the good citizen to understand this point of view, and many things conspire to make it hard for him to act upon it. He is more or less a victim to that curious feeling so often possessed by the good man, that the righteous do not need to be agreeable, that their goodness alone is sufficient, and that they can leave the arts and wiles of securing popular favor to the self-seeking. This results in a certain repellent manner commonly regarded as the apparel of righteousness, and is further responsible for the fatal mistake of making the surroundings of "good influences" singularly unattractive; a mistake which really deserves a reprimand quite as severe as the equally reprehensible deed of making the surroundings of "evil influences" so beguiling. Both are akin to that state of mind which narrows the entrance into a wider morality to the eye of a needle, and accounts for the fact that new moral movements have ever and again been inaugurated by those who have found themselves in revolt against the conventionalized good.

The success of the reforming politician who insists upon mere purity of administration and upon the control and suppression of the unruly elements in the community, may be the easy result of a narrowing and selfish process. For the painful condition of endeavoring to minister to genuine social needs, through the political machinery, and at the same time to remodel that machinery so that it shall be adequate to its new task, is to encounter the inevitable discomfort of a transition into a new type of democratic relation. The perplexing experiences of the actual administration, however, have a genuine value of their own. The economist who treats the individual cases as mere data, and the social reformer who labors to make such cases impossible, solely because of the appeal to his reason, may have to share these perplexities before they feel themselves within the grasp of a principle of growth, working outward from within; before they can gain the exhilaration and uplift which comes when the individual sympathy and intelligence is caught into the forward intuitive movement of the mass. This general movement is not without its intellectual aspects, but it has to be transferred from the region of perception to that of emotion before it is really apprehended. The mass of men seldom move together without an emotional incentive. The man who chooses to stand aside, avoids much of the perplexity, but at the same time he loses contact with a great source of vitality.

SAMUEL P. HAYS

The Politics of Reform in Municipal Government in the Progressive Era

In this important essay Samuel P. Hays, professor of history at the University of Pittsburgh, challenges the notions that reform was primarily the product of either middle- or lower-class efforts and leadership, and also seeks to show that it was hardly a disinterested crusade to improve the lot of the downtrodden. The reader should closely examine Professor Hays' definition of the "upper class" (what does he mean by the term? does it clarify our understanding of the origins of "reform"?), and the implications of his conclusions with respect to the purposes of reform, the character of the "Progressive Movement," and the role of the political boss. One could also relate Hays' interpretation to Robert H. Wiebe's thesis that the centralization and bureaucratization of political and economic authority in these years were major man-

Reprinted with permission from *Pacific Northwest Quarterly*, 55 (October, 1964), 157–169.

ifestations of a "search for order" in American society. If such a search was underway, who were the searchers and what kinds of "order" did they seek?

Largely because of the questions it raises, Professor Hays' essay serves as a fitting conclusion to our discussion of urban "reform movements" in this period, and an equally appropriate introduction to the consideration of contributions by political bosses to the process of socioeconomic change in the city.

In order to achieve a more complete understanding of social change in the Progressive Era, historians must now undertake a deeper analysis of the practices of economic, political, and social groups. Political ideology alone is no longer satisfactory evidence to describe social patterns because generalizations based upon it, which tend to divide political groups into the moral and the immoral, the rational and the irrational, the efficient and the inefficient, do not square with political practice. Behind this contemporary rhetoric concerning the nature of reform lay patterns of political behavior which were at variance with it. Since an extensive gap separated ideology and practice, we can no longer take the former as an accurate description of the latter, but must reconstruct social behavior from other types of evidence.

Reform in urban government provides one of the most striking examples of this problem of analysis. The demand for change in municipal affairs, whether in terms of over-all reform, such as the commission and city-manager plans, or of more piecemeal modifications, such as the development of city-wide school boards, deeply involved reform ideology. Reformers loudly proclaimed a new structure of municipal government as more moral, more rational, and more efficient and, because it was so, self-evidently more desirable. But precisely because of this emphasis, there seemed to be no need to analyze the political forces behind change. Because the goals of reform were good, its causes were obvious; rather than being the product of particular people and particular ideas in particular situations, they were deeply imbedded in the universal impulses and truths of "progress." Consequently, historians have rarely tried to determine precisely who the municipal reformers were or what they did, but instead have relied on reform ideology as an accurate description of reform practice.

The reform ideology which became the basis of historical analysis is well known. It appears in classic form in Lincoln Steffens' *Shame of the Cities*. The urban political struggle of the Progressive Era, so the argument goes, involved a conflict between public impulses for "good government" against a corrupt alliance of "machine politicans" and "special interests."

During the rapid urbanization of the late 19th century, the latter had been free to aggrandize themselves, especially through franchise grants, at the expense of the public. Their power lay primarily in their ability to manipulate the political process, by bribery and corruption, for their own ends. Against such arrangements there gradually arose a public protest, a demand by the public for honest government, for officials who would act for the public rather than for themselves. To accomplish their goals, reformers sought basic modifications in the political system, both in the structure of government and in the manner of selecting public officials. These changes, successful in city after city, enabled the "public interest" to triumph.[1]

Recently, George Mowry, Alfred Chandler, Jr., and Richard Hofstadter have modified this analysis by emphasizing the fact that the impulse for reform did not come from the working class.[2] This might have been suspected from the rather strained efforts of National Municipal League writers in the "Era of Reform" to go out of their way to demonstrate working-class support for commission and city-manager governments.[3] We now know that they clutched at straws, and often erroneously, in order to prove to themselves as well as to the public that municipal reform was a mass movement.

The Mowry-Chandler-Hofstadter writings have further modified older views by asserting that reform in general and municipal reform in particular sprang from a distinctively middle-class movement. This has now become the prevailing view. Its popularity is surprising not only because it is based upon faulty logic and extremely limited evidence, but also because it, too, emphasizes the analysis of ideology rather than practice and fails to contribute much to the understanding of who distinctively were involved in reform and why.

Ostensibly, the "middle-class" theory of reform is based upon a new type of behavioral evidence, the collective biography, in studies by Mowry of California Progressive party leaders, by Chandler of a nationwide group of that party's leading figures, and by Hofstadter of four professions—ministers, lawyers, teachers, editors. These studies demonstrate the middle-class nature of reform, but they fail to determine if reformers were distinctively middle class, specifically if they differed from their opponents. One study of 300 political leaders in the state of Iowa, for example, discovered that Progressive party, Old Guard, and Cummins Republicans were all substantially alike, the Progressives differing only in that they were slightly younger than the others and had less political experience.[4] If its opponents were also middle class, then one cannot describe Progressive reform as a phenomenon, the special nature of which can be explained in terms of middle-class characteristics. One cannot explain the distinctive behavior of people in terms of characteristics which are not distinctive to them.

Hofstadter's evidence concerning professional men fails in yet another way to determine the peculiar characteristics of reformers. For he describes ministers, lawyers, teachers, and editors without determining who within these professions became reformers and who did not. Two analytical distinctions might be made. Ministers involved in municipal reform, it appears, came not from all segments of religion, but peculiarly from upper-class churches. They enjoyed the highest prestige and salaries in the religious community and had no reason to feel a loss of "status," as Hofstadter argues. Their role in reform arose from the class character of their religious organizations rather than from the mere fact of their occupation as ministers.[5] Professional men involved in reform (many of whom—engineers, architects, and doctors—Hofstadter did not examine at all) seem to have come especially from the more advanced segments of their professions, from those who sought to apply their specialized knowledge to a wider range of public affairs.[6] Their role in reform is related not to their attempt to defend earlier patterns of culture, but to the working out of the inner dynamics of professionalization in modern society.

The weakness of the "middle-class" theory of reform stems from the fact that it rests primarily upon ideological evidence, not on a thoroughgoing description of political practice. Although the studies of Mowry, Chandler, and Hofstadter ostensibly derive from behavioral evidence, they actually derive largely from the extensive expressions of middle-ground ideological position, of the reformers' own descriptions of their contemporary society, and of their expressed fears of both the lower and the upper classes, of the fright of being ground between the millstones of labor and capital.[7]

Such evidence, though it accurately portrays what people thought, does not accurately describe what they did. The great majority of Americans look upon themselves as "middle class" and subscribe to a middle-ground ideology, even though in practice they belong to a great variety of distinct social classes. Such ideologies are not rationalizations or deliberate attempts to deceive. They are natural phenomena of human behavior. But the historian should be especially sensitive to their role so that he will not take evidence of political ideology as an accurate representation of political practice.

In the following account I will summarize evidence in both secondary and primary works concerning the political practices in which municipal reformers were involved. Such an analysis logically can be broken down into three parts, each one corresponding to a step in the traditional argument.

First, what was the source of reform? Did it lie in the general public rather than in particular groups? Was it middle class, working class, or perhaps of other composition? Second, what was the reform target of attack? Were reformers primarily interested in ousting the corrupt individual, the political or business leader who made private arrangements at the expense of the public, or were they interested in something else? Third, what political innovations did reformers bring about? Did they seek to expand popular participation in the governmental process?

There is now sufficient evidence to determine the validity of these specific elements of the more general argument. Some of it has been available for several decades; some has appeared more recently; some is presented here for the first time. All of it adds up to the conclusion that reform in municipal government involved a political development far different from what we have assumed in the past.

Available evidence indicates that the source of support for reform in municipal government did not come from the lower or middle classes, but from the upper class. The leading business groups in each city and professional men closely allied with them initiated and dominated municipal movements. Leonard White, in his study of the city manager published in 1927, wrote:

> The opposition to bad government usually comes to a head in the local chamber of commerce. Business men finally acquire the conviction that the growth of their city is being seriously impaired by the failures of city officials to perform their duties efficiently. Looking about for a remedy, they are captivated by the resemblance of the city-manager plan to their corporate form of business organization.[8]

In the 1930's White directed a number of studies of the origin of city-manager government. The resulting reports invariably begin with such statements as, "the Chamber of Commerce spearheaded the movement," or commission government in this city was a "businessmen's government."[9] Of thirty-two cases of city-manager government in Oklahoma examined by Jewell C. Phillips, twenty-nine were initiated either by chambers of commerce or by community committees dominated by businessmen.[10] More recently James Weinstein has presented almost irrefutable evidence that the business community, represented largely by chambers of commerce, was the overwhelming force behind both commission and city-manager movements.[11]

Dominant elements of the business community played a prominent role in another crucial aspect of municipal reform: the Municipal Research

Bureau movement.[12] Especially in the larger cities, where they had less success in shaping the structure of government, reformers established centers to conduct research in municipal affairs as a springboard for influence.

The first such organization, the Bureau of Municipal Research of New York City, was founded in 1906; it was financed largely through the efforts of Andrew Carnegie and John D. Rockefeller. An investment banker provided the crucial support in Philadelphia, where a Bureau was founded in 1908. A group of wealthy Chicagoans in 1910 established the Bureau of Public Efficiency, a research agency. John H. Patterson of the National Cash Register Company, the leading figure in Dayton municipal reform, financed the Dayton Bureau, founded in 1912. And George Eastman was the driving force behind both the Bureau of Municipal Research and city-manager government in Rochester. In smaller cities data about city government was collected by interested individuals in a more informal way or by chambers of commerce, but in larger cities the task required special support, and prominent businessmen supplied it.

The character of municipal reform is demonstrated more precisely by a brief examination of the movements in Des Moines and Pittsburgh. The Des Moines Commercial Club inaugurated and carefully controlled the drive for the commission form of government.[13] In January, 1906, the Club held a so-called "mass meeting" of business and professional men to secure an enabling act from the state legislature. P. C. Kenyon, president of the Club, selected a Committee of 300, composed principally of business and professional men, to draw up a specific proposal. After the legislature approved their plan, the same committee managed the campaign which persuaded the electorate to accept the commission form of government by a narrow margin in June, 1907.

In this election the lower-income wards of the city opposed the change, the upper-income wards supported it strongly, and the middle-income wards were more evenly divided. In order to control the new government, the Committee of 300, now expanded to 530, sought to determine the nomination and election of the five new commissioners, and to this end they selected an avowedly businessman's slate. Their plans backfired when the voters swept into office a slate of anticommission candidates who now controlled the new commission government.

Proponents of the commission form of government in Des Moines spoke frequently in the name of the "people." But their more explicit statements emphasized their intent that the new plan be a "business system" of government, run by businessmen. The slate of candidates for commissioner endorsed by advocates of the plan was known as the "businessman's ticket." J. W. Hill, president of the committees of 300 and 530, bluntly declared: "The professional politician must be ousted and in his place capable business men chosen to conduct the affairs of the city." I. M. Earle, general counsel of the Bankers Life Association and a prominent figure in the movement, put the point more precisely: "When the plan was adopted it was the intention to get businessmen to run it."

Although reformers used the ideology of popular government, they in no sense meant that all segments of society should be involved equally in municipal decision-making. They meant that their concept of the city's welfare would be best achieved if the business community controlled city government. As one businessman told a labor audience, the businessman's slate represented labor "better than you do yourself."

The composition of the municipal reform movement in Pittsburgh demonstrates its upper-class and professional as well as its business sources.[14] Here the two principal reform organizations were the Civic Club and the Voters' League. The 745 members of these two organizations came primarily from the upper class. Sixty-five per cent appeared in upper-class directories which contained the names of only 2 per cent of the city's families. Furthermore, many who were not listed in these directories lived in upper-class areas. These reformers, it should be stressed, comprised not an old but a new upper class. Few came from earlier industrial and mercantile families. Most of them had risen to social position from wealth created after 1870 in the iron, steel, electrical equipment, and other industries, and they lived in the newer rather than the older fashionable areas.

Almost half (48 per cent) of the reformers were professional men: doctors, lawyers, ministers, directors of libraries and museums, engineers, architects, private and public school teachers, and college professors. Some of these belonged to the upper class as well, especially the lawyers, ministers, and private school teachers. But for the most part their interest in reform stemmed from the inherent dynamics of their professions rather than from their class connections. They came from the more advanced segments of their organizations, from those in the forefront of the acquisition and application of knowledge. They were not the older professional men, seeking to preserve the past against change; they were in the vanguard of professional life, actively seeking to apply expertise more widely to public affairs.

Pittsburgh reformers included a large segment of businessmen; 52 per cent were bankers and corporation officials or their wives. Among them were the presidents of fourteen large banks and officials of Westinghouse,

Pittsburgh Plate Glass, U.S. Steel and its component parts (such as Carnegie Steel, American Bridge, and National Tube), Jones and Laughlin, lesser steel companies (such as Crucible, Pittsburgh, Superior, Lockhart, and H. K. Porter), the H. J. Heinz Company, and the Pittsburgh Coal Company, as well as officials of the Pennsylvania Railroad and the Pittsburgh and Lake Erie. These men were not small businessmen; they directed the most powerful banking and industrial organizations of the city. They represented not the old business community, but industries which had developed and grown primarily within the past fifty years and which had come to dominate the city's economic life.

These business, professional, and upper-class groups who dominated municipal reform movements were all involved in the rationalization and systematization of modern life; they wished a form of government which would be more consistent with the objectives inherent in those developments. The most important single feature of their perspective was the rapid expansion of the geographical scope of affairs which they wished to influence and manipulate, a scope which was no longer limited and narrow, no longer within the confines of pedestrian communities, but was now broad and city-wide, covering the whole range of activities of the metropolitan area.

The migration of the upper class from central to outlying areas created a geographical distance between its residential communities and its economic institutions. To protect the latter required involvement both in local ward affairs and in the larger city government as well. Moreover, upper-class cultural institutions, such as museums, libraries, and symphony orchestras, required an active interest in the larger municipal context from which these institutions drew much of their clientele.

Professional groups, broadening the scope of affairs which they sought to study, measure, or manipulate, also sought to influence the public health, the educational system, or the physical arrangements of the entire city. Their concerns were limitless, not bounded by geography, but as expansive as the professional imagination. Finally, the new industrial community greatly broadened its perspective in governmental affairs because of its new recognition of the way in which factors throughout the city affected business growth. The increasing size and scope of industry, the greater stake in more varied and geographically dispersed facets of city life, the effect of floods on many business concerns, the need to promote traffic flows to and from work for both blue-collar and managerial employees—all contributed to this larger interest. The geographically larger private perspectives of upper-class, professional, and business groups gave rise to a geographically larger public perspective.

These reformers were dissatisfied with existing systems of municipal government. They did not oppose corruption per se—although there was plenty of that. They objected to the structure of government which enabled local and particularistic interests to dominate. Prior to the reforms of the Progressive Era, city government consisted primarily of confederations of local wards, each of which was represented on the city's legislative body. Each ward frequently had its own elementary schools and ward-elected school boards which administered them.

These particularistic interests were the focus of a decentralized political life. City councilmen were local leaders. They spoke for their local areas, the economic interests of their inhabitants, their residential concerns, their educational, recreational, and religious interests—i.e., for those aspects of community life which mattered most to those they represented. They rolled logs in the city council to provide streets, sewers, and other public works for their local areas. They defended the community's cultural practices, its distinctive languages or national customs, its liberal attitude toward liquor, and its saloons and dance halls which served as centers of community life. One observer described this process of representation in Seattle:

> The residents of the hill-tops and the suburbs may not fully appreciate the faithfulness of certain downtown ward councilmen to the interests of their constituents. . . . The people of a state would rise in arms against a senator or representative in Congress who deliberately misrepresented their wishes and imperilled their interests, though he might plead a higher regard for national good. Yet people in other parts of the city seem to forget that under the old system the ward elected councilmen with the idea of procuring service of special benefit to that ward.[15]

In short, pre-reform officials spoke for their constituencies, inevitably their own wards which had elected them, rather than for other sections or groups of the city.

The ward system of government especially gave representation in city affairs to lower- and middle-class groups. Most elected ward officials were from these groups, and they, in turn, constituted the major opposition to reforms in municipal government. In Pittsburgh, for example, immediately prior to the changes in both the city council and the school board in 1911 in which city-wide representation replaced ward representation, only 24 per cent of the 387 members of those bodies represented the same managerial, professional, and banker occupations which dominated the membership of the Civic Club and the Voters' League.

The great majority (67 per cent) were small businessmen—grocers, saloon-keepers, and skilled and unskilled workmen.[16]

This decentralized system of urban growth and the institutions which arose from it reformers now opposed. Social, professional, and economic life had developed not only in the local wards in a small community context, but also on a larger scale had become highly integrated and organized, giving rise to a superstructure of social organization which lay far above that of ward life and which was sharply divorced from it in both personal contacts and perspective.

By the late 19th century, those involved in these larger institutions found that the decentralized system of political life limited their larger objectives. The movement for reform in municipal government, therefore, constituted an attempt by upper-class, advanced professional, and large business groups to take formal political power from the previously dominant lower- and middle-class elements so that they might advance their own conceptions of desirable public policy. These two groups came from entirely different urban worlds, and the politcal system fashioned by one was no longer acceptable to the other.

Lower- and middle-class groups not only dominated the pre-reform governments, but vigorously opposed reform. It is significant that none of the occupational groups among them, for example, small businessmen or white-collar workers, skilled or unskilled artisans, had important representation in reform organizations thus far examined. The case studies of city-manager government undertaken in the 1930's under the direction of Leonard White detailed in city after city the particular opposition of labor. In their analysis of Jackson, Michigan, the authors of these studies wrote:

> The *Square Deal*, oldest Labor paper in the state, has been consistently against manager government, perhaps largely because labor has felt that with a decentralized government elected on a ward basis it was more likely to have some voice and to receive its share of privileges.[17]

In Janesville, Wisconsin, the small shopkeepers and workingmen on the west and south sides, heavily Catholic and often Irish, opposed the commission plan in 1911 and in 1912 and the city-manager plan when adopted in 1923.[18] "In Dallas there is hardly a trace of class consciousness in the Marxian sense," one investigator declared, "yet in city elections the division has been to a great extent along class lines."[19] The commission and city-manager elections were no exceptions. To these authors it seemed a logical reaction, rather than an embarrassing fact that had to be swept away, that workingmen should have opposed municipal reform.[20]

In Des Moines working-class representatives, who in previous years might have been council members, were conspicuously absent from the "businessman's slate." Workingmen acceptable to reformers could not be found. A workingman's slate of candidates, therefore, appeared to challenge the reform slate. Organized labor, and especially the mineworkers, took the lead; one of their number, Wesley Ash, a deputy sheriff and union member, made "an astonishing run" in the primary, coming in second among a field of more than twenty candidates.[21] In fact, the strength of anticommission candidates in the primary so alarmed reformers that they frantically sought to appease labor.

The day before the final election they modified their platform to pledge both an eight-hour day and an "American standard of wages." They attempted to persuade the voters that their slate consisted of men who represented labor because they had "begun at the bottom of the ladder and made a good climb toward success by their own unaided efforts."[22] But their tactics failed. In the election of March 30, 1908, voters swept into office the entire "opposition" slate. The business and professional community had succeeded in changing the form of government, but not in securing its control. A cartoon in the leading reform newspaper illustrated their disappointment; John Q. Public sat dejectedly and muttered, "Aw, What's the Use?"

The most visible opposition to reform and the most readily available target of reform attack was the so-called "machine," for through the "machine" many different ward communities as well as lower- and middle-income groups joined effectively to influence the central city government. Their private occupational and social life did not naturally involve these groups in larger city-wide activities in the same way as the upper class was involved; hence they lacked access to privately organized economic and social power on which they could construct political power. The "machine" filled this organizational gap.

Yet it should never be forgotten that the social and economic institutions in the wards themselves provided the "machine's" sustaining support and gave it larger significance. When reformers attacked the "machine" as the most visible institutional element of the ward system, they attacked the entire ward form of political organization and the political power of lower- and middle-income groups which lay behind it.

Reformers often gave the impression that they opposed merely the corrupt politician and his "machine." But in a more fundamental way they looked upon the deficiencies of pre-reform political leaders in terms not of their personal shortcomings, but of the limitations inherent in their occupational, institutional, and class positions. In 1911 the Voters' League of Pittsburgh wrote in its pamphlet analyzing the qualifications of candidates that "a man's occupation ought to give a strong indication of his qualifications for membership on a school board."[23] Certain occupations inherently disqualified a man from serving:

Employment as ordinary laborer and in the lowest class of mill work would naturally lead to the conclusion that such men did not have sufficient education or business training to act as school directors. . . . Objection might also be made to small shopkeepers, clerks, workmen at many trades, who by lack of educational advantages and business training, could not, no matter how honest, be expected to administer properly the affairs of an educational system, requiring special knowledge, and where millions are spent each year.

These, of course, were precisely the groups which did dominate Pittsburgh government prior to reform. The League deplored the fact that school boards contained only a small number of "men prominent throughout the city in business life . . . in professional occupations . . . holding positions as managers, secretaries, auditors, superintendents and foremen" and exhorted these classes to participate more actively as candidates for office.

Reformers, therefore, wished not simply to replace bad men with good; they proposed to change the occupational and class origins of decision-makers. Toward this end they sought innovations in the formal machinery of government which would concentrate political power by sharply centralizing the processes of decision-making rather than distribute it through more popular participation in public affairs. According to the liberal view of the Progressive Era, the major political innovations of reform involved the equalization of political power through the primary, the direct election of public officials, and the initiative, referendum, and recall. These measures played a large role in the political ideology of the time and were frequently incorporated into new municipal charters. But they provided at best only an occasional and often incidental process of decision-making. Far more important in continuous, sustained, day-to-day processes of government were those innovations which centralized decision-making in the hands of fewer and fewer people.

The systematization of municipal government took place on both the executive and the legislative levels. The strong-mayor and city-manager types became the most widely used examples of the former. In the first decade of the 20th century, the commission plan had considerable appeal, but its distribution of administrative responsibility among five people gave rise to a demand for a form with more centralized executive power; consequently, the city-manager or the commission-manager variant often replaced it.[24]

A far more pervasive and significant change, however, lay in the centralization of the system of representation, the shift from ward to city-wide election of councils and school boards. Governing bodies so selected, reformers argued, would give less attention to local and particularistic matters and more to affairs of city-wide scope. This shift, an invariable feature of both commission and city-manager plans, was often adopted by itself. In Pittsburgh, for example, the new charter of 1911 provided as the major innovation that a council of twenty-seven, each member elected from a separate ward, be replaced by a council of nine, each elected by the city as a whole.

Cities displayed wide variations in this innovation. Some regrouped wards into larger units but kept the principle of areas of representation smaller than the entire city. Some combined a majority of councilmen elected by wards with additional ones elected at large. All such innovations, however, constituted steps toward the centralization of the system of representation.

Liberal historians have not appreciated the extent to which municipal reform in the Progressive Era involved a debate over the system of representation. The ward form of representation was universally condemned on the grounds that it gave too much influence to the separate units and not enough attention to the larger problems of the city. Harry A. Toulmin, whose book, *The City Manager,* was published by the National Municipal League, stated the case:

> The spirit of sectionalism had dominated the political life of every city. Ward pitted against ward, alderman against alderman, and legislation only effected by "log-rolling" extravagant measures into operation, mulcting the city, but gratifying the greed of constituents, has too long stung the conscience of decent citizenship. This constant treaty-making of factionalism has been no less than a curse. The city manager plan proposes the commendable thing of abolishing wards. The plan is not unique in this for it has been common to many forms of commission government. . . .[25]

Such a system should be supplanted, the argument usually went, with city-wide representation in which elected officials could consider the city "as a unit." "The new officers are elected," wrote Toulmin, "each to represent all the people. Their duties are so defined that they must administer the corporate business in its entirety, not as a hodgepodge of associated localities."

Behind the debate over the method of representation, however, lay a debate over who should be represented, over whose views of public policy should prevail. Many reform leaders often explicitly, if not implicitly, expressed fear that lower- and middle-income groups had too much influence in decision-making. One Galveston leader, for example, complained about the movement for initiative, referendum, and recall:

We have in our city a very large number of negroes employed on the docks; we also have a very large number of unskilled white laborers; this city also has more barrooms, according to its population, than any other city in Texas. Under these circumstances it would be extremely difficult to maintain a satisfactory city government where all ordinances must be submitted back to the voters of the city for their ratification and approval.[26]

At the National Municipal League convention of 1907, Rear Admiral F. E. Chadwick (USN Ret.), a leader in the Newport, Rhode Island, movement for municipal reform, spoke to this question even more directly:

Our present system has excluded in large degree the representation of those who have the city's well-being most at heart. It has brought, in municipalities . . . a government established by the least educated, the least interested class of citizens.

It stands to reason that a man paying $5,000 taxes in a town is more interested in the well-being and development of his town than the man who pays no taxes. . . . It equally stands to reason that the man of the $5,000 tax should be assured a representation in the committee which lays the tax and spends the money which he contributes. . . Shall we be truly democratic and give the property owner a fair show or shall we develop a tyranny of ignorance which shall crush him.[27]

Municipal reformers thus debated frequently the question of who should be represented as well as the question of what method of representation should be employed.

That these two questions were intimately connected was revealed in other reform proposals for representation, proposals which were rarely taken seriously. One suggestion was that a class system of representation be substituted for ward representation. For example, in 1908 one of the prominent candidates for commissioner in Des Moines proposed that the city council be composed of representatives of five classes: educational and ministerial organizations, manufacturers and jobbers, public utility corporations, retail merchants including liquor men, and the Des Moines

Trades and Labor Assembly. Such a system would have greatly reduced the influence in the council of both middle- and lower-class groups. The proposal revealed the basic problem confronting business and professional leaders: how to reduce the influence in government of the majority of voters among middle- and lower-income groups.[28]

A growing imbalance between population and representation sharpened the desire of reformers to change from ward to city-wide elections. Despite shifts in population within most cities, neither ward district lines nor the apportionment of city council and school board seats changed frequently. Consequently, older areas of the city, with wards that were small in geographical size and held declining populations (usually lower and middle class in composition), continued to be overrepresented, and newer upper-class areas, where population was growing, became increasingly underrepresented. This intensified the reformers' conviction that the structure of government must be changed to give them the voice they needed to make their views on public policy prevail.[29]

It is not insignificant that in some cities (by no means a majority) municipal reform came about outside of the urban electoral process. The original commission government in Galveston was appointed rather than elected. The failure of previous attempts to secure an efficient city government through the local electorate made the business men of Galveston willing to put the conduct of the city's affairs in the hands of a commission dominated by state-appointed officials."[30] Only in 1903 did the courts force Galveston to elect the members of the commission, an innovation which one writer described as "an abandonment of the commission idea," and which led to the decline of the influence of the business community in the commission government.[31]

In 1911 Pittsburgh voters were not permitted to approve either the new city charter or the new school board plan, both of which provided for city-wide representation: they were a result of state legislative enactment. The governor appointed the first members of the new city council, but thereafter they were elected. The judges of the court of common pleas, however, and not the voters, selected members of the new school board.

The composition of the new city council and new school board in Pittsburgh, both of which were inaugurated in 1911, revealed the degree to which the shift from ward to city-wide representation produced a change in group representation.[32] Members of the upper class, the advanced professional men, and the large business groups dominated both. Of the fifteen members of the Pittsburgh Board of Education appointed in 1911 and the nine members of the new city council, none were small businessmen or white-collar workers. Each body contained only one person who could remotely be classified as a blue-collar worker; each of these men filled a position specifically but unofficially designed as reserved for a "representative of labor," and each was an official of the Amalgamated Association of Iron, Steel, and Tin Workers. Six of the nine members of the new city council were prominent businessmen, and all six were listed in upper-class directories. Two others were doctors closely associated with the upper class in both professional and social life. The fifteen members of the Board of Education included ten businessmen with city-wide interests, one doctor associated with the upper class, and three women previously active in upper-class public welfare.

Lower- and middle-class elements felt that the new city governments did not represent them.[33] The studies carried out under the direction of Leonard White contain numerous expressions of the way in which the change in the structure of government produced not only a change in the geographical scope of representation, but also in the groups represented. "It is not the policies of the manager or the council they oppose," one researcher declared, "as much as the lack of representation for their economic level and social groups."[34] And another wrote:

> There had been nothing unapproachable about the old ward aldermen. Every voter had a neighbor on the common council who was interested in serving him. The new councilmen, however, made an unfavorable impression on the less well-to-do voters. . . . Election at large made a change that, however desirable in other ways, left the voters in the poorer wards with a feeling that they had been deprived of their share of political importance.[35]

The success of the drive for centralization of administration and representation varied with the size of the city. In the smaller cities, business, professional, and elite groups could easily exercise a dominant influence. Their close ties readily enabled them to shape informal political power which they could transform into formal political power. After the mid-1890's the widespread organization of chambers of commerce provided a base for political action to reform municipal government, resulting in a host of small-city commission and city-manager innovations. In the larger, more heterogeneous cities, whose subcommunities were more dispersed, such community-wide action was extremely difficult. Few commission or city-manager proposals materialized here. Mayors became stronger, and steps were taken toward centralization of representation, but the ward system or some modified version usually persisted. Reformers in large cities often had to rest content with their Municipal Research Bureaus through which they could exert political influence from outside the municipal government.

A central element in the analysis of municipal reform in the Progressive Era is governmental corruption. Should it be understood in moral or political terms? Was it a product of evil men or of particular socio-political circumstances? Reform historians have adopted the former view. Selfish and evil men arose to take advantage of a political arrangement whereby unsystematic government offered many opportunities for personal gain at public expense. The system thrived until the "better elements," "men of intelligence and civic responsibility," or "right-thinking people" ousted the culprits and fashioned a political force which produced decisions in the "public interest." In this scheme of things, corruption in public affairs grew out of individual personal failings and a deficient governmental structure which could not hold those predispositions in check, rather than from the peculiar nature of social forces. The contestants involved were morally defined: evil men who must be driven from power, and good men who must be activated politically to secure control of municipal affairs.

Public corruption, however, involves political even more than moral considerations. It arises more out of the particular distribution of political power than of personal morality. For corruption is a device to exercise control and influence outside the legal channels of decision-making when those channels are not readily responsive. Most generally, corruption stems from an inconsistency between control of the instruments of formal governmental power and the exercise of informal influence in the community. If powerful groups are denied access to formal power in legitimate ways, they seek access through procedures which the community considers illegitimate. Corrupt government, therefore, does not reflect the genius of evil men, but rather the lack of acceptable means for those who exercise power in the private community to wield the same influence in governmental affairs. It can be understood in the Progressive Era not simply by the preponderance of evil men over good, but by the peculiar nature of the distribution of political power.

The political corruption of the "Era of Reform" arose from the inaccessibility of municipal government to those who were rising in power and influence. Municipal government in the United States developed in the 19th century within a context of universal manhood suffrage which decentralized political control. Because all men, whatever their economic, social, or cultural conditions, could vote, leaders who reflected a wide variety of community interests and who represented the views of people of every circumstance arose to guide and direct municipal affairs. Since the majority of urban voters were workingmen or immigrants, the views of those groups carried great and often decisive weight in governmental affairs. Thus, as Herbert Gutman has shown, during strikes in the 1870's city officials were usually friendly to workingmen and refused to use police power to protect strikebreakers.[36]

Ward representation on city councils was an integral part of grass-roots influence, for it enabled diverse urban communities, invariably identified with particular geographical areas of the city, to express their views more clearly through councilmen peculiarly receptive to their concerns. There was a direct, reciprocal flow of power between wards and the center of city affairs in which voters felt a relatively close connection with public matters and city leaders gave special attention to their needs.

Within this political system the community's business leaders grew in influence and power as industrialism advanced, only to find that their economic position did not readily admit them to the formal machinery of government. Thus, during strikes, they had to rely on either their own private police, Pinkertons, or the state militia to enforce their use of strike-breakers. They frequently found that city officials did not accept their views of what was best for the city and what direction municipal policies should take. They had developed a common outlook, closely related to their economic activities, that the city's economic expansion should become the prime concern of municipal government, and yet they found that this view had to compete with even more influential views of public policy. They found that political tendencies which arose from universal manhood suffrage and ward representation were not always friendly to their political conceptions and goals and had produced a political system over which they had little control, despite the fact that their economic ventures were the core of the city's prosperity and the hope for future urban growth.

Under such circumstances, businessmen sought other methods of influencing municipal affairs. They did not restrict themselves to the channels of popular election and representation, but frequently applied direct influence—if not verbal persuasion, then bribery and corruption. Thereby arose the graft which Lincoln Steffens recounted in his *Shame of the Cities*. Utilities were only the largest of those business groups and individuals who requested special favors, and the franchises they sought were only the most sensational of the prizes which included such items as favorable tax assessments and rates, the vacating of streets wanted for factory expansion, or permission to operate amid antiliquor and other laws regulating personal behavior. The relationships between business and formal government became a maze of accommodations, a set of political arrangements which grew up because effective power had few legitimate means of accomplishing its ends.

Steffens and subsequent liberal historians, however, misread the significance of these arrangements, emphasizing their personal rather than their more fundamental institutional elements. To them corruption involved personal arrangements between powerful business leaders and powerful "machine" politicians. Just as they did not fully appreciate the significance of the search for political influence by the rising business community as a whole, so they did not see fully the role of the "ward politician." They stressed the argument that the political leader manipulated voters to his own personal ends, that he used constituents rather than reflected their views.

A different approach is now taking root, namely, that the urban political organization was an integral part of community life, expressing its needs and its goals. As Oscar Handlin has said, for example, the "machine" not only fulfilled specific wants, but provided one of the few avenues to success and public recognition available to the immigrant.[37] The political leader's arrangements with businessmen, therefore, were not simply personal agreements between conniving individuals; they were far-reaching accommodations between powerful sets of institutions in industrial America.

These accommodations, however, proved to be burdensome and unsatisfactory to the business community and to the upper third of socio-economic groups in general. They were expensive; they were wasteful; they were uncertain. Toward the end of the 19th century, therefore, business and professional men sought more direct control over municipal government in order to exercise political influence more effectively. They realized their goals in the early 20th century in the new commission and city-manager forms of government and in the shift from ward to city-wide representation.

These innovations did not always accomplish the objectives that the business community desired because other forces could and often did adjust to the change in governmental structure and reëstablish their influence. But businessmen hoped that reform would enable them to increase their political power, and most frequently it did. In most cases the innovations which were introduced between 1901, when Galveston adopted a commission form of government, and the Great Depression, and especially the city-manager form which reached a height of popularity in the mid-1920's, served as vehicles whereby business and professional leaders moved directly into the inner circles of government, brought into one political system their own power and the formal machinery of government, and dominated municipal affairs for two decades.

Municipal reform in the early 20th century involves a paradox: the ideology of an extension of political control and the practice of its concentration. While reformers maintained that their movement rested on a wave of popular demands, called their gatherings of business and professional leaders "mass meetings," described their reforms as "part of a world-wide trend toward popular government," and proclaimed an ideology of a popular upheaval against a selfish few, they were in practice shaping the structure of municipal government so that political power would no longer be broadly distributed, but would in fact be more centralized in the hands of a relatively small segment of the population. The paradox became even sharper when new city charters included provisions for the initiative, referendum, and recall. How does the historian cope with this paradox? Does it represent deliberate deception or simply political strategy? Or does it reflect a phenomenon which should be understood rather than explained away?

The expansion of popular involvement in decision-making was frequently a political tactic, not a political system to be established permanently, but a device to secure immediate political victory. The prohibitionist advocacy of the referendum, one of the most extensive sources of support for such a measure, came from the belief that the referendum would provide the opportunity to outlaw liquor more rapidly. The Anti-Saloon League, therefore, urged local option. But the League was not consistent. Towns which were wet, when faced with a county-wide local-option decision to outlaw liquor, demanded town or township local option to reinstate it. The League objected to this as not the proper application of the referendum idea.

Again, "Progressive" reformers often espoused the direct primary when fighting for nominations for their candidates within the party, but once in control they often became cool to it because it might result in their own defeat. By the same token, many municipal reformers attached the initiative, referendum, and recall to municipal charters often as a device to appease voters who opposed the centralization of representation and executive authority. But, by requiring a high percentage of voters to sign petitions—often 25 to 30 per cent—these innovations could be and were rendered relatively harmless.

More fundamentally, however, the distinction between ideology and practice in municipal reform arose from the different roles which each played. The ideology of democratization of decision-making was negative rather than positive; it served as an instrument of attack against the existing political system rather than as a guide to alternative action. Those who wished to destroy the "machine" and to eliminate party competition in local government widely utilized the theory that these political instruments thwarted public impulses, and thereby shaped the tone of their attack.

But there is little evidence that the ideology represented a faith in a purely democratic system of decision-making or that reformers actually wished, in practice, to substitute direct democracy as a continuing system of sustained decision-making in place of the old. It was used to destroy the political institutions of the lower and middle classes and the political power which those institutions gave rise to, rather than to provide a clear-cut guide for alternative action.[38]

The guide to alternative action lay in the model of the business enterprise. In describing new conditions which they wished to create, reformers drew on the analogy of the "efficient business enterprise," criticizing current practices with the argument that "no business could conduct its affairs that way and remain in business," and calling upon business practices as the guides to improvement. As one student remarked:

> The folklore of the business elite came by gradual transition to be the symbols of governmental reformers. Efficiency, system, orderliness, budgets, economy, saving, were all injected into the efforts of reformers who sought to remodel municipal government in terms of the great impersonality of corporate enterprise.[39]

Clinton Rodgers Woodruff of the National Municipal League explained that the commission form was "a simple, direct, businesslike way of administering the business affairs of the city . . . an application to city administration of that type of business organization which has been so common and so successful in the field of commerce and industry."[40] The centralization of decision-making which developed in the business corporation was now applied in municipal reform.

The model of the efficient business enterprise, then, rather than the New England town meeting, provided the positive inspiration for the municipal reformer. In giving concrete shape to this model in the strong-mayor, commission, and city-manager plans, reformers engaged in the elaboration of the processes of rationalization and systematization inherent in modern science and technology. For in many areas of society, industrialization brought a gradual shift upward in the location of decision-making and the geographical extension of the scope of the area affected by decisions.

Experts in business, in government, and in the professions measured, studied, analyzed, and manipulated ever wider realms of human life, and devices which they used to control such affairs constituted the most fundamental and far-reaching innovations in decision-making in modern America, whether in formal government or in the informal exercise of power in private life. Reformers in the Progressive Era played a major role in shaping this new system. While they expressed an ideology of restoring a previous order, they in fact helped to bring forth a system drastically new.[41]

The drama of reform lay in the competition for supremacy between two systems of decision-making. One system, based upon ward representation and growing out of the practices and ideas of representative government, involved wide latitude for the expression of grass-roots impulses and their involvement in the political process. The other grew out of the rationalization of life which came with science and technology, in which decisions arose from expert analysis and flowed from fewer and smaller centers outward to the rest of society. Those who espoused the former looked with fear upon the loss of influence which the latter involved, and those who espoused the latter looked only with disdain upon the wastefulness and inefficiency of the former.

The Progressive Era witnessed rapid strides toward a more centralized system and a relative decline for a more decentralized system. This development constituted an accommodation of forces outside the business community to the political trends within business and professional life rather than vice versa. It involved a tendency for the decision-making processes inherent in science and technology to prevail over those inherent in representative government.

Reformers in the Progressive Era and liberal historians since then misread the nature of the movement to change municipal government because they concentrated upon dramatic and sensational episodes and ignored the analysis of more fundamental political structure, of the persistent relationships of influence and power which grew out of the community's social, ideological, economic, and cultural activities. The reconstruction of these patterns of human relationships and of the changes in them is the historian's most crucial task, for they constitute the central context of historical development. History consists not of erratic and spasmodic fluctuations, of a series of random thoughts and actions, but of patterns of activity and change in which people hold thoughts and actions in common and in which there are close connections between sequences of events. These contexts give rise to a structure of human relationships which pervade all areas of life; for the political historian the most important of these is the structure of the distribution of power and influence.

The structure of political relationships however, cannot be adequately understood if we concentrate on evidence concerning ideology rather than practice. For it is becoming increasingly clear that ideological evidence is no safe guide to the understanding of practice, that what people thought and said about their society is not necessarily an accurate representation of what they did. The current task of the historian of the Progressive Era is to quit taking the reformers' own description of political practice at its face value and to utilize a wide variety of new types of evidence to reconstruct political practice in its own terms. This is not to argue that ideology is either important or unimportant. It is merely to state that ideological evidence is not appropriate to the discovery of the nature of political practice.

Only by maintaining this clear distinction can the historian successfully investigate the structure of political life in the Progressive Era. And only then can he begin to cope with the most fundamental problem of all: the relationship between political ideology and political practice. For each of these facets of political life must be understood in its own terms, through its own historical record. Each involves a distinct set of historical phenomena. The relationship between them for the Progressive Era is not now clear; it has not been investigated. But it cannot be explored until the conceptual distinction is made clear and evidence tapped which is pertinent to each. Because the nature of political practice has so long been distorted by the use of ideological evidence, the most pressing task is for its investigation through new types of evidence appropriate to it. The reconstruction of the movement for municipal reform can constitute a major step forward toward that goal.

NOTES

[1]See, for example, Clifford W. Patton, *Battle for Municipal Reform* (Washington, D.C., 1940), and Frank Mann Stewart, *A Half-Century of Municipal Reform* (Berkeley, 1950).

[2]George E. Mowry, *The California Progressives* (Berkeley and Los Angeles, 1951), 86-104; Richard Hofstadter, *The Age of Reform* (New York, 1955), 131-269; Alfred D. Chandler, Jr., "The Origins of Progressive Leadership," in Elting Morrison *et al.*, eds. *Letters of Theodore Roosevelt* (Cambridge, 1951-54), VIII, Appendix III, 1462-64.

[3]Harry A. Toulmin, *The City Manager* (New York, 1915), 156-68; Clinton R. Woodruff, *City Government by Commission* (New York, 1911), 243-53.

[4]Eli Daniel Potts, "A Comparative Study of the Leadership of Republican Factions in Iowa, 1904-1914," M.A. thesis (State University of Iowa, 1956). Another satisfactory comparative analysis is contained in William T. Kerr, Jr., "The Progressives of Washington, 1910-12," *PNQ*, Vol. 55 (1964), 16-27.

[5]Based upon a study of eleven ministers involved in municipal reform in Pittsburgh, who represented exclusively the upper-class Presbyterian and Episcopal churches.

[6]Based upon a study of professional men involved in municipal reform in Pittsburgh, comprising eighty-three doctors, twelve architects, twenty-five educators, and thirteen engineers.

[7]See especially Mowry, *The California Progressives*.

[8]Leonard White, *The City Manager* (Chicago, 1927), ix-x.

[9]Harold A. Stone *et al.*, *City Manager Government in Nine Cities* (Chicago, 1940); Frederick C. Mosher *et al.*, *City Manager Government in Seven Cities* (Chicago, 1940); Harold A. Stone *et al.*, *City Manager Government in the United States* (Chicago, 1940). Cities covered by these studies include: Austin, Texas; Charlotte, North Carolina; Dallas, Texas; Dayton, Ohio; Fredericksburg, Virginia; Jackson, Michigan; Janesville, Wisconsin; Kingsport, Tennessee; Lynchburg, Virginia; Rochester, New York; San Diego, California.

[10]Jewell Cass Phillips, *Operation of the Council-Manager Plan of Government in Oklahoma Cities* (Philadelphia, 1935), 31-39.

[11]James Weinstein, "Organized Business and the City Commission and Manager Movements," *Journal of Southern History*, XXVIII (1962), 166-82.

[12]Norman N. Gill, *Municipal Research Bureaus* (Washington, 1944).

[13]This account of the movement for commission government in Des Moines is derived from items in the Des Moines *Register* during the years from 1905 through 1908.

[14]Biographical data constitutes the main source of evidence for this study of Pittsburgh reform leaders. It was found in city directories, social registers, directories of corporate directors, biographical compilations, reports of boards of education, settlement houses, welfare organizations, and similar types of material. Especially valuable was the clipping file maintained at the Carnegie Library of Pittsburgh.

[15]*Town Crier* (Seattle), Feb. 18, 1911, p. 13.

[16]Information derived from same sources as cited in footnote 14.

[17]Stone *et al.*, *Nine Cities*, 212.

[18]*Ibid.*, 3-13.

[19]*Ibid.*, 329.

[20]Stone *et al.*, *City Manager Government*, 26, 237-41, for analysis of opposition to city-manager government.

[21]Des Moines *Register and Leader*, March 17, 1908.

[22]*Ibid.*, March 30, March 28, 1908.

[23]Voters' Civic League of Allegheny County, "Bulletin of the Voters' Civic League of Allegheny County Concerning the Public School System of Pittsburgh," Feb. 14, 1911, pp. 2-3.

[24]In the decade 1911 to 1920, 43 per cent of the municipal charters adopted in eleven home rule states involved the commission form and 35 per cent the city-manager form; in the following decade the figures stood at 6 per cent and 71 per cent respectively. The adoption of city-manager charters reached a peak in the years 1918 through 1923 and declined sharply after 1933. See Leonard D. White, "The Future of Public Administration," *Public Management*, XV (1933), 12.

[25]Toulmin, *The City Manager*, 42.

[26]Woodruff, *City Government*, 315. The Galveston commission plan did not contain provisions for the initiative, referendum, or recall, and Galveston commercial groups which had fathered the commission plan opposed movements to include them. In 1911 Governor Colquitt of Texas vetoed a charter bill for Texarkana because it contained such provisions; he maintained that they were "undemocratic" and unnecessary to the success of commission government. *Ibid.*, 314-15.

[27]*Ibid.*, 207-208.

[28]Des Moines *Register and Leader*, Jan. 15, 1908.

[29]Voters' Civic League of Allegheny County, "Report on the Voters' League in the Redistricting of the Wards of the City of Pittsburgh" (Pittsburgh, n.d.).

[30]Horace E. Deming, "The Government of American Cities," in Woodruff, *City Government*, 167.

[31]*Ibid.*, 168.

[32]Information derived from same sources as cited in footnote 14.

[33]W. R. Hopkins, city manager of Cleveland, indicated the degree to which the new type of government was more responsive to the business community: "It is undoubtedly easier for a city manager to insist upon acting in accordance with the business interests of the city than it is for a mayor to do the same thing." Quoted in White, *The City Manager*, 13.

[34]Stone *et al.*, *Nine Cities*, 20.

[35]*Ibid.*, 225.

[36]Herbert Gutman, "An Iron Workers' Strike in the Ohio Valley, 1873-74," *Ohio Historical Quarterly*, LXVIII (1959), 353-70; "Trouble on the Railroads, 1873-1874: Prelude to the 1877 Crisis," *Labor History*, II (Spring, 1961), 215-36.

[37]Oscar Handlin, *The Uprooted* (Boston, 1951), 209-17.

[38]Clinton Rodgers Woodruff of the National Municipal League even argued that the initiative, referendum, and recall were rarely used. "Their value lies in their existence

rather than in their use." Woodruff, *City Government*, 314. It seems apparent that the most widely used of these devices, the referendum, was popularized by legislative bodies when they could not agree or did not want to take responsibility for a decision and sought to pass that responsibility to the general public, rather than because of a faith in the wisdom of popular will.

[39]J. B. Shannon, "County Consolidation," *Annals of the American Academy of Political and Social Science*, Vol. 207 (January, 1940), 168.

[40]Woodruff, *City Government,* 29-30.

[41]Several recent studies emphasize various aspects of this movement. See, for example, Loren Baritz, *Servants of Power* (Middletown, 1960); Raymond E. Callahan, *Education and the Cult of Efficiency* (Chicago, 1962); Samuel P. Hays, *Conservation and the Gospel of Efficiency* (Cambridge, 1959); Dwight Waldo, *The Administrative State* (New York, 1948), 3-61.

III The City Boss and Urban Reform

Neither the "boss" nor the "reformer" have lived up to their reputations as venal crooks or saintly paragons. Certainly, the reformers were frequently motivated by desires to achieve order, progress, and a greater degree of political democracy, while lessening the conflict between classes and special interest groups. Yet they have often been justly indicted for their elitism, their tendency to conceive of problems in moral dichotomies, and their narrow middle- and upper-class biases and concerns. "When they said, as they consistently did, that power must be taken away from the bosses and given back to the people, the word *people* did not mean everybody," Henry F. May observed. "It did not mean, for instance, the people who had given their power to the bosses in the first place or allowed them to take it. It meant the sound people, under the right leadership."[1]

On the other hand, while the staid editor and civil service advocate E. L. Godkin might justifiably have looked upon professional politicians as men "whom no one would make guardians of his children or trustees of his property," the traditional urban boss played in many respects a constructive role in easing the tensions of urban society, aiding the assimilation of millions of newcomers to a strange urban environment, and in providing a voice—however diluted by graft and corruption—for the city's dispossessed and downtrodden. It would not be accurate, of course, to claim that the ward or city boss was an unsung hero of American democracy; bribes that passed under the table in payment of franchise agreements were, after all, signs of the boss's alliance with powerful and entrenched interests in the city, not necessarily with the urban masses. But the boss was hardly altogether malevolent in his impact upon American society.

There were, in fact, a number of middle-class reformers at that time who recognized the real bases for the urban political machine, even though they vilified the boss's corruption and immorality. Harold L. Ickes, a Chicago newspaperman in the 1890s and later Secretary of the Interior under Franklin D. Roosevelt and Harry S. Truman, for example, recalled that in the late nineteenth century "it was the plug-ugly, the heavy-handed manipulator of ballots, the man who could smell out the loot and get to it first, who was in the saddle.'' Yet Ickes also admitted that he liked the company of the ward bosses and respected their effectiveness. "The reformers,'' he wrote, "were aloof and austere, and contrasted unfavorably with the warm joviality of the Irish political chieftains. I am grateful that I was never in a position where I felt I had to go either to the politicians or to the reformers for help. But had I needed help I am sure that I would have been more certain of getting it from the politicians.''[2] Even Herbert Croly, a principal spokesman of reform theory in the first decades of the twentieth century, concluded that the urban boss "has been a genuine and within limits a useful product of the American democracy; and it would be fatal either to undervalue or misunderstand him.''[3]

Indeed, some of the most effective leaders in instituting widespread social and economic change and protecting the public interest in this period were not only "reformers" but "bosses" as well—men who organized political "machines" that effectively brought power to bear on entrenched political and economic interests and carved stability and order out of urban chaos. Perhaps the most notable of those urban politicos recently described by Charles N. Glaab and A. Theodore Brown as "reform bosses" were Tom L. Johnson of Cleveland, Samuel "Golden Rule" Jones of Toledo, and Hazen S. Pingree of Detroit.[4] Johnson called for a reduction in the streetcar fare and the public ownership of utilities, and tended to overlook the "evils" of the saloon and the gaming table. Much of his support came from the politically oppressed, economically deprived, foreign-born wards of Cleveland's West Side, support that was galvanized by a smoothly-functioning machine. Jones instituted the eight-hour day in several city departments and projects, increased public services by providing playgrounds, musical entertainment, and public kindergartens, and favored the municipal ownership of public utilities. It is significant that Jones was consistently opposed by virtually every leading businessman, "respectable" civic group, and newspaper in Toledo, and just as consistently returned to office by the mass of urban citizens until his death in 1904. Similarly, Hazen Pingree established an effective organization on the basis of a largely immigrant, lower-class constituency, and focused his fire on the corruption of big business, the inequality of excessive utility rates, the paucity of public services, and the quest for "home rule." The methods of Pingree's "reform machine" were similar to those of machines everywhere, including threats of economic reprisal against citizens and city employees as a means of insuring their political loyalty.

While reform bosses were adopting the methods and practices of the urban political machine in advocating social and economic change in the Midwest, New York's Tammany Hall was engaged in activities that Boss

Plunkitt might have found unusual in all but method. Under the leadership of Charles F. Murphy, Tammany brought to national prominence two of the most notable liberal reformers of the twentieth century—Alfred E. Smith and Robert F. Wagner—and supported a variety of measures including the regulation of banking and insurance companies, a strengthening of the tenement house laws, and the public ownership of utilities. Although the machine maintained its traditional lack of interest in moralistic reforms and continued to hold power through the effective use of patronage and a strong ward organization, it supported woman suffrage, the direct election of United States Senators, the direct primary, and "home rule." In addition, it succeeded in expanding state and city services, creating a public employment office, and establishing old-age pensions and a six-day week. Furthermore, the political successor in New York City to Murphy's Tammany Hall was a maverick insurgent named Fiorello La Guardia—elected Mayor in 1933—who rose to power by building an effective organization, catering to the demands of the city's polyglot districts, and creating a coalition of significant interest groups. Speaking any one of seven languages, La Guardia became the most powerful and successful ethnic politician in American history, known for his masterful use of the techniques long practiced by the "bosses" he derided.

The nineteenth-century urban political machine was forced by the necessity of survival to adjust to new circumstances. The increasing sophistication of the electorate, the assimilation of ethnic groups, and the coming of age of the urban masses—indeed, the entire process of urban growth itself—turned the political machine toward new methods and concerns. City bosses looked to state legislatures for economic and social welfare legislation to aid their immigrant, working-class constituencies, and gradually became the distributors and administrators of state and, eventually, federal programs. While they instinctively feared political reform, the urban bosses soon realized that certain innovations could be used for their own advantage. It would not be too much to say that the successful urban politician, regardless of his background or his motives, simply could not maintain power in the complex world of the American city without cultivating the bases of power or responding in some way to the demands for social change—whether he be George Washington Plunkitt or Hazen Pingree. In a very real sense, for the reformer to be effective he had to become a "boss"; and for the boss to survive he usually found it necessary to become in some ways a "reformer."

Thus, the formerly clear-cut distinction between the corrupt, reactionary boss and the honest, progressive reformer has become hopelessly blurred, in large part because, as Lyle Dorsett recently concluded, "the goals, accomplishments, and methods of both 'bosses' and political 'reformers' were strikingly similar.''[5] The elimination of outworn conceptions is not enough, however; an understanding of the immensely varied urban political world demands that valid distinctions in goals and methods be appreciated. We must be able to distinguish, for example, not only between the administrations of "Golden Rule" Jones and Frank Hague, but also between the business-oriented reorganizations of municipal government and the settlement house activity of Jane Addams; between the "reform" administrations of men like Seth Low in New York and James D. Phelan in San Francisco, and those of Tom Johnson and Hazen Pingree; between attacks on the saloon and those on fundamental economic inequities. Certainly, venality and degrees of self-interest have ceased to be effective analytical tools for examining the viability and ultimate consequences of political activity or for distinguishing between those who accomplished constructive reform and those who did not.

Both the traditional political machine and those who sought to replace it with something more honest, efficient, and responsible were apparently seeking means of establishing order and stability through the centralization and rationalization of the decision-making process—whether order was achieved through the hard-fisted rule of the ward boss or through the election or appointment of experts to the councils of city government. The search for order in the city continues, of course, even though the traditional urban boss has become an anachronism in many localities. Many reforms begun in the early twentieth century largely succeeded in erecting centralized and bureaucratized municipal governments that took many of the traditional powers away from the local boss. As a result, modern city governments now tend to draw strength more from their ability to bargain with the federal government than from their political connections at the ward level. Yet it would be a mistake to assume that the powerful political leader and local organization have vanished. Though welfare, social security, and unemployment compensation undermined the boss's previous monopoly on services to those in need, the boss clearly retained a prominent role in the *distribution* of these services—as recent studies in Kansas City and Pittsburgh have demonstrated. And many of the older organizations have adapted substantially to modern conditions—a phenomenon of which Mayor Richard J. Daley's Chicago machine is perhaps the best example.

It would also be a mistake to conclude that the centralization and bureaucratization of municipal government have succeeded in providing responsive government; the opposite, in fact, often appears to be the case. The bureaucrat, secure in the protection of civil service, frequently does not identify with the plight of those who come to him for help. Compared with the complexity and red tape of city hall, the older urban boss often seems a far more personal and perhaps even more efficient political agent, whose survival depended in the final analysis on how well he was able to satisfy his constituents.

Ultimately, our definition of *reform* will probably rest upon the distinction between those changes that were constructive and successful in meeting the needs of our cities and their people, and those that were not. Judgments of this kind vary, of course, from generation to generation, and from scholar to scholar, and will surely be debated for some time to come.

NOTES

[1]Henry F. May, *The End of American Innocence: A Study of the First Years of Our Time, 1912–1917* (New York: Knopf, 1959), p. 26.

[2]Harold L. Ickes, *The Autobiography of a Curmudgeon* (New York: McClelland, 1943), pp. 33, 38.

[3]Herbert Croly, *The Promise of American Life* (New York: Macmillan, 1909), pp. 117–126.

[4]Charles N. Glaab and A. Theodore Brown, *A History of Urban America* (New York: Macmillan, 1967), pp. 213–215.

[5]Lyle W. Dorsett, "The City Boss and the Reformer: A Reappraisal" (unpublished paper presented to the annual meeting of the Organization of American Historians, Los Angeles, Calif., April, 1970). The editors wish particularly to thank Professor Dorsett for providing them with a copy of his paper, which contains many of the major points presented in this volume.

ZANE L. MILLER

Boss Cox's Cincinnati: A Study of Urbanization and Politics, 1880–1914

Regardless of conflicting opinions concerning the urban political boss, it is certain that his rise in the late nineteenth century was fundamentally tied to the socioeconomic reality of the emerging industrial city. In the following essay, Zane L. Miller of the University of Cincinnati challenges the view that the boss and his machine were simply sores on the body politic. He argues that "Boss" George B. Cox's reign in Cincinnati cannot be understood apart from the chaos and confusion of the time, or without attention to Cox's responses to the urban situation. The reader should therefore not only note the political activities of the boss and his machine, but also attempt to relate these to the social and economic realities of the city. Beyond that, one must ask whether some form of tightly-organized "machine politics" was an inevitable response to the social conditions of the period, and whether men like Cox did indeed make significant contributions to the development of urban America.

Many observers of the turn-of-the-century urban scene have depicted boss-ism as one of the great unmitigated evils of the American city, as a tyrannical, authoritarian, relentlessly efficient and virtually invulnerable political system. Between 1904 and 1912, for example, George B. Cox was castigated by writers in four national magazines. Gustav Karger called him the "Proprietor of Cincinnati." Lincoln Steffens declared that "Cox's System" was "one great graft," "the most perfect thing of the kind in this country." Frank Parker Stockbridge claimed that "The Biggest Boss of Them All" had an organization "more compact and closely knit than any of the political machines which have dominated New York, Philadelphia, Chicago, St. Louis or San Francisco." And George Kibbe Turner concluded that in the 1890s "the man from Dead Man's Corner . . . seated himself over the city of Cincinnati. For twenty years he remained there—a figure like no other in the United States, or in the world."[1] Yet these knowledgable and sensitive journalists obscured as much as they revealed about the nature of Queen City politics in the Progressive era. A new kind of city had developed, and "the boss" comprised only a fraction of its novel political system.

From *The Journal of American History*, 54 (March, 1968), 823-838. Copyright 1968 by *The Journal of American History*. Reprinted by permission.

Paradoxically, Cox and his machine[2] were produced by, fed on, and ultimately helped dispel the spectacular disorder which engulfed Cincinnati in the late-nineteenth century and threatened the very survival of the democratic political process. In these years, increasing industrialization, technological innovations in communication and transportation—especially the coming of rapid transit—and continued foreign and domestic migration had reversed the physical pattern of the mid-century walking city and transformed Cincinnati into a physically enlarged, divided, and potentially explosive metropolis.[3]

Old citizens were shocked as familiar landmarks and neighborhoods vanished. By 1900, railroads and warehouses had monopolized the Ohio River bottoms. The financial and retail districts had moved up into the Basin around Fountain Square, the focus of the street railway system; new club, theater, and tenderloin districts had developed; and industries had plunged up Mill Creek Valley, converting Mohawk-Brighton into "the undisputed industrial bee-hive of the Great Queen City of the West," surrounding once fashionable Dayton Street, creating a new community called Ivorydale, and reaching out to the villages of Norwood and Oakley in search of cheap land, ready access to railroads, and less congested and more cheerful surroundings.[4]

The Over-the-Rhine entertainment section along Vine Street became tawdry with commercialism. It now had, complained one habitue, "all the tarnished tinsel of a Bohemianism with the trimmings of a gutter and the morals of a sewer"—a repulsive contrast, he felt, to "the old-time concert and music halls . . . where one could take wife, sister, or sweetheart and feel secure . . . that not one obnoxious word would profane their ears."[5]

The fashionable residential districts which had flanked the center of the walking city began to disintegrate. One family after another fled the East End for the hills around the Basin, leaving only a small coterie led by the Charles P. Tafts to stave off the advance of factories and slums.[6] The elite West End seemed to disappear overnight. It "did not go down imperceptibly," recalled one old resident. "It went to ruin almost as if a bombshell sent it to destruction."[7]

The Hilltops, at mid-century the private preserve of cemeteries, colleges, and a handful of wealthy families,[8] became the prime residential district in the new city. The crush to get in generated new tensions. In 1899 one observer acidly remarked: "when rapid transit came the Hebrews . . . flocked to" Walnut Hills

until it was known by the name of New Jerusalem. Avondale was then heralded as the suburb of deliverance, but again rapid transit brought the wealthy Hebrews . . . in numbers greater than the flock of crows that every morning and evening darkens her skies, until now it has been facetiously said that the congregation has assembled in force and . . . when Avondale is roofed over the synagogue will be complete.[9]

The diffusion of wealthy families, the reduction in casual social and business contacts, and the construction of new communities made ardent joiners of the Hilltops elite. Each neighborhood had an improvement association, and between 1880 and 1905 five new businessmen's organizations devoted to boosting the city's lethargic economy had appeared. In the same period six social clubs opened downtown facilities, and three country clubs were started. By 1913, moreover, there were twenty-two exclusive clubs and patriotic societies and innumerable women's groups.[10] These developments helped counteract the disruptive effects of the "country movement," as one visitor labeled it, which was "so general that church-going became an affair of some difficulty" and "society itself . . . more or less disintegrated."[11]

But not all those moving out were affluent. Liberated by rapid transit, skilled and semiskilled workers and moderately prosperous professional and white-collar men with life savings, the courage to take out a mortgage, an equity in a building and loan association, or a willingness to rent a flat in a double or triple decker, also fled the Basin.[12] They took refuge in a no-man's-land between the center of the city and the Hilltops frontier which was similar to an area dubbed the Zone of Emergence by Boston social workers.[13]

Zone residents formed what the Cincinnati *Post* referred to as "the so-called middle class . . ., the class that makes any city . . . what it is . . .[,] the class that takes in the great body of people between wealth and poverty" and builds up "many organizations, societies, associations, fraternities and clubs that bring together people who are striving upward, trying to uplift themselves, and hence human society."[14]

They, too, found life in the new city a novel experience. A retired leather factory porter who moved into the Zone lamented:

When I lived down on Richmond in a little house we cooked the corn beef and cabbage in the house and ate in there, and when we wanted to go to the toilet we went out into the yard, now I live in a fine house, I am made to eat . . . out in the yard, and when I want to go to the toilet I have to go into the house.[15]

Graham R. Taylor had noted that since most Zone residents commuted they suffered a severe "dislocation of the normal routine of factory and home": they had to adjust to "the need for travel and its curtailment of leisure and income . . .," to eating lunches away from home, to doing without "customary city facilities," and to knowing the feeling of "isolation from their fellows."[16] Price Hill—like the rest of the Zone a heavily Catholic area—felt itself conspicuously cut off. In the 1890s the editor of the *Catholic-Telegraph*, denouncing the traction company as the "octopus," joined the Price Hill Improvement Association in begging both city and traction company officials to bring the area "within range of the civilized world" and suggested secession as a means of dramatizing to the "people east of Millcreek" that a new public school, "granted by the unbounded munificence of the City of Cincinnati," did not amount to a redemption of the city's annexation pledges.[17]

The exodus, however, did not depopulate the Basin. Instead, a great residential Circle formed around the central business district. It filled with newcomers and those who lacked the means to get out—rural whites and Negroes from the South, Germans, Irish, Greeks, Italians, and Jews from eastern Europe. Working at the poorest paying jobs available, they were jammed into the most congested quarters. The Circle led all other areas of the city in arrests, mortality, and disease.[18]

Although the pressure to escape was enormous, the barriers were formidable. Ignorant of the ways of the city, as an Associated Charities report put it, Circle dwellers had to be "shown how to buy, how to cook, how to make the home attractive, how to find employment." Many, "utterly friendless and discouraged," succumbed to "the damnable absence of want or desire" and grew "indifferent . . . to their own elevation."[19] Plagued by "physical bankruptcy,"[20] they found it difficult to find and hold jobs, let alone form and maintain the kind of organizations which enabled Zone residents to shield themselves from economic disaster, legal pitfalls, social isolation, and apathy.[21]

The immediate impact of the emergence of the new city pushed Cincinnati to the brink of anarchy. In March 1884, the *Enquirer* complained that the police had failed to choke off a crime wave although, in the last year alone, there had been twelve arrests for malicious shooting, twenty-nine for malicious cutting, forty-seven for cutting with intent to wound, 284 for shooting with intent to kill, ninety-two for murder and manslaughter, and 948 for carrying a concealed weapon. The total number of arrests came to 56,784. The city's population was 250,000.[22] Later that same month, a lynch mob descended on the county jail. While police and militia fought off the mob, gangs looted stores and shops on the fringe of the downtown district. In three days of riot the courthouse was burned to the ground, fifty-four people were killed, and an estimated 200 people wounded.[23]

During the fall elections, violence erupted in the lower wards; two policemen and one Negro were killed. Congressman Benjamin Butterworth remarked that he had "never witnessed anywhere such coarse brutality and such riotous demonstrations. . . ." Cincinnati, he concluded, "seems . . . doomed to perdition."[24]

Less than two years later the city faced another major crisis. On May 1, 1886, Cincinnati workers joined in nationwide demonstrations for the eight-hour day. These were followed by a series of strikes. The militia was called out, and for two weeks the city resembled an armed camp. Only the show of force and, perhaps, the memory of the courthouse catastrophe prevented another riot.[25]

Yet labor remained restive, and a rash of strikes followed. By 1892, the paternalistic system which had dominated the breweries was smashed.[26] And in 1894, Judge William Howard Taft spent the hot days of June and July "trying to say nothing to reporters" and "issuing injunctions" in an effort to control and prevent the railroad strike from leading to mass violence.[27]

The Sunday-closing question was another explosive issue. The *Post*, the *Catholic-Telegraph*, a Committee of Five Hundred, and many Protestant clergymen all leveled scathing attacks on the continental Sabbath. "Sunday in Cincinnati," asserted one Methodist minister, "is a high carnival of drunkenness, base sensuality, reeking debauchery and bloody, often fatal crime." Other spokesmen tied the open Sunday to anarchism, atheism, corrupt politicians, a decadent daily press, indifferent public officials, and the ruthless exploitation of labor.[28] "The modern Puritan," insisted Charles P. Taft, "intends to rise up and oppose to the uttermost this kind of Sunday."[29]

When, in 1889, the mayor announced his intention to enforce the Sunday-closing law for saloons, the city almost faced another riot. Some 1,000 saloonkeepers vowed to ignore the new policy. When a cadre of police and firemen marched over the Rhine to close Kissell's saloon, an unruly crowd gathered, epithets were hurled, but no violence occurred. Kissell's was closed; the "era of the back door," with "front doors locked and curtains up, but back doors widened," had opened.[30]

These spectacular outbreaks plus other pressures overwhelmed city hall. Indeed, scarcely a residential area, economic interest, or social or occupational group was left unscathed by the multidimensional disorder. As the physical area of the city expanded, officials were besieged by demands for the extension, improvement, and inauguration of public services of all kinds and for lower taxes. Simultaneously, the relative decline of the city heightened the urgency of the agitation. Municipal institutions and agencies, established to meet the needs of the walking city, became overburdened, outmoded, and dilapidated.[31]

The new city, with old ways shattered, provided a fertile breeding ground for turmoil and discontent and, as it turned out, for innovation and creative reconstruction. Initially, however, this unprecedented change accompanied by unprecedented demands for government action produced only the hope of reform. In 1885, on the eve of the repudiation of a Democratic administration, William Howard Taft predicted that "the clouds are beginning to break over this Sodom of ours and the sun of decency is beginning to dispel the moral miasma that has rested on us now for so many years. It's the beginning of an era of reform."[32]

Yet for almost a decade no party could put together a decisive ruling majority.[33] The city's political processes seemed frozen by a paralyzing factionalism. The division of the city into residential districts which roughly coincided with socio-economic lines made it difficult for the wealthy and well-educated[34] to keep in contact with and control ward politics. As a result, extreme factionalism developed which could, apparently, be surmounted only by appealing to a host of neighborhood leaders and by constructing alliances which crossed party lines.

According to close observers, the chief products of this system were the use of money in city conventions and the rise of what Charles P. Taft called the "bummer," a "queer creature" who "evolves somehow from the slums. . . ." In youth "a bootblack, a newsboy or a general loafer," he matured into "an Arab" who needed only "a good standing with a saloon that has a fine layout during the day." A "hustler at the polls and conventions," the bummer was in such demand that he could accept money from competing candidates, thus lengthening the convention and contributing to interfactional dealing. After studying the influence of the "bummer," Taft gloomily concluded that the "day of pure politics can never be . . . until a riot, a plague or flood kills off all the ward bummers."[35]

By 1897, however, and without divine intervention, all this had changed. In January of that year, three months before the city election, the *Post* gravely announced its intention to describe "impassionately and without bias the means employed" in Cincinnati's "superior and unrecorded government." It was controlled by "the boss, whose power is absolute"—George B. Cox.[36]

The *Post*'s analysis closely paralleled those made after the turn of the century. It dissected the patronage system, outlined the sources of financial support, and noted the attempted appeasement of the city's various special groups—the soldiers, the Germans, the Republican clubs, the Reform Jews, the legal and medical professions, the socially prominent Hilltops businessmen, and certain cooperative Democrats. It excitedly reported the effectiveness of the organization's intelligence system, the way the "plugger" and the "knocker" wore "beaten paths to the office of the boss to urge the appointment of this man, the discharge of that [,] or to report some feature of misconduct or expression. . . ." The paper noted that Cox was always available for consultation with any citizen regardless of station or status and that he had been little more than one of several important factional leaders until, in 1886, Governor Joseph B. Foraker selected him to serve as chief adviser on patronage and political affairs in Hamilton County.[37]

Foraker made a shrewd choice; Cox had grown up with the new city and received a liberal education in its ways. The son of British immigrants, he was born in 1853 and reared in the Eighteenth Ward, a district which by the 1880s contained fashionable as well as slum housing, factories, and its share of saloons and brothels. His father died when Cox was eight. Successively, Cox worked as a bootblack, newsboy, lookout for a gambling joint, grocery deliveryman, bartender, and tobacco salesman. His school principal, who later became superintendent of schools, claimed that Cox was frequently in boyish trouble in classes, exhibited an "undisguised love for his mother," and "never lied . . . bore malice, sulked, whined or moped." Cox had also been exposed to religion. Although not a churchgoer, as an adult he had, according to one journalist, "dormant powerful sentiments, which rest on foundations of the firmest faith."[38]

In the mid-1870s Cox acquired a saloon in his home neighborhood. He entered politics and served on the city council from 1878 until 1885 when, after joining forces with the Republican reform mayoralty candidate, he ran unsuccessfully for county clerk. He tried for the same post in 1888, failed, and never again stood for public office.[39]

At that time, moving away politically from the Circle, Cox worked with George Moerlein, perhaps the strongest of the GOP professionals in the Zone. In 1890, he and Moerlein quarreled over patronage; and in the city convention of 1891, Cox was able, with the support of the Blaine Club, a kind of political settlement house that he had helped to establish, to defeat Moerlein's candidate for police judge and nominate his own man.[40] Moerlein men now became Cox men. So, too, did Charles P. Taft and the *Times-Star*, which had been one of the last, the most influential, and the most outspoken of Cox's critics in the Hilltops

Republican ranks. It accepted Cox, the paper announced, to secure a "New Order" for Cincinnati.[41] And the president of the gas company, sensing the political drift, confided to his diary that he had "concluded [an] arrangement with Geo. B. Cox for services at $3500 per year quarterly to last for three years."[42] In the spring election of 1894 the Republicans carried the city with a plurality of over 6,500 votes, the first decisive municipal election in a decade.[43] In 1897, Cox was the honest broker in a coalition composed of Circle and Zone Negroes, Zone politicians, the gas and traction companies, and Hilltops Republican reformers.[44]

Election returns after 1885 disclose a clear pattern. The GOP won five successive contests by uniting powerful Hilltops support with enough strength in the Zone to overcome the Democratic grip on the Circle.[45] Until 1894 the margins of victory were perilously thin. The substantial triumph of that year merely marked the completion of the alliance which pitted a united periphery against the center of the city.

The heart of the Republican "New Order" coalition, and the critical factor in the election of 1894, was its appeal to voters in the Hilltops fringe who demanded order and reform. To satisfy the Hilltops, Cox and his associates eliminated the bummer, provided brief and decorous conventions, enfranchised Negroes by suppressing violence at the polls, reduced the rapid turnover in office, and cut down the incidence of petty graft and corporation raiding.

Moreover, the "machine" heeded the advice of its reform allies from the Hilltops. Cox accepted the secret ballot, voter registration, and a series of state laws which, though retaining the mayor-council form of government with ward representation, were designed to give the city a stable and more centralized government. The administrations which he indorsed started to build a professional police force, expanded and reequipped the fire department, pushed through a $6,000,000 water-works program, renovated municipal institutions, supported the growth of the University of Cincinnati, launched extensive street-paving and sewer-constructing projects, and tried to reduce the smoke problem and expand the city's park acreage. They also opened the door to housing regulation, suppressed the Sunday saloon, flagrant public gambling, and disorderly brothels (the city was never really closed), began to bring order into the chaotic public-utilities field by favoring privately owned, publicly regulated monopolies under progressive management, and succeeded in keeping the tax rate low. The Republican regime, in short, brought positive government to Cincinnati.[46]

While this program also won votes in the Zone, it was not the sole basis for the party's popularity there. Many of the lieutenants and captains closest to Cox were Zone residents. They composed a colorful group known variously as "the gang," "the sports," or the "bonifaces"—a clique which met nightly Over-the-Rhine either at Schubert and Pels, where each had a special beer mug with his name gilded on it, or at the round table in Wielert's beer garden. Three of them owned or operated combination saloons, gambling joints, and dance halls; one was prominent in German charitable associations and the author of several textbooks used in the elementary schools; another served twenty consecutive terms as president of the Hamilton County League of Building Associations; and one was a former catcher for the Cincinnati Redlegs.[47]

Their tastes, behavior, and attitudes were conveniently summarized in the biographical sketches of ward leaders and city officials in the 1901 *Police and Municipal Guide*. All were characterized as friendly, well-known, "All Around Good-Fellows" who liked a story, belonged to several social and fraternal groups, gave generously to charity, and treated the poor and sick with special kindness. They were all among the most ardent supporters of any project to boost the city.

Cox is pictured in the *Guide* as an adherent to the code of the Zone who had risen to the top. He was a *bon vivant* who enjoyed good cigars and good jokes, a man of wealth whose recently completed Clifton mansion was luxuriously decorated and adorned with expensive works of art, a man of impressive but quiet and private charity. Above all, he was true to his word, loyal to his friends, yet quick to reprimand and replace those who betrayed his trust by misusing public office.[48]

Cox and his top civil servants—surrounded by a motley crowd of newspaper reporters, former boxers and ball players, vaudeville and burlesque performers, and other Vine Street characters—provided an attractive model for men awed by the glamor, wealth, and power which was so visible yet so elusive in the new city. Cox's opponents in the Zone seldom attacked him or this inside group directly. Even in the heat of the 1897 campaign, the *Volksfreund*, the German Catholic Democratic daily, carefully described Cox as an "amiable man" who had to be "admired" for his "success" and, either ignoring or unaware of the process of negotiation and mediation by which he ruled, criticized him only for his illiberality in imposing "dictatorial methods" on the GOP.[49] Indeed, most Zone residents, like those of the Hilltops, found it difficult to object to a government which seemed humane, efficient, and progressive.

Yet it would be a mistake to overestimate the strength of the "New Order" Republican coalition. Its victories from 1885 to 1894 were won by perilously close pluralities. The organization, moreover, failed to carry a referendum for the sale of the city-owned Southern Railroad in 1896 and lost the municipal contest in 1897 to a reform fusion ticket, and the fall elections of 1897, 1898, and 1899 to the Democrats.[50] In all these reversals, crucial defections occurred in both the Hilltops and the Zone. Skittish voters grew indignant over alleged corruption, outraged by inaction on the traction and gas questions, piqued by the rising cost of new city projects, annoyed by the slow expansion of the educational program, or uneasy over the partial sacrifice of democracy to efficiency within the Republican organization.[51]

Thereafter, however, the Republicans rallied and won three of the next four city elections by unprecedented margins. The strategy and tactics remained essentially the same. Although not wholly averse to raising national issues, Cox's group gave local affairs the most emphasis.[52] The organization was occasionally purged of its less savory elements. Cox and his Zone advisors continued to consult with their Hilltops allies on nominations. The party promised and, in fact, tried to deliver order and reform. Without abolishing ward representation in the city council, it strengthened the mayor and streamlined the administration. The party also broadened and deepened its program as civic associations, women's clubs, social workers, social gospellers, and spokesmen for the new unionism—all novel forces in urban politics—expanded and elaborated their demands.[53]

But voting patterns underwent a fundamental and, for the GOP, an ultimately disastrous change. By 1903 the Republicans dominated the entire city, carrying not only the Zone and Hilltops but also the center. The Circle was now the invincible bulwark of Cox's power.[54]

There were several factors involved in the conversion of Circle Democrats to Republicanism. First, Cox had extensive personal contacts with them which dated back to his unsuccessful races for county clerk in the 1880s. Second, the Democrats had been unable to put down factionalism. By the late 1890s there were two reform elements in the party, both of which belabored the regulars from the center of the city as tainted with corruption, too cozy with Cox, and perhaps worst of all, as a discredit and burden to the party because they wore the charred shirt of the courthouse riot.[55]

In the wake of the fusionist victory of 1897, Mike Mullen, the leader of a riverfront Democratic ward, explained why he would henceforth work with the Republican party.

> I have worked hard [for the Democratic party] have suffered much and have won for it many victories. Yet all the while there was a certain element . . . that looked on me with distrust. . . . [L]eaders of the Fusionist Party did not think enough of me to let me look after the voting in my own ward, but sent down a lot of people to watch the count. That decided me.[56]

He was later joined by Colonel Bob O'Brien who, like Mullen, specialized in Christmas turkey, soupline, and family-service politics.[57] These Democrats led their constituents into the Republican fold.

It was this alliance with the Circle which ultimately destroyed Cox. Anti-machine spokesmen were convinced that they had to educate the city before they could redeem it. They felt, too, that politics was a potent educational tool. But campaigns had to be spectacular in order to engage the voters' attention and participation. As A. Julius Freiberg notes, the "psychology" of the electorate was such that years of "speaking, writing, explaining, even begging and imploring" had been "to no purpose." The "reformer and his fellow students may sit about the table and evolve high principles for action, but the people . . . will not be fed by those principles unless there is a dramatic setting, and the favorite dramatic setting is the killing of a dragon." And all the people "love the dramatic; not merely the poor, but the rich, and the middle class as well." All that was needed was a situation which would enable the right man to "bring to book the boss himself."[58]

Reformers hammered relentlessly at the theme that Cox was not a good boss; he was the head of a "syndicate" which included the worst products of slum life.[59] In "that part of the city where vice and infamy hold high revel," went one version of the charge, "the boss-made ticket finds its most numerous supporters. Every dive keeper, every creature who fattens upon the wages of sin . . ., all the elements at war with society have enlisted." Men "who claim to be respectable," the chief "beneficiaries of this unholy alliance . . ., go down into the gutter and accept office from hands that are reeking with the filth of the slums." Worse still, this "alliance of the hosts of iniquity with the greed of special privilege and ambition for power and place" plays so successfully "upon the prejudices and . . . superstition of the many that wrong is often espoused by those who in the end are the victims of the wrong."[60]

The reformers also impugned Cox's personal integrity. Democratic County Prosecutor Henry T. Hunt secured evidence that Cox had perjured himself in 1906 when he said he had not received a cent of some $250,000 of interest on public funds which Republican county treasurers had been paid by bankers. In the spring of 1911, Hunt and the grand jury indicted Cox and 123 others during a broad investigation of politics, corruption, and vice.[61]

Finally, Hunt, stressing the issue of moral indignation, ran for mayor in the fall of 1911 on a Democratic reform ticket. Using the moral rhetoric of the muckraker, Hunt and his associates tied bossism, the chaos, poverty, and vice of the slums, and the malefactors of great wealth together and pictured them as a threat to the welfare of the whole city. Once again the Hilltops and Zone voted for order and reform. Hunt's progressive coalition swept the periphery, lost only in the Circle wards, and won the election.[62]

By that time, however, Cox was no longer boss. President Taft and Charles P. Taft had wanted Cox to step aside as early as 1905, but they found him indispensable. After the grand jury revelations, however, they were able to convince the "bonifaces" that Cox was a liability. With the organization against him, Cox retired. For a time, he insisted that his two chief assistants, August Herrmann, and Rudolph Hynicka, should also quit, apparently convinced that they, like himself, could no longer command the confidence of the periphery. Charles P. Taft's *Times-Star* agreed. The two men, backed by the Blaine Club, merely resigned their offical party positions but refused to get out of politics entirely.[63]

What, then, was Cox's role in politics and government in the new city? He helped create and manage a voluntary political-action organization which bridged the racial and cultural chasms between the Circle, Zone, and Hilltops. He and his allies were able to bring positive and moderate reform government to Cincinnati and to mitigate the conflict and disorder which accompanied the emergence of the new city. With the crisis atmosphere muted, ardent reformers could develop more sophisticated programs and agitate, educate, and organize without arousing the kind of divisive, emotional, and hysterical response which had immobilized municipal statesmen in the 1880s. In the process, while battering at the boss, the slums, and the special-privilege syndicate, they shattered the bonds of confidence which linked the Zone "bonifaces" and the moderate reformers of the Hilltops to Cox's organization. Cox, it seems, said more than he realized when, in 1892, he remarked that a boss was "not necessarily a public enemy."[64]

NOTES

[1]Gustav J. Karger, "George Barnesdale Cox: Proprietor of Cincinnati," *Frank Leslie's Popular Monthly*, LVII (Jan. 1904), 273; Lincoln Steffens, "Ohio: A Tale of Two Cities," *McClure's Magazine*, XXV (June 1905), 309; Frank Parker Stockbridge, "The Biggest Boss of Them All," *Hampton's Magazine*, XXVI (Jan.-June 1911), 616; George Kibbe Turner, "The Thing Above the Law: The Rise and Rule of George B. Cox, and His Overthrow by Young Hunt and the Fighting Idealists of Cincinnati," *McClure's Magazine*, XXXVIII (March 1912), 580. See also Wallace S. Sayre and Nelson W. Polsby, "American Political Science and the Study of Urbanization," Philip M. Hauser and Leo F. Schnore, eds., *The Study of Urbanization* (New York, 1965), 115-23.

[2]It operated, according to William Howard Taft, "as smoothly . . . as a nicely adjusted Corliss engine. . . ." Cincinnati *Enquirer*, Oct. 22, 1905.

[3]Zane L. Miller, "Boss Cox and the Municipal Reformers: Cincinnati Progressivism, 1880-1914" (doctoral dissertation, University of Chicago, 1966), Part I. Introduction, 2-5.

[4]For the quotation see Max Mosler, Jacob Hoffman, and James D. Smith, *Historic Brighton: Its Origin, Growth and Development* (Cincinnati, 1902), 91. See also James A. Green to Joseph C. Green, March 28, 1913, James A. Green Papers (Cincinnati Historical Society); Andrew Hickenlooper, "Reminiscences," 524, Andrew Hickenlooper Papers (Cincinnati Historical Society); Graham Romeyn Taylor, *Satellite Cities: A Study of Industrial Suburbs* (New York, 1915), 91-93; Willard Glazier, *Peculiarities of American Cities* (Philadelphia, 1886), 135.

[5]Frank Y. Grayson, *Pioneers of Night Life on Vine Street* (Cincinnati, Aug. 1924), 63-65, 123-25. Interviews: William C. Smith, Dec. 19, 1962; Alfred Segal, Nov. 2, 1962; Robert Heuck, Nov. 27, 1962; and Edward F. Alexander, Nov. 13, 1962.

[6]Cincinnati *Post*, June 20, 1912; Ruth M. Heistand, "A Social History of Cincinnati's Eastern Basin Area: An Inquiry into the Character, Interests, Attitudes, and Social Services of this Primary Neighborhood" (master's thesis, University of Cincinnati, 1936), 55, 72-75.

[7]James Albert Green, *History of the Associated Charities of Cincinnati, 1879-1937: A Record of Service* (Cincinnati, n.d.), 18-19.

[8]Sidney D. Maxwell, *The Suburbs of Cincinnati: Sketches Historical and Descriptive* (Cincinnati, 1870), 2, 96-97, 99-100, 118-28, 148, 177-85.

[9]Cincinnati *American Israelite*, Oct. 26, 1899.

[10]Cincinnati *Civic News*, I (Oct. 1911), 3; Frank F. Dinsmore, Chas. W. Dupuis, Martin H. Fischer, and Walter A. Draper, *History of the Queen City Optimists Club* (Cincinnati, Jan. 1955), 1-2; *Mrs. Devereux's Blue Book of Cincinnati Society for the Year 1912-1913* (Cincinnati [1912?]), 183-241.

[11]Charles Dudley Warner, "Studies of the Great West, Cincinnati and Louisville," *Harper's New Monthly Magazine*, LXXVII (Aug. 1888), 430.

[12]For a full analysis of this region see Miller, "Boss Cox and the Municipal Reformers," Part I, 58-124.

[13]Robert A. Woods and Albert J. Kennedy, *The Zone of Emergence* (Cambridge, 1962), 31-183.

[14]Cincinnati *Post*, June 11, 1913.

[15]Quoted in Joseph Stacy Hill, "Further Chats With My Descendants," Typescript ca. 1933, p. 42 (Cincinnati Historical Society).

[16]Taylor, *Satellite Cities*, 95-96.

[17]Cincinnati *Catholic-Telegraph*, March 20, 1890, Nov. 2, 16, 1893.

[18]For a detailed analysis see Miller, "Boss Cox and the Municipal Reformers," Part I, 15-57.

[19]Cincinnati *Charities Review*, I (April 1908), 8; United Jewish Charities, *Fourteenth Annual Report, 1910* (Cincinnati, n.d.), 59.

[20]One social worker speculated that the Circle dwellers' "lack of energy and initiative" was due "to physical bankruptcy . . . which, although largely imaginative, is the result of [a] neurotic and temperamental condition . . . and incapacitates . . . as effectively as real physical disability." See United Jewish Charities, *Eighteenth Annual Report, 1914* (Cincinnati, n.d.), 7-8.

[21]Boris D. Bogen, "Politics in Jewish Settlements," *Jewish Charities*, II (Sept. 1911), 10-11.

[22]Cincinnati *Enquirer*, March 9, 1884. See also Joseph D. Emery, *Thirty-Five Years Among the Poor and Public Institutions of Cincinnati* (Cincinnati, 1887), 16.

[23]Perhaps the best among the many contemporary accounts of the riot is J. S. Tunison, *The Cincinnati Riot: Its Causes and Results* (Cincinnati, 1886). The casualty totals are from "Annual Report of the Department of Police," *Annual Reports of the City Departments of the City of Cincinnati for the Fiscal Year Ending December 31, 1884* (Cincinnati, 1885), 311.

²⁴Benjamin Butterworth to Alphonso Taft, June 5, 1885, Taft Papers, Family Correspondence, Box 25 (Manuscript Division, Library of Congress). For other accounts of the election disorders in the fall of 1884 see Cincinnati *Catholic-Telegraph*, Oct. 16, 1884; Butterworth to Joseph B. Foraker, Jan. 5, 9, 1885, Joseph B. Foraker Papers, Box 31 (Cincinnati Historical Society).

²⁵Oscar Ameringer, *If You Don't Weaken: The Autobiography of Oscar Ameringer* (New York, 1940), 44-47; Sidney D. Maxwell to Mrs. Emma Maxwell, May 5, 6, 11, 12, 1886, Sidney D. Maxwell Papers (Cincinnati Historical Society); Cincinnati *Times-Star*, May 3, 13, 1886.

²⁶Cincinnati *Freie Presse*, Jan. 23, 1921. For the strikes see Cincinnati *Times-Star*, Feb. 3, Oct. 6, 1892; Cincinnati Central Labor Council *Chronicle*, June 5, 1886, Sept. 29, 1901.

²⁷Henry F. Pringle, *The Life and Times of William Howard Taft: A Biography* (2 vols., New York, 1939), I, 134-36.

²⁸Rev. T. H. Pearne, *What Shall Be Done with the Cincinnati Sunday Saloon? An Address Before the Cincinnati Methodist Preachers' Meeting, May 13th and May 19th, 1887* (Cincinnati, 1887), 7. See also Cincinnati *Times-Star*, March 29, 1889; Cincinnati *Post*, March 29, 1889; Cincinnati *Catholic-Telegraph*, June 5, 1884; *Address of the Bund für Freiheit und Recht* (Cincinnati, May 1886), 4, 5, 6-7.

²⁹Cincinnati *Times-Star*, Dec. 2, 1889.

³⁰Jno. Pearson to Foraker, July 26, 1889; Foraker to John B. Mosby, July 26, 1889, Foraker Papers, Boxes 38, 29; "Report of the Non-Partisan Board of Police Commissioners," *Annual Reports of the City Departments of the City of Cincinnati for the Fiscal Year Ending December 31, 1889* (Cincinnati, 1889), 199-200; Joseph Benson Foraker, *Notes of a Busy Life* (2 vols., Cincinnati, 1916), I, 411-16. For the "era of the back door" see Grayson, *Pioneers of Night Life*, 18.

³¹See the reports of the city boards, departments, and agencies, and the mayor's annual messages in the *Annual Reports* of the city, 1884-1891. See also Cincinnati Commercial Club, *Report of [the] Special Committee to [the] Commercial Club . . . on Deficient Water Supply to the City, Aug. 25, 1890* (Cincinnati, n.d.); Cincinnati Chamber of Commerce, *A Canal Town in a Railroad Era* (Cincinnati, Feb. 1887); Charles B. Wilby, "What is the Matter with Cincinnati?" *Extracts of a Paper Read before the Young Business Men's Club, Nov. 30, 1886* (Cincinnati, n.d.).

³²William Howard Taft to Mother [Louisa Taft], March 27, 1885, Taft Papers, Family Correspondence, Box 25.

³³In 1885 the Republican reform mayoralty candidate won by 4,000 votes out of a total of nearly 53,000. See Cincinnati *Times-Star*, April 6, 1885. But the elections of 1887 and 1889 were three-cornered affairs resulting in a total Republican plurality of 1,153. In 1891, with only two strong tickets in the field, the Republican mayoralty nominee won by a margin of 138 votes over his Democratic opponent. Cincinnati *Times-Star*, April 5, 1887; Hamilton County Board of Elections, "Record of City Elections, Commencing in 1888" (Offices of the Hamilton County Board of Elections, Cincinnati).

³⁴Richard C. Wade, *The Urban Frontier: The Rise of Western Cities, 1790-1830* (Cambridge, 1959), 112-17, 204-06.

³⁵Cincinnati *Times-Star*, Sept. 27, 29, 1890.

³⁶Cincinnati *Post*, Jan. 2, 1897.

³⁷*Ibid.*, Jan. 2, 8, 15, 20, 26, 30, Feb. 1, 1897.

³⁸Karger, "George Barnesdale Cox," 274.

³⁹See notes 1 and 37.

⁴⁰George B. Cox to Foraker, Dec. 24, 1888; Foraker to T. W. Graydon, March 16, 1889; Foraker to Murat Halstead, March 18, 1889, Foraker Papers, Boxes 32, 29; Diaries, Feb. 2, 16, March 23, 25, 1891, Hickenlooper Papers; Cincinnati *Post*, Feb. 3, March 4, 1891; Hickenlooper to Milton A. McRae, March 26, 1891, Hickenlooper Papers.

[41]Cincinnati *Times-Star*, April 4, 1891.

[42]Diaries, May 8, 1891, Hickenlooper Papers.

[43]Hamilton County Board of Elections, "Record of City Elections."

[44]Although Cox avoided publicity, his few public statements succinctly summarize his technique. Bossism, he believed, evolved with the modern city. He never consciously aspired to leadership but acquired it naturally—or had it thrust upon him. A good and successful boss, he felt, claimed and held power by adhering to a few principles. He kept graft at a minimum, kept his word, and demanded that those responsible for securing nominations and winning elections receive consideration when favors were passed out. See Cincinnati *Commercial-Gazette*, Jan. 29, 1892; Cincinnati *Post*, Feb. 22, 1911, May 20, 1916.

[45]Election returns from Cincinnati *Times-Star*, April 6, 1885, April 5, 1887; Hamilton County Board of Elections, "Record of City Elections."

[46]See *Annual Reports of the City Departments of the City of Cincinnati . . .*, 1885-1897; Cincinnati Municipal Reference Bureau, *The March of City Government, City of Cincinnati (1802-1936)* (Cincinnati, 1937), 15-16.

[47]The Cincinnati *Times-Star*, March 27, 30, 1891, lists all the Republican councilmen, gives their occupations, and comments on their backgrounds. See also Cincinnati *Citizens' Bulletin*, Aug. 29, 1903.

[48]Cincinnati Police Department, *Police and Municipal Guide, 1901* (Cincinnati, n.d.). Perhaps the best description of the "bonifaces" and the Vine Street characters is in Grayson, *Pioneers of Night Life*, 63-65. Grayson was a reporter for the Cincinnati *Times-Star* and a member of the coterie.

[49]Cincinnati *Volksfreund*, March 8, 1897. The Cincinnati *Catholic-Telegraph* and the *Chronicle*, the Cincinnati Central Labor Council organ, both spoke essentially to a Zone constituency. Even when in a reform mood they did not attack the "bonifaces" personally in these years.

[50]In the 1899 gubernatorial election the Zone, apparently attracted by the Democratic reform platform, went Democratic along with the Circle. The Hilltops, however, voted Republican. See Hamilton County Board of Elections, "Abstract of Votes Cast from 1896-1899, Incl., . . . 1899" (Offices of Hamilton County Board of Elections, n.d.). In 1897 both the Zone and the Hilltops went for the fusion reformers against the GOP. See Hamilton County Board of Elections, "Record of City Elections."

[51]The accumulation of Zone grievances is quite clearly seen in the 1897 election which the fusionists won by 7,400 votes out of a total of 64,000. For the campaign and post-election analyses see Miller, "Boss Cox and the Reformers," 818-81. Nonetheless, it was the massive defection of the heretofore solidly Republican Hilltops which put the fusionists on top in 1897.

[52]Although national issues were irrelevant, the general pattern of politics in Cincinnati was similar to national developments. Carl N. Degler has suggested that the Republican party attained national dominance after 1884 in part because it was identified by urban voters as the party of positive action. See Carl N. Degler, "American Political Parties and the Rise of the City: An Interpretation," *Journal of American History*, LI (June 1964), 41-50.

[53]For the new forces in politics see Miller, "Boss Cox and the Reformers," 305-37. The Cincinnati *Citizens' Bulletin*, Aug. 15, 29, 1908, Oct. 23, 1909, Sept. 30, 1911, among other contemporary sources, recorded Republican strategy. For the policy of the Republican administrations see the *Annual Reports of the City Departments of the City of Cincinnati . . .* for the years 1900-1905 and 1907-1911.

[54]Before this time, only two Circle wards had been reliably Republican. One, the Eighteenth, was Cox's former district; and the other, the old Ninth, was entrusted to Rudolph K. Hynicka who, with August Herrmann, served as Cox's closest associates. See also Hamilton County Board of Elections, "Record of City Elections."

[55]Cincinnati *Times-Star*, Nov. 7, 1888. For the Democratic factions see *ibid.*, March 25, 1885; C. W. Woolley to John Sherman, April 7, 1885, John Sherman Papers (Manuscript Division, Library of Congress); Cincinnati *Volksfreund*, April 8, 1887; Cincinnati *Times-Star*,

April 2, 1889; Cincinnati *Post*, April 2, 1889, Feb. 26, 1894; and especially R. B. Bowler to Charles T. Greve, Sept. 13, 19, 20, Oct. 8, 29, Dec. 19, 26, 1893, Jan. 6, 12, March 23, 1894, Charles T. Greve Papers (Cincinnati Historical Society).

[56]Cincinnati *Post*, April 12, 1897.

[57]Cincinnati *Citizens' Bulletin*, April 11, May 9, Aug. 29, 1903; Cincinnati *Volksblatt*, April 7, 1903; Henry C. Wright, *Bossism in Cincinnati* (Cincinnati, 1905), 48-49.

[58]A. Julius Freiberg, "Mayor Hunt's Administration in Cincinnati," *National Municipal Review*, III (July 1914), 518.

[59]See, for example, Cincinnati *Post*, Oct. 5, 11, 13, 1905; Cincinnati *Enquirer*, Nov. 1, 17, 1905; Cincinnati *Citizens' Bulletin*, May 6, July 8, Sept. 30, 1905, April 27, 1907.

[60]Cincinnati *Citizens' Bulletin*, Oct. 19, 1907.

[61]Ohio General Assembly, Joint Committee on the Investigation of Cincinnati and Hamilton County, *Who got the quarter million graft and who paid it back? . . . History and Work of the Special Committee Created Under and by Virtue of Senate Joint Resolution No. 54 and House Bill No. 1287* (Columbus, n.d.), 6-11; Cincinnati *Citizens' Bulletin*, Feb. 22, 1908, April 8, 1911; Charles P. Taft to William Howard Taft, Feb. 28, 1911, Taft Papers, Presidential Series, No. 3, Box 523.

[62]Henry T. Hunt, *An Account of My Stewardship of the Office of Prosecuting Attorney* (Cincinnati, n.d.), 1-11; Cincinnati *Citizens' Bulletin*, Sept. 30, 1911; Cincinnati *Post*, Oct. 25, 1911; Hamilton County Board of Elections, "Abstract of Votes . . . 1908-1911" (Offices of the Hamilton County Board of Elections). The language of the Cincinnati reformers regarding democracy, morality, and politics was very much like that of the Muckrakers as described in Stanley K. Schultz, "The Morality of Politics: The Muckrakers' Vision of Democracy," *Journal of American History*, LII (Dec. 1965), 527-47. Yet they were primarily interested in devising institutions, including a positive government, which would mold moral citizens and make politics democratic. Their goal was not destructive, nor their rhetoric ceremonial.

[63]Cincinnati *Times-Star*, Nov. 8, 1905; William Howard Taft to Rudolph K. Hynicka, July 15, 1910, Taft Papers, Presidential Series 8, Letterbooks; William Howard Taft to Horace D. Taft, Nov. [?], 1911, Taft Papers, Presidential Series 8, Letterbook; Cincinnati *Post*, May 22, 1911; Cincinnati *Commercial-Tribune*, Nov. 5, 1911.

[64]Cincinnati *Commercial-Gazette*, Jan. 29, 1892; Cincinnati *Post*, Feb. 22, 1911.

JOHN D. BUENKER

The Urban Political Machine
and the Seventeenth Amendment

Representing one of the major constitutional changes in twentieth-century America, the direct election of United States Senators is usually depicted as a victory of middle-class progressive reformers over the immigrant-dominated, boss-controlled urban political machines. John D. Buenker, associate professor of history at the University of Wisconsin-Parkside, persuasively refutes this view in the following selection. Why did the urban political machines suddenly and openly endorse and provide leadership

From *The Journal of American History*, 56 (September, 1969), 305-322. Copyright 1969 by *The Journal of American History*. Reprinted by permission.

for a reform which supposedly was aimed directly at the "boss-immigrant-machine complex"? Since the boss's support of progressive measures was by no means limited to the Seventeenth Amendment, the answer to this question is crucial to Buenker's argument that the urban political machine of the nineteenth century evolved and accommodated itself to the demands of a new, diverse, and complex era.

With the possible exception of the giant corporation, no institution was so severely castigated by the middle-class progressive as the urban political machine. Viewing such civic virtues as honesty, efficiency, and economy in government as workable solutions for the complex problems of urban, industrial America, these genteel reformers often looked with horror upon the activities of the urban political machine and its constituents, who seemed preoccupied with such mundane realities as food, clothing, jobs, and votes. Historians have usually assumed that the urban political organizations were unabashed opponents of any political change which might challenge their authority.[1]

Yet the proof of this assertion must be sought in detailed analysis of the machine politician's attitude toward specific reform proposals. A clear-cut test case is the enactment of the Seventeenth Amendment to the Constitution—a measure which, theoretically, struck at the big city organization's control of patronage by removing the selection of United States senators from the state legislatures, where it could be readily manipulated, and placing it in the hands of the voters where, presumably, it could not. Here, certainly, was one of the cardinal achievements of the Progressive era, one which transformed the upper chamber from a bastion of private privilege into the more liberal of the two houses of Congress; yet, almost without exception, it was one which had the overwhelming support of the urban machines' minions in the major industrial states.

To understand this, it is necessary to identify the kinds of lawmakers who are under consideration. The urban political machine developed in the nineteenth century as a response to the industrialization, urbanization, and immigration which transformed the nature of American society and created a multitude of largely new stock wage earners who were often unable to cope with the circumstances of their new existence. By providing jobs, protection from the law, and various welfare activities, the political boss came to command large blocs of minority-group votes. Alliances between a number of ward politicians ultimately produced an organization which was able to dominate the politics of the entire city and even to exert influence at the state and national level. Generally, this amalgamation resulted in one machine and one boss, as in New York City; but sometimes it fragmented into two or three machines under different bosses, as in Chicago or Boston. The fealty of the immigrant voter was partly secured by the judicious dispensation of economic and political favors, but it also depended upon a rough sense of identification with the organization and its constituents. A study of twenty city bosses disclosed that five of them were immigrants and ten others second-generation Americans and that "there seems to be some relationship between the racial stock of municipal bosses and the dominant racial group of foreign origin in their cities."[2] This ethnic confluence was even more apparent in the backgrounds of the urban lawmakers who considered ratification of the Seventeenth Amendment in 1913. For example, among the thirty-five Chicago Democrats who participated, there were no fourth-generation Americans; all of them were of Irish, German, Polish, Norwegian, Danish, Italian, Bohemian, Canadian, or Russian Jewish ancestry.[3]

New stock origins alone did not automatically make a lawmaker a spokesman for the urban machine any more than an old stock background made him an independent. The correlation was high enough, however, and the chief spokesmen for the political machine generally turned out to be members of ethnic minorities—a circumstance which often caused the native, middle-class reformer to suspect the existence of a monolith. Mindful of this tendency, Richard Hofstadter has "singled out, as a phenomenon of the Progressive era, the antipathy between the ethos of the boss-machine-immigrant complex and that of the reformer-individualist-Anglo-Saxon complex . . . ," identified the latter group with progressivism, and styled the former as part of the "potent mass that limited the range and achievements of Progressivism." More specifically, Hofstadter has cited the popular election of senators as one of those reforms sponsored by "Progressives" to end the power of the urban political machine—an interpretation which clearly does not square with the circumstances of the Seventeenth Amendment's ratification in the major industrial states.[4]

Since many of the political machines were Democratic, the easy triumph of the measure in the industrial states can be attributed primarily to the party's sweeping victories in the 1912 elections. Of the eleven major industrial states, eight elected Democratic governors in 1912. In six states, both houses of the legislatures were Democratic, while in three others, the party captured one chamber and narrowly missed control of the other. Only in Pennsylvania and California was Republican rule intact, and even there it was severely shaken by Progressive incursions.[5] Clearly, then, the attitude of the machine-oriented Democrats was crucial to the fate of the amendment.

Actually, machine support for the measure was demonstrated even when the proposal was discussed in Congress, although the nature of the matter was somewhat confused. The complicating factor was a side argument concerning the right of Congress to regulate elections for United States senators, which intruded when Senator George Sutherland, a standpat Republican from Utah, introduced an amendment to that effect. Southern congressmen, who generally favored the idea of direct, popular election of senators, were fearful that granting such control to the federal government would open the door to enfranchisement of the Negro; and they regarded it as "a price greater than the South is willing to pay." As a consequence, they voted against the Sutherland amendment and, when it passed, either abstained or voted against the basic measure. Their attitude disturbed the northern Democrats who also favored the direct election of senators but who did not wish to alienate their southern colleagues. In the final vote, however, the majority of the northerners supported the proposed amendment, and most of the rest abstained.[6]

The real opponents of direct election were the standpat Republicans, and they employed the divide-and-conquer technique to prevent its passage. They voted for the Sutherland amendment in order to insure southern distaste for the basic measure and later joined southern Democrats in voting against submission. In the Senate, the final test on the proposal saw the opposition emerge as a coalition of southern Democrats and Republican conservatives such as Henry Cabot Lodge, Frank Brandegee, William Lorimer, Boies Penrose, Reed Smoot, and Elihu Root. In the House, where the conservative Republicans were less influential, the proposed article passed over the objections of the southern Democrats.[7]

Very few machine Democrats were members of the Senate, but they all voted for adoption—including James Martine of New Jersey, James O'Gorman of New York, and Atlee Pomerene of Ohio. The situation was slightly more complex in the House, where Democratic urban machine politicians were more numerous, but the great majority of the Democrats also voted in favor of the proposal. There were some notable exceptions, such as James Cox of Ohio, William Sulzer of New York, James Michael Curley of Massachusetts, George O'Shaunessey of Rhode Island, and Adolph Sabath of Illinois, all of whom abstained; and it seems highly likely, given the extraneous issue of states rights, that their hesitancy was not due to any distaste for the idea of the direct election of senators, but rather to a desire to placate the peculiar sensibilities of the southern members of their party. The Republican machine politicians, who were free from this disability, like Martin Madden of Chicago and Julius Kahn of San Francisco, supported the resolution. Moreover, one of the more stirring speeches in favor of the principle of direct election, given before the issue of federal control of elections intruded, was made by Sulzer—a readily recognizable minion of Tammany Hall—who was soon to be his party's successful candidate for governor, a post which enabled him to recommend the ratification of the amendment.[8]

The most convincing evidence of urban machine approval of the Seventeenth Amendment is provided by an analysis of the support which it won in the various legislatures of the industrial states. There, the measure received the almost unanimous endorsement of the representatives of the urban machines. They not only acquiesced in the triumph of the proposal but they also actually seized the initiative in sponsoring it. This was clearly the case in New York. The resolution to ratify in the senate was introduced by Robert F. Wagner of New York City, a German immigrant, associate of Tammany Hall, and the Democratic majority leader. All thirty-two Democratic members of the senate voted in favor of ratification, and the twenty-two representatives of metropolitan New York City formed the bulk of that total. Of these, all but four were Irish, German, or Jewish. In addition, Buffalo's three Democratic senators added their support. The four dissenting votes were cast by upstate Republicans of old stock lineage—Elon Brown of Watertown, Henry Sage of Menands, Herbert Coots of Saranac Lake, and John Stivers of Middletown. Sage had previously denounced the measure as a "step toward pure democracy," and Brown had stigmatized it as an "act of stultification" and an admission that the legislature was unworthy.[9]

Neither Democratic favor nor Republican distaste was as evident in the assembly, but the general outlines remained the same. The resolution to ratify was once again introduced by a Tammany Democrat, Aaron J. Levy. In the main, the party's delegation from the metropolitan area concurred with his stand—thirty-two of New York County's thirty-five Democrats and seventeen of Kings County's twenty-three voted yes. The number of abstentions, especially in Kings County, was significant and probably indicates the desire of individual Democrats to express their personal displeasure at the amendment without risking outright opposition to the party's policy. Buffalo's nine Democrats were unanimous in their approval.[10] In the final analysis, Democrats cast 70 percent of the votes in favor of ratification, and New York City contributed about 70 percent of them. Four "nay" votes were once again cast by upstate Republicans—Simon Adler of Rochester, John Jones of Carthage, John Malone of Albany, and Ransom Richardson of Fillmore. Six other Republicans abstained—including the party's candidate for speaker of the assembly, Harold J. Hinman of Albany. Still, thirty-two of the lower chamber's forty-two Republicans favored the resolution, a result which demonstrates its general popularity and contrasts sharply with the performance in the senate where over half of the party spokesmen had either opposed or abstained.[11]

A clash between the urban-based Democrats and the more traditionally oriented Republicans over the Seventeenth Amendment was also evident in Rhode Island, where the Republicans succeeded in blocking passage mostly because of the apportionment system. General Charles R. Brayton had built an almost invincible organization upon a system of representation which allowed each town only one senator regardless of population and thus discriminated against Providence and its environs. It was estimated that twenty towns with a total population of 41,000, about 7 percent of the state's total, could actually control the upper house, a circumstance which guaranteed the selection of business-oriented Republican United States senators. Most of the population of the gerrymandered urban areas around Providence were wage earners and members of ethnic minorities—Irish, German, Italian, French Canadian, and various East European nationalities. By 1912, large numbers of these urban, new stock workers were voting Democratic and sending like-descended representatives to the state capital. Twenty-three of the party's thirty-eight representatives in 1913 were of new stock origin. Only eight of the sixty-four Republicans and Progressives in the lower house were of new stock origin, although more than 70 percent of the state's population was foreign born or second generation.[12]

From the outset, Democrats urged ratification upon the Republicans. The resolution to ratify was introduced by James J. Dunn, an Irish Catholic Democrat of East Providence. The Republican majority promptly referred it to a committee on special legislation which consisted of five Republicans, two Democrats, and one Progressive. Predictably, the committee recommended rejection of the measure, and a spirited debate followed. Republican spokesmen argued that the existing system was devised by the Founding Fathers and that it had worked especially well in Rhode Island. The heartiest denunciations of this view were voiced by Patrick Dillon of Cumberland, who insisted that the system allowed the election of corporation men like Nelson Aldrich. Dillon was vigorously seconded by Thomas O'Niel and Albert West, both Providence Democrats. In the end, the house rejected the committee report 39-54; and it ratified the amendment.[13]

Thirty-seven of the thirty-eight Democrats made up the largest segment of the negative votes, and only James Cummiskey of Warwick voted for the majority report. The remainder of the thirty-eight votes recorded for the motion to reject, and hence against the direct election of senators, were cast by Republicans. Almost two thirds of the Republicans opposed ratification. The bulk of Republican votes in favor were those of minority-group legislators from Providence and its environs. On balance, the contest was clearly one between the urban-based Democrats, aided by a few Progressives and Republicans from similar constituencies, and the rural and small-town based Republican organization.[14]

In the senate, where the apportionment system virtually disfranchised urban voters, the Seventeenth Amendment was not even able to get on the floor. The resolution was smothered in a committee where the Republicans had a six-to-one majority, approximately the same ratio which obtained in the chamber as a whole.[15] Rhode Island became one of only three states to reject the proposed amendment, and the result was clearly a triumph of the Brayton combine over the urban Democrats.

This conflict was even more intense in neighboring Connecticut. Again the apportionment system, this time in the lower house, operated against the urban areas by requiring that no town could have less than one nor more than two representatives, regardless of its population. This discriminated against the state's new stock wage earners who comprised the bulk of the population of New Haven, Hartford, Bridgeport, and the other industrial cities, and who generally sent lawmakers of similar antecedents and Democratic leanings to the legislature. This enabled the Republicans under the leadership of J. Henry Rorabach to retain much of their strength in the lower house in spite of the general Democratic victory in 1912.[16]

The division in the lower house over ratification was one of the most clear-cut. The resolution was introduced by James Lynch, an Irish-born lawyer and Democrat from Waterbury. The final vote was 151-77—a coalition of Democrats and Progressive Republicans defeated the regular Republicans. All 119 Democrats present voted yes, but the Republicans showed only thirty-two in favor and seventy-seven against. In Hartford County only ten of the thirty-two Republicans favored ratification; in New Haven County, only three of eighteen; in New London County, one of six; in Fairfield, six of fourteen; in Windham, five of seventeen; in Litchfield, ten of twenty-two; in Middlesex, seven of ten; and in Tolland County, seven of ten. Nearly all of the Republicans were old stock legislators from rural areas who were protecting their position from the challenge of the Democrats.[17]

In the senate, where the Democrats had a three-to-two majority, the measure easily passed, but it was once again the urban lawmakers who took the lead. Ratification was proposed by Democratic Senator John Hurley of Waterbury, an Irish immigrant, and seconded by another Irish Democrat, Arch McNiel of Bridgeport. The amendment was adopted by voice vote. The results in the lower house, the identity of the sponsors, and the Democratic control of the senate clearly indicate that ratification was victory for the state's urban Democrats.[18]

In Massachusetts the same general lines of division obtained. The Republican party in Massachusetts had been dominant for several decades and had only recently been challenged by the resurgent Democrats. The Democratic party was largely controlled by Irish-Americans and had its greatest strength in the general area of Boston. Although some of the more recent immigrant groups such as the Italians, Poles, and French Canadians who inhabited the mill towns sometimes tended to vote Republican, the Irish, according to the foremost students of Massachusetts politics, claimed to be representative of all the minority groups in the state. Moreover, the Republican delegations to the legislature were preponderantly old stock and rural, and the Democratic delegations were overwhelmingly new stock and urban.[19] Republican control of the legislature usually resulted in the selection of Yankee-descended, corporation-conscious Republicans like Lodge and Winthrop Murray Crane, and the Democrats saw a remedy for this situation in direct, popular election.

Actually, the Democrats began their campaign for this reform even before Congress officially proposed the amendment. In a resolution prepared by Secretary of State Frank Donahue, the Democrats called upon Congress to summon a constitutional convention in order to amend the Constitution to allow for the direct election of senators. The Republicans, endorsing a motion by Yankee George Barnes of suburban Norfolk County, proposed to amend the Donahue resolution so that it merely petitioned Congress to effect the reform in any way it saw fit. Although many Republicans undoubtedly favored direct election and were leery of the calling of a general constitutional convention which might open the door to other amendments, it is clear that many party regulars were actually opposed to the idea and that Barnes introduced his amendment as a face-saving gesture in the light of the popular sentiment for the change. When Democrat John Mack of North Adams asked Barnes point-blank if he favored the direct election of senators, the Republican admitted that he had "grave doubts" about its wisdom, was skeptical that it would produce men of the same calibre as the existing system, and would support the reform only because it "reflects the sentiment of the people."[20]

The vote on the Barnes amendment was the nearest thing to an outright test of the policy of the two parties, and the Democrats clearly established themselves as the staunchest supporters of direct election. All thirteen Democrats, mostly Irish-Americans from the Boston vicinity, voted against the Barnes amendment and demonstrated their desire for the strongest possible position on the question. They were joined by four of the so-called "labor legislators"—Republicans with labor backgrounds and working-class constituencies. The remaining Republicans, regulars like Barnes and Calvin Coolidge, voted for the Barnes amendment, and it passed. The Democrats and their labor legislator allies, believing that "half a loaf is better than none," voted for the amended resolution which passed 35-3. Two Republican regulars apparently refused to agree to even the more modest resolution, while Democrat Francis Quigley presumably held out for the original proposal.[21]

The same question was raised in the lower house, but the Democrats carried the day by virtue of superior numbers. The resolution calling for a convention was introduced by John Meany of Blackstone, the Democratic leader, who argued that the people had already proven their capacity to govern. Some Republicans, like Roger Wolcott of Milton and Robert Washburn of Worcester, stated their objections to popular government, but most of the party joined the Democrats. They even refused to alter the language to read "requests" instead of "demands." The resolution passed resoundingly—162-37. All thirty-seven negative votes were cast by Republicans. With the exception of a few members who were absent, the Irish-American delegates from Suffolk, Middlesex, and Worcester Counties were unanimous in their approval—even the prototype of the Boston machine politico, Martin Lomasney.[22]

Clearly, the urban Democrats had demonstrated a far greater preference for direct election than had their Yankee Republican opponents before the Seventeenth Amendment was proposed by Congress. Since the Republicans admitted the overwhelming sympathy of the people of Massachusetts for the reform, the legislature ratified the amendment within ten days after it had been submitted. The measure passed the lower house by a voice vote. The only inkling of opposition in the senate was provided by nine abstentions—three Democrats who apparently felt the amendment too modest and six Republicans who could not bring themselves to vote for any measure advocating direct election. The contest over the direct election of senators in Massachusetts is a concrete illustration of Richard Abram's contention that the "truly 'insurgent' groups" in the state were "the large Irish-American segment of the population, who purported to represent the newer Americans generally," aided by a few labor unionists.[23]

Democratic machine support for the direct election of senators was also evidenced in Illinois, and the lack of any serious opposition from the Republicans resulted in an easy triumph for ratification. The urgency of the reform was all the more pressing in Illinois because of two incidents which had marred the selection of the state's senators. In 1909, the election of Republican Lorimer had been effected by bribery which allegedly involved some fifty-seven lawmakers and made the Illinois legislature a symbol for all those who desired the change to direct election. In the same 1913 session at which ratification of the amendment was being considered, the task of selecting Lorimer's successor and another full-term senator consumed almost four months of the legislature's time and interfered with other business.[24]

At the outset, support for ratification appeared bipartisan. The ratification resolutions in both houses were introduced by downstate Republicans, and firm endorsement was given by Democratic Governor Edward F. Dunne of Chicago, an Irish Catholic and a member of the so-called Hearst-Harrison faction of the party. Dunne, in his own history of Illinois, refers to the amendment as one of his most important recommendations to the legislature and to its ratification as "the greatest victory for popular government in fifty years."[25] Despite this apparent agreement, however, senate Republicans did make one unsuccessful attempt at blocking consideration of the amendment by trying to table a motion by Democratic Senator John Denvir—an Irish Catholic labor leader—to refer the measure to the Committee on Constitutional Amendments. The maneuver failed on an almost completely partisan vote, and the measure was referred to a committee where the Democrats had a narrow majority. After a favorable report, it was approved by the senate 50-0.[26] No Illinois state senator was willing to declare against ratification in the light of the state's past history, although some Republicans were reluctant to allow the amendment to come to a vote.

The vote in the lower house was an equally decisive 146-1; only downstate Democrat Lee O'Niel Browne of La Salle opposed. The affirmative votes represented both factions of the Democratic party. The followers of the Chicago boss Roger Sullivan—R. E. "Bob" Wilson, John J. McLaughlin, and "Bennie" Mitchell—agreed with Michael Igoe and James Ryan of the Harrison-Dunne group.[27] The support of the Chicago Democratic machine for the Seventeenth Amendment was at least as great as that of any other political faction in Illinois.

In two other major industrial states, Ohio and New Jersey, ratification was easily effected after a major Democratic electoral victory which temporarily strengthened the position of the urban political machine complex. In Ohio, traditionally a Republican state, the 1912 election had resulted in a Democratic sweep. Cox, a protégé of Toledo Democratic boss Edward

Hanley, was elected governor; William Greenlund, a Danish-American from Cleveland and a former state senator, was chosen lieutenant governor; and two Irish Catholics, John Brennan and Timothy Hogan, were selected treasurer and attorney-general respectively. More significantly for the future of the Seventeenth Amendment, both houses of the legislature were solidly controlled by the Democrats, and even such usually Republican strongholds as Cincinnati produced Democratic lawmakers.[28]

Ratification in the senate came on a motion introduced by Maurice Bernstein of Cleveland. The other four Cleveland senators supported the motion, and they were joined by two of Cincinnati's three Democratic delegates; one was absent. The amendment was also approved by President Pro Tempore of the Senate William Green of Coshocton, well-known leader of the state's mine workers and future head of the American Federation of Labor, and by such acknowledged machine Democrats as Daniel F. Mooney of St. Marys and Michael Cahill of Eaton. The lone negative vote out of the thirty-one cast was that of Michael A. Broadstone of Xenia, whose biographer describes him as "an uncompromising republican."[29]

Easy ratification, 114-0, also followed in the lower house, after the introduction of the amendment by Democrat Robert Black of Cincinnati. Floor leader Lawrence Brennan and future Senator Stephen Young were among twelve of the thirteen-man Cleveland delegation which voted yes. Except for Young and Don P. Mills, the remainder of the delegates were products of the city's Irish, German, Bohemian, and Polish minorities. Speaker Charles Swain joined seven of the ten Cincinnati Democrats to vote yes, and so did the Democratic representatives of other urban areas such as Toledo, Dayton, and Columbus.[30]

In New Jersey the Democratic trend had begun with election of Woodrow Wilson as governor in 1910. After the 1912 contest, the party controlled the assembly 51-8. In the senate, the margin was much narrower, 12-9, because of an apportionment law which gave each county one senator regardless of population. In the lower house especially, most of the party's strength was composed of new stock, Jersey City, and Newark lawmakers who were normally considered to be the servants of the machines bossed by Robert "Little Bob" Davis and James "Big Jim" Smith. The Democrats also dominated the two next largest delegations, those of Passaic and Union Counties.[31]

The sponsorship of the amendment in the assembly was undertaken by Charles O'Connor Hennessy, an Irish-born lawyer from Haworth in Bergen County. In the final vote, 42-0, thirty-six Democrats and six Republicans were recorded in favor. Twelve of the thirteen Essex County

(Newark) Democrats and nine of the Hudson County (Jersey City) delegation voted yes. Four of Passaic's five delegates, two of Bergen's three, and all three of Union County's assemblymen were recorded in favor of ratification. The floor leader, Charles Egan of Hudson, voted yes, but most of the abstainers were Democrats from rural areas. The machine Democrats in New Jersey's lower legislative house provided the largest bloc of votes for the direct election of senators.[32]

Machine influence was less noticeable in the New Jersey senate, where the measure passed 18-1. The lone dissenter was Democrat Richard Fitzherbert of Dover. The Democratic senators from Bergen, Union, Passaic, and Hudson Counties and an Essex County Republican lawmaker voted yes. One member of each party abstained.[33] Thus, in New Jersey, as in Ohio, a Democratic legislature dominated by politicians who were normally considered spokesmen for the state's urban political machines effected passage of a reform widely regarded as a blow at one of the organization's prerogatives.

The representatives of other urban Democratic organizations in somewhat less populous states also endorsed the Seventeenth Amendment. In Delaware, for example, sponsorship of the measure was undertaken by two Democrats from Wilmington, Senator John Gormley and Representative Timothy Mooney. In the lower house, where the Democrats were in control after the 1912 election, ratification occurred by an easy vote, 30-0; and Timothy Mooney and Speaker Chauncey Holcomb of Wilmington were the leading proponents. In the senate, where the Republicans held a nine-to-seven edge, the amendment was rejected by an almost perfectly partisan division, 6-10. Delaware joined Rhode Island and Utah as the only states where Republican control of the senate was the deciding factor in the rejection of the Seventeenth Amendment.[34]

In Missouri, too, the sizeable Democratic delegations from St. Louis and Kansas City generally supported ratification. In the lower house, where the measure passed 128-1, all fourteen Democrats from the St. Louis area were recorded in favor; and all but two of them were of Irish or German extraction. Five of Kansas City's six Democrats also voted yes, and the sixth was absent due to illness. In the senate, however, nearly all the Democrats from those two cities were absent on the day the vote was taken, a development which might have portended disapproval on their part.[35] Nevertheless, the fact that they chose to abstain rather than openly oppose, coupled with the nearly unanimous backing which the measure received from their colleagues in the house, would seem to indicate widespread approbation of the Seventeenth Amendment on the part of the machine and its constituents.

A somewhat different pattern was evident in Wisconsin, although the support of Milwaukee's Democrats was equally clear. All twelve of them voted for ratification in the lower house, as did both the city's Republicans and Social Democrats. Nearly all of these men were of new stock extraction, regardless of party label. The city's lone Democratic senator, George Weissleder, was not recorded in the vote on the Seventeenth Amendment, but since three of four Republicans and the single Social Democrat did vote in favor of ratification, the measure was obviously popular among all political factions in Milwaukee.[36]

It seems safe to assert that the Seventeenth Amendment received an overwhelming degree of support from the representatives of urban Democratic political machines. The same assertion can be made about the Republican political machines in Pennsylvania and California, but only with certain clarifications. In both Philadelphia and Pittsburgh, the Republican party had succeeded in preventing, or at least slowing, the drift of new stock voters into the Democratic party. By collusion and other methods, they had reduced the Democratic party to the status of a subsidiary organization, which often accepted favors and took orders from the dominant Republican group headed in 1912 by Senator Penrose. The Democrats occasionally sent lawmakers from Philadelphia or Pittsburgh to Harrisburg during this period, but the Republicans retained control. However, this virtual monopoly led to factionalism within the Republican ranks and, ultimately, to a power struggle between Penrose and Philadelphia boss Edwin Vare.[37]

This factionalism was evident in the struggle over the Seventeenth Amendment because Edwin "Duke" Vare's lieutenants apparently supported ratification more enthusiastically than did Penrose's followers. This was particularly obvious in the senate, where, despite a unanimous vote, there were some significant abstentions. Only five of Philadelphia's nine senators voted for the measure, and two of these, Richard Farley and James Nulty, were Democrats and Irish Catholic labor leaders. The three Republicans who favored ratification were in Vare's faction. The four Penrose people in the senate, however, including the senator's personal representative, James "Strawberry Jim" McNichol, abstained. All but one of the six-man Republican delegation from Pittsburgh also concurred.[38] Thus, despite its apparent dislike for the measure, even the powerful Penrose machine was reluctant to oppose it openly.

This split in the Pennsylvania Republican ranks was less evident in the lower house, where thirty-seven of the thirty-nine Philadelphia lawmakers voted for ratification. There were two dissenters—Edward Fahey and Harry Bass, the only Negro member. The other negative vote was cast by Richard Baldwin of suburban Delaware County. Four of Pittsburgh's twenty-four-man delegation abstained, but the support of the measure among urban machine Republicans in both major cities was nevertheless clearly established.[39]

San Francisco's Republican machine also favored ratification. In the lower house the entire Republican delegation from the Bay City area voted in favor of the amendment. Three of the four San Francisco Democrats, all Irish-Americans with labor backgrounds, voted yes. In the senate, however, two of the five city Republicans abstained, and there was no overt attempt by the machine to block ratification.[40]

The fate of the Seventeenth Amendment in the major industrial states amply demonstrates that the urban political machine was one of the most consistent and influential supporters of this reform. In some states the machine was simply one of several political factions favoring ratification. In others—New York, New Jersey, Connecticut, and Massachusetts—machine support was unquestionably the major force behind the success of the measure. In Rhode Island and Delaware, the urban-based Democrats sponsored the amendment in the face of overwhelming Republican opposition, and it went down to defeat. No urban machine or its representatives openly opposed ratification.

The enthusiasm of the urban political machines for the Seventeenth Amendment raises a serious question about the overall attitude of these organizations toward reform in the Progressive era. It may be that ratification of the Seventeenth Amendment was a solitary exception, or that the machines had to acquiesce in the inevitable because of the clamor of public opinion, but the overwhelming nature of their support makes such an interpretation highly unlikely. It seems far more credible that the issue is a concrete illustration of the contention, first set forward by J. Joseph Huthmacher, that the machine politician's attitude toward political reform was not uniformly reactionary, but selectively pragmatic. Indeed, Huthmacher cites the ratification of the Seventeenth Amendment by the New York General Assembly as an example of his thesis.[41] The apportionment system in the legislatures of most of the major industrial states was so weighted in favor of the non-metropolitan areas that it all but guaranteed the selection of senators who were rural, old stock, business-oriented, and Republican. This was certainly true in New England, and the difference in most of the other more populous states was only one of degree. The change to a system of direct, popular election would greatly enhance the chances of candidates who were urban, new stock, and more attuned to the needs of the industrial wage earner. This was explicit in Congressman Sulzer's contention that the apportionment system made it impossible to secure selection of a Democratic senator in New York unless that party won by a margin of at least 100,000 votes.[42] It was clearly expressed by state representative Dillon of Rhode Island, when he asserted repeatedly that Aldrich could never be victorious in a popular election. It was strongly implied in Republican denunciations of the measure in Massachusetts, Rhode Island, and New York. It was patently obvious when Penrose, who controlled virtually all of Pennsylvania, opposed ratification and Vare, who dominated only Philadelphia, supported it. It was also clearly indicated by the fact that the Democrats immediately began to produce urban, new stock candidates under the new system of election. The first Massachusetts Democrat to try for the Senate after the ratification of the Seventeenth Amendment was John F. Fitzgerald, and the next was David I. Walsh. In Illinois, Roger Sullivan, in Indiana, boss Thomas Taggart, and in Ohio, Timothy Hogan all entered senatorial contests.[43] Only a few were successful, but the potential for producing future Kennedys, Wagners, and Ribicoffs was clearly established.

Although there were political advantages for the machine in direct election, many machine spokesmen also believed that more significant issues were involved. The selection of United States senators by malapportioned legislatures clearly violated the idea of American democracy and representative government. The fact that this system so uniformly discriminated against the chances of candidates with urban, industrial, immigrant backgrounds seemed to be a denial of the equality of opportunity which American life was supposed to provide. Little wonder that it was the people who were most affected by these inequities who developed the keenest sense of appreciation of the principles involved. It was, after all, the suffragettes who felt most strongly about the full participation of women in American life; and, despite the substantial contributions of white liberals, it has been Negro leaders who have demonstrated the greatest anguish about racial inequality. Moreover, as Hofstadter has observed, it was at least partly concern for their own waning power and prestige which awakened the members of the "reformer-individualist-Anglo-Saxon complex" to the full meaning of such ideals as patriotism and democracy. In any event, the spokesmen for the urban machines voiced their concern about the democratic process as eloquently as did the good-government reformer. Governor Dunne of Illinois asserted that true democracy could only be realized when all important state and national officials were elected by popular vote. Congressman Sulzer of New York maintained that the people "can and ought to be trusted." Assemblyman Dillon of Rhode Island demanded that the people and not the corporations select United States senators, and Democratic majority leader Meany of Massachusetts insisted that the people had already demonstrated their capacity to act wisely in the selection of other public officials.[44] The urban machine politician supported the Seventeenth Amendment out of a healthy mixture of idealism and self-interest, and it is difficult to separate the one from the other.

Until recently, much of the activity of historians of the Progressive era has centered around the delineation of a movement called "Progressivism" and a group of people deemed "progressives." It has generally been assumed that the solid legislative achievements of those years flowed somehow from that movement and that group of people. Few would deny that the Seventeenth Amendment was one of the cardinal achievements of the era, yet its success was owed in large measure to the support of an entirely different segment of society—one generally considered antagonistic to the aims of the Progressive movement. It would seem appropriate, therefore, for historians to concentrate their attention less on the concept of a movement and more on the method by which the important legislation was enacted. To do this they must also heed Huthmacher's advice and "modify the 'middle class' emphasis which has come to dominate the field and devote more attention to exploring hitherto neglected elements of the American social structure."[45]

NOTES

[1]The best exposition of this view can be found in Richard Hofstadter, *The Age of Reform: From Bryan to F.D.R.* (New York, 1955), 257-69. He also provides a perceptive critique, 269-71.

[2]For the development of the political machine, see Oscar Handlin, *The Uprooted: The Epic Story of the Great Migrations that Made the American People* (New York, 1951), 201-26; J. Joseph Huthmacher, *Massachusetts People and Politics: 1919-1933* (Cambridge, 1959), 4-18; Harold Zink, *City Bosses in the United States: A Study of Twenty Municipal Bosses* (Durham, 1930), 4-5; Elmer E. Cornwell, Jr., "Bosses, Machines, and Ethnic Groups," *Annals of the Academy of Political and Social Science*, 353 (May 1964), 27-33.

[3]These conclusions about the ethno-religious makeup of the machine and its representatives are based upon a study of the biographical sketches in the following sources: Edgar J. Murlin, *The New York Red Book: Containing the Portraits and Biographies of the United States Senators, Governors, State Officers and Members of the Legislature, . . . and General Facts of Interest* (Albany, 1913), 85-190; Harry Woods, comp., *Blue Book of the State of Illinois, 1913-1914* (Danville, 1914), 240-340; The Commonwealth of Massachusetts, *Manual for the Use of the General Court Containing the Rules of the Two Branches . . . and Other Statistical Information* (Boston, 1913), 425-85; *Legislative History and Souvenir of Connecticut, VIII, 1911-1912* (Hartford, 1912), 12-288; J. Fred Parker, comp., *Manual, With Rules and Orders, for the Use of the General Assembly of the State of Rhode Island, 1913-1914* (Providence, 1913), 380-410; W. V. Goshorn and John R. Cassidy, comps., *Legislative Manual of the State of Ohio, Eightieth General Assembly, 1913-1914* (Columbus, 1914), 29-41, 117-58; Herman P. Miller and W. Harry Baker, comps., *Smull's Legislative Handbook and Manual of the State of Pennsylvania, 1913* (Harrisburg, 1913), 729-54;

Cornelius Roach, comp., *Official Manual of the State of Missouri for the Years 1913-1914* (Jefferson City, 1914), 41-136; Wisconsin, General Assembly, *The Wisconsin Blue Book* (Madison, 1913), 638-90.

[4]Hofstadter, *Age of Reform*, 186n, 182, 257, 9.

[5]New York *Times*, Nov. 6, 1912.

[6]For the best account of the congressional struggle over proposal of the amendment, see George H. Haynes, *The Senate of the United States: Its History and Practice* (2 vols., Boston, 1938), I, 106-17.

[7]*Cong. Record*, 62 Cong., 1 Sess., 1924 (June 12, 1911); *ibid.*, 62 Cong., 2 Sess., 6366-67 (May 13, 1912).

[8]For William Sulzer's speech, see *ibid.*, 62 Cong., 2 Sess., Appendix, 161 (May 13, 1912).

[9]*Journal of the Senate of the State of New York at Their One Hundred and Thirty-Six Session* (2 vols., Albany, 1913), I, 58; Murlin, *Red Book*, 85-190; New York *Times*, Jan. 16, 1913.

[10]*Journal of the General Assembly of the State of New York at Their One Hundred and Thirty-Six Session* (Albany, 1913), 50, 74-75; Murlin, *Red Book*, 85-190.

[11]There is no specific evidence concerning the attitude of Tammany Hall boss Charles F. Murphy toward the Seventeenth Amendment, but his chief lieutenants, including his son-in-law James Foley, voted for ratification. In addition, it was later asserted by Bronx boss Ed Flynn that "nothing could have been done at Albany [from 1911 to 1914] unless Charles F. Murphy permitted or encouraged it." J. Joseph Huthmacher argues that Murphy developed a penchant for many progressive reforms, including the direct election of senators. See J. Joseph Huthmacher, "Charles Evans Hughes and Charles Francis Murphy: The Metamorphosis of Progressivism," *New York History*, XLVI (Jan. 1965), 25-40.

[12]Dept. of Commerce, Bureau of the Census, *Abstract of the Fourteenth Census of the United States, 1920* (Washington, 1923), 107; Parker, *Manual*, 385-410; Chester Lloyd Jones, "The Rotten Boroughs of New England," *North American Review*, CXCVII (April 1913), 489; Duane Lockard, *New England Politics* (Princeton, 1959), 174-77. Elmer E. Cornwell, Jr., "Party Absorption of Ethnic Groups: The Case of Providence, Rhode Island," *Social Forces*, 38 (March 1960), 205-10; Murray S. Stedman, Jr., and Susan W. Stedman, "The Rise of the Democratic Party of Rhode Island," *New England Quarterly*, XXIV (Sept. 1951), 329-41.

[13]Providence *Daily Journal*, March 14, 1913.

[14]*Ibid.*, Parker, *Manual*, 385-410.

[15]State of Rhode Island and Providence Plantations, *Journal of the Senate, Vol. 7, No. 40, March 14, 1913* (Providence, 1913).

[16]Jones, "Rotten Boroughs of New England," 488; *Legislative History and Souvenir of Connecticut*, 12-288; Lockard, *New England Politics*, 228-43; Joseph I. Lieberman, *The Power Broker: A Biography of John M. Bailey, Modern Political Boss* (Boston, 1966), 17-68.

[17]*Journal of the House of Representatives of the State of Connecticut, January Session, 1913* (Hartford, 1913), 97-98, 727-30.

[18]*Journal of the Senate of the State of Connecticut, January Session, 1913* (Hartford, 1913), 648.

[19]See Huthmacher, *Massachusetts People and Politics*, 4-18; Richard M. Abrams, *Conservatism in a Progressive Era: Massachusetts Politics, 1900-1912* (Cambridge, 1964), 50, 182-84, 234-48; Donald B. Cole, *Immigrant City* (Chapel Hill, 1963), 88-92, 168-70; Massachusetts, *Manual for the Use of the General Court*, 425-70.

[20]Boston *Daily Globe*, April 17, 1912.

[21]*Ibid.*, Commonwealth of Massachusetts, *The Journal of the Senate for the Year 1912* (Boston, 1912), 1149.

[22]Boston *Daily Globe*, March 28, 1912; Commonwealth of Massachusetts, *Journal of the House of Representatives of the Commonwealth of Massachusetts, 1912* (Boston, 1913), 1134-36.

²³Massachusetts, *Journal of the House* . . . *1912*, p. 1717; Massachusetts, *Journal of the Senate* . . . *1912*, p. 1491; Abrams, *Conservatism in a Progressive Era*, 132-33.

²⁴*Journal of the House of Representatives of the 48th General Assembly of the State of Illinois* (Springfield, 1914). For a discussion of the William Lorimer case, see Edward F. Dunne, *Illinois: The Heart of the Nation* (5 vols., Chicago, 1933), II, 181-87; Haynes, *Senate of the United States*, I, 131-35.

²⁵Dunne, *Illinois*, II, 365; William Sullivan, *Dunne: Judge, Mayor, Governor* (Chicago, 1916), 547.

²⁶Illinois General Assembly, *Journal of the Senate* . . . *1913* (Springfield, 1913), 383-85, 440; Woods, *Blue Book of the State of Illinois*, 240-340.

²⁷*Journal of the House* . . . *Illinois, 1913*, p. 232; Woods, *Blue Book of the State of Illinois*, 240-340. There is no specific evidence that Chicago boss Roger Sullivan backed ratification, but his lieutenants in the general assembly voted for it. He himself was the first candidate of his party to run in a popular election for senator. Governor Edward F. Dunne, a political rival, credited Sullivan with support for many reform measures and asserted that the Chicagoan had "more personal influence than probably any other citizen of Illinois." Dunne, *Illinois*, III, 275. It is at least certain that he did not use his considerable influence in opposition to the amendment. When Sullivan died, even the Chicago *Tribune*, which had long and bitterly opposed him, acknowledged that "it is not too much to say that the so-called 'reform laws' of the last ten or fifteen years bear more of Sullivan's thumb print than of the professional reformers." Harold Zink concurred with this judgment. Dunne, *Illinois*, III, 275; Chicago *Tribune*, April 15, 1920; Zink, *City Bosses*, 61, 299.

²⁸Goshorn and Cassidy, *Legislative Manual of* . . . *Ohio*, 16-20, 29-41, 117-58.

²⁹Ohio General Assembly, *Journal of the Senate* . . . *1913* (Columbus, 1913), 228; Goshorn and Cassidy, *Legislative Manual of* . . . *Ohio*, 29-41, especially 31.

³⁰Ohio General Assembly, *Journal of the House* . . . *1913* (Columbus, 1913), 54; Goshorn and Cassidy, *Legislative Manual of* . . . *Ohio*, 117-58. About half the Cincinnati delegation were German-Americans.

³¹Parker, *Manual*, 320-65; Arthur S. Link, *Wilson: The Road to the White House* (Princeton, 1947), 140-45. John Morton Blum, *Joe Tumulty and the Wilson Era* (Boston, 1951), 1-41; Rudolph Vecoli, *The People of New Jersey* (Princeton, 1965), 100-10.

³²*Minutes of the Votes and Proceedings of the One Hundred and Thirty-Seventh General Assembly of the State of New Jersey* (Trenton, 1913), 335.

³³*Journal of the Sixty-Ninth Senate of the State of New Jersey Being the One Hundred and Thirty-Seventh Session of the Legislature* (Trenton, 1913), 595.

³⁴State of Delaware, *Journal of the House of Representatives At a Session of the General Assembly* . . . (Dover, 1913), 329-30; State of Delaware, *Journal of the Senate At a Session of the General Assembly* . . . (Dover, 1913), 1017.

³⁵*Journal of the House of Representatives of the 47th General Assembly of the State of Missouri, 1913* (Jefferson City, 1913), 197; *Journal of the Senate of the Forty-Seventh General Assembly of the State of Missouri, 1913* (Jefferson City, 1913), 749; *Official Manual* . . . *of Missouri* . . . *1913-1914*, pp. 41-136.

³⁶*In Assembly, Journal of the Proceedings of the Fifty-First Session of the Wisconsin Legislature, 1913* (Madison, 1913), 194; *In Senate, Journal of Proceedings of the Fifty-First Session of the Wisconsin Legislature, 1913* (Madison, 1913), 194; *The Wisconsin Blue Book* (Madison, 1913), 638-90.

³⁷Wayland F. Dunaway, *A History of Pennsylvania* (Englewood Cliffs, 1945), 479-82; Robert Bowden, *Boies Penrose: Symbol of an Era* (New York, 1937), 240-42; Miller and Baker, *Smull's Legislative Handbook, 1913*, pp. 729-54; J. T. Salter, *Boss Rule* (New York, 1935), 21-22n.

³⁸*Journal of the Senate of the Commonwealth of Pennsylvania* . . . , *1913* (Harrisburg, 1913), Pt. 1, p. 878; Miller and Baker, *Smull's Legislative Handbook, 1913* pp. 729-42. It should be remembered that Boies Penrose had voted against the amendment.

³⁹State of Pennsylvania, *Journal of the House of Representatives of the Commonwealth of Pennsylvania* . . . , *1913* (Harrisburg, 1914), Pt. 1, pp. 585-86; Miller and Baker,

Smull's Legislative Handbook, 1913, pp. 743-54. The Vare organization controlled over three fourths of the Philadelphia seats in the assembly. Zink, *City Bosses*, 227.

[40]*Journal of the Assembly During the Fortieth Session of the Legislature of the State of California, 1913* (Sacramento, 1913), 183; *Journal of the Senate During the Fortieth Session of the Legislature of the State of California, 1913* (Sacramento, 1913), 323; Frank C. Jordan, comp., *Roster of State, County, City and Township Officials* . . . (Sacramento, 1913), 1-3.

[41]J. Joseph Huthmacher, "Urban Liberalism and the Age of Reform," *Mississippi Valley Historical Review*, XLIX (Sept. 1962), 231-41; Huthmacher, "Charles Evans Hughes and Charles Francis Murphy," 25-40.

[42]*Cong. Record*, 62 Cong., 2 Sess., Appendix, 161 (May 13, 1912).

[43]Democratic dominated legislatures had already selected Irish immigrant William Hughes in New Jersey and James O'Gorman in New York. Since Democratic control of the legislature was a rarity, however, direct election was much more likely to produce the type of senator desired by the urban machines.

[44]Dunne, *Illinois*, II, 365; *Cong. Record*, 62 Cong., 2 Sess., Appendix, 161 (May 13, 1912); Providence *Daily Journal*, March 14, 1913; Boston *Daily Globe*, March 28, 1912.

[45]Huthmacher, "Urban Liberalism and the Age of Reform," 240-41. For additional evidence of machine support for progressive measures, see John D. Buenker, "Urban Immigrant Lawmakers and Progressive Reform In Illinois," Donald F. Tingley, ed., *Essays In Illinois History: In Honor of Glenn Huron Seymour* (Carbondale, 1968), 55-74; Michael Rogin, "Progressivism and the California Electorate," *Journal of America History*, LX (Sept. 1968), 297-314.

FREDERIC C. HOWE

The Confessions of a Reformer

Frederic C. Howe was born in 1867 in Meadville, Pennsylvania. Reacting against the constrictions of small-town life, he eventually left Meadville to attend the Johns Hopkins University in Baltimore, where he received a doctorate in 1892. Two years later he took a position in Cleveland with the law firm of Harry and James Garfield, sons of the late President. Howe was deeply impressed with the need for a higher level of public service in the city—the kind that could be rendered by the professionals, experts, and educated men of "his class." He lived in a settlement house, became active in the "good government" Municipal Association, and concocted various plans to beautify the city with Morris Black, a young attorney, Harvard graduate, and close friend who was elected to the City Council.

At the turn of the century, Howe was still deeply impressed with the standards he had learned at the Johns Hopkins. "I still believed that America would be aroused only through disinterested service," he wrote. "But this faith was strangely confused by new human equations. . . ." After Black's

From Frederic C. Howe, *The Confessions of a Reformer* (New York: Charles Scribner's Sons, 1925).

death in 1900, Howe decided to enter politics himself. Determined to rid the city of the boss politics of Mayors McKisson and "Honest John" Farley, and the "notorious thirteen" who sat on the City Council, Howe was elected to the Council as a Republican in 1901. His experience as a councilman and his relationship with Cleveland's remarkable "reform mayor" Tom Johnson had a profound influence on his life. Howe became a proponent of the municipal ownership of public utilities and a confirmed follower of Henry George, who proposed to solve the nation's ills through his famous "single tax" on rent—the "unearned increment" or profit derived from the value of land which society, not the landowner, had created. Confronted with a myriad of "new human equations" he began to lose his faith in some of the old standards. Gradually, Howe came to understand that the city was more complex than he had realized; reluctantly, he concluded that the issues of "bossism" and "reform" were equally complex.

Howe was appointed Commissioner of Immigration of the Port of New York by Woodrow Wilson in 1914, and served in various minor capacities in the New Deal. He is most noted, however, for his writings, which are among the most candid and sensitive of the reform literature in this period even if they are not among the most brilliant or learned. His books include *The City, The Hope of Democracy* (1905), *The Modern City and Its Problems* (1915), *Revolution and Democracy* (1921), and *The Confessions of a Reformer* (1925), from which the following selections are taken.

I had heard about Tom Johnson ever since I had been in the city. He was a dramatic personality; every one had a story about him. I knew about his life what every one knew: that he had come to Cleveland as a young man with no capital and had bought out an old horse-car line of no particular value on the west side, thereby coming into conflict with Mark Hanna,* who looked upon the west side of the city as his own. He and his brother Albert had driven their own cars and collected fares. When he wanted to extend his car-line into the public square, he went before a Republican council and promised to carry passengers over his entire system for a single fare. The extension was granted in the teeth of Mark Hanna's opposition. In time he was recognized by other street-railway magnates; and he induced them to form a consolidation, capitalized far in excess of the capitalization of the constituent companies. Then he sold out his holdings and went to Brooklyn, where he repeated the operation. He

*Marcus A. Hanna was a Cleveland industrialist and Senator from Ohio, 1897-1904. At the turn of the century he was an important political figure at the local, state, and national levels. [Editors' note.]

repeated it again in Detroit and Philadelphia. He acquired steel-mills in Johnstown, Pa., and Lorain, Ohio, and sold them out to the Steel Trust. He had made most of his money by stock manipulations of this kind and was reputed to be many times a millionaire. He had a palatial home on Euclid Avenue, where he entertained generously. Although he was an intimate friend of many of the rich people of Cleveland, he was distrusted because of his unusual opinions and the apparent discrepancy between his social position and the things he advocated. He was a Democrat and an absolute free-trader. He had been elected to Congress by advocating free trade in a city in the heart of the iron and steel district. He had advocated it in Congress, protesting against a protective tariff on iron and steel, which he said would add new millions to his wealth for which others would have to pay. He advocated the public ownership of street railways, although he had made most of his fortune out of them. He had a devoted following wherever he went; many people loved him. Among the poor he was known for his generosity. Waiters, doorkeepers, cab-drivers knew him as the man whose smallest change was a dollar bill.

Odd among other oddities was the fact that Henry George had lived with him in Washington. *Protection and Free Trade* had been written by Henry George as a series of speeches which Mr. Johnson delivered in Congress. They were then reprinted in pamphlet form by the Government Printing Office, and a million copies distributed by Mr. Johnson under his congressional frank.

When I heard one day that this puzzling, contradictory, much-talked-of Tom Johnson had arrived and would announce his candidacy that evening at the Hollenden House, I freed myself from engagements and was there at eight o'clock. There was a stir outside and the crowd surged in. A short, pudgy man was pushed on to the cigar-stand above me. He stood round and smiling, hands in his pockets, he looked like a boy out for a lark. Politicians shouted like mad around him; evidently they expected a "barrel" campaign.

Surely, I thought, a man of wealth and position is not going to run for mayor in this undignified way. Politics is a serious business, a crusade against politicians and spoilsmen. Tom Johnson should have had a committee of prominent citizens to wait on him and ask him to run. He should have conferred with the Municipal Association and the Chamber of Commerce. That would have given dignity to his campaign.

When the crowd grew quiet Mr. Johnson began to speak. He started in the middle of things. He had permanently given up the making of money, he said, and had come back from New York to run for mayor. He had sold out all his railways and his iron and steel plants, and intended to devote the rest of his life to politics. He talked about the city. The steam railroads had gotten possession of the lake front and held it illegally. The lake-front land was worth millions of dollars. The city was contesting the railroad occupancy in the United States courts, where the case had lain for a dozen years. Mayor Farley was attempting to jam legislation through the council to validate these illegal holdings. In addition, he was doing everything he could to give the street railways a very valuable franchise; a franchise, Mr. Johnson said, worth many millions of dollars. He knew how much it was worth, because he had been in the street-railway business and had made millions out of just such franchise grants. He told how he had gone before the city council when seeking a grant for his company, and had said to the council that it was foolish for the city to give away such franchises. He had urged that the public should own the street railways and operate them, just as the water-works were operated, but if the city insisted on being foolish, he hoped it would be foolish to him. As a business man he had made money out of the city's stupidity. Now he intended to see to it that nobody got what he himself had gotten, without paying for it. Under municipal ownership the city could carry passengers for three cents, if the water was squeezed out of the capital stock. Much of this water, he admitted, had been put into the companies by himself.

It was all very simple, very winning. But I could see why my friends distrusted him. Was he as candid and honest as he seemed, or was he using his frankness merely as a political blind? I was at sea. Everybody said that the city needed a business man's administration, and Mr. Johnson was certainly an eminent business man. But he was not going at it the way I felt he should. He did not seem to be a reformer. He was not indignant enough. He said nothing about waste and extravagance; about bad men; about politicians; about the spoils system. He made no personal attacks on any one. He seemed not to have a high opinion of the kind of men on whom I counted to save democracy. He held a cigar in his hand while he spoke and went away with a crowd of riotous politicians. He was not at all like my picture of the business man who was to redeem politics.

I walked slowly homeward that night pondering on the enigma of Tom Johnson's personality, as I was to ponder on it for weeks to come. But a few days later something happened to divert my attention from him and centre it on my own affairs. One evening a group of men called on me at the University Club. Some of them I knew by name; they were residents of the brownstone ward in which the club was situated, the same ward that had sent Morris Black to the council. They came to ask me to run as Republican candidate for the council. They promised me support, management of my campaign, funds, everything needful. They spoke of the disclosures of corruption in the city government, of the "notorious thirteen." They reminded me that as secretary of the Municipal Association I had been appealing to other men to organize, to clean up the city, and hinted that there was a moral obligation on me not to refuse the candidacy offered. The situation, they implied, was one that demanded sacrifices.

I put them off for a day, talked to my law partners, reflected that I could not afford the expense or the distraction of campaigning, but waited eagerly for the gentlemen to reappear the next evening, and, when they came, consented to run. I liked being called from my law practice as Cincinnatus was called from the fields by the old Romans, liked being thought "a good citizen." And I was eager again to take part in the renaissance of politics which I felt was coming; the renaissance started by Morris Black and myself.

I plunged into the campaign whole-heartedly. Bill Crawford met Harry Garfield at the club at lunch one day and told him that he would wipe me off the earth. I sent word to him to go to it, we would have a good fight. And we did. I was out every night, making speeches in the saloons, visiting from house to house, as Black and I had done in his campaign. I spent more money than I could afford, but much more was being spent by some one else for my election. The other candidate spent more than we did, and that was comforting; moreover, I argued that one must beat the devil with his own tools. I had my photograph taken in a frock coat, and liked to see it on telegraph-poles, in shops, and in the windows of private homes. I looked thoroughly the good citizen. To my surprise, I found that many of the ward politicians were working for me. They distributed my literature, arranged meetings, and never called on me for money. I wondered at the time who had raised the money and gathered together such a motley array of workers. They don't realize that I am a civil-service reformer, I thought, at the same time disturbed and pleased by their assistance; and that what I stand for will put them out of business. For civil-service reform seemed very important to me; it would break the power of the boss, strip the mayor of power at the primaries, and make it possible to nominate good men for office. Although I took the support of the politicians, I did not disguise my opinions. In fact, I emphasized them. When I talked about these things, they smiled. I remembered that afterward.

The issue in the people's minds was the councilmanic scandal. The street-railway question made good campaign material, especially in the poorer sections of the district, which consisted of Euclid Avenue flanked by a strip of tenements on either side. It was known that I had taken a prominent part in the fight against the franchise. I urged the necessity of cleaning up the council, of electing a new sort of men to public office, of getting rid of the spoilsman. City administration, I said, should be taken out of party politics. The city was merely housekeeping, and housekeeping should be done on a business basis. In talking about the franchise, I denounced Mayor Farley's change of front; his "business men's settlement" with the street railways.

The principal issue in my mind, too, was corruption. The old gang should be cleaned out, a new kind of men put in. The kind of men I had in mind were business men, trained, university men. They were my friends. The others, the bad ones, lived principally down under the hill. They were immigrants. The Thirteenth Ward was the worst; it was controlled by a Polish immigrant named Harry Bernstein. He delivered, to a man, the number of votes he promised to deliver, to whoever would purchase them. He was the city scandal. It was Bernsteinism that ruled the city and Bernsteinism that must be wiped out. The risk of being dirtied by politics had to be taken; the sacrifice involved in running for office had to be made. And I was proud to have been selected by my friends, by the good people of my district, to make the sacrifice.

But the riddle of Tom Johnson remained. When I could spare time from my own campaigning, I went to his meetings. He would go to a Republican meeting and ask permission to talk from the same platform with the Republican candidate for mayor. When permission was denied him, the crowd followed him out into the street, almost emptying the hall. One night he talked about poverty, about how to be rid of it. He said that society should be changed not by getting good men into office, but by making it possible for all men to be good. He said that most men would be reasonably good if they had a chance. We had evil in the world because people were poor. The trouble was not with people, it was with poverty. Poverty was the cause of vice and crime. It was social conditions that were bad rather than people. These conditions could be changed only through politics.

This bothered me, as did most of his speeches. Surely some people were good, while others were bad. My classifications were simple. Roughly, the members of the University Club and the Chamber of Commerce were good; McKisson, Bernstein, and the politician were bad. The bad were commonly in power; they held offices and controlled elections. They did not do their work well and were paid very much more than they should receive. At the primaries they elected their own kind to office.

The way to change this vicious circle, I thought, was to get the good people to form committees in each ward as had been done in my own. If these committees nominated men who would go out and fight the politicians, if we gave enough thought to politics—as we were under a moral obligation to do—we should drive out the spoilsmen. It was all quite clear to me and very simple. It was the choice between the good and the bad.

But here was a man who said that bad people were not bad; they were merely poor and had to fight for a living. They got an easier living out of politics than they did working twelve hours a day in the steel-mills. So they went into politics. And being in the majority, they won out.

I resented what Mr. Johnson said, resented too the issues he ignored. He made my work in the Municipal Association seem false; made it seem as if we were trying to patch up something that ought not to be patched, that ought to be done away with entirely. I think there was a time when I might have turned against him. He was an enemy of my opinions, of my education, of my superior position. It hurt my ego, my self-respect, to be told that I was really not much better than the politician and that my class was not as important as I thought it was.

But I continued to go to his meetings while I listened to the criticisms of my friends who branded him as insincere. I could not understand why a man should make so much money out of business and then admit that the way he made it was wrong; why a rich man should advocate the things that he advocated, especially as what he proposed would take money away from his old friends. Still, much of what he said seemed true to me. Perhaps his personality was winning me; perhaps somewhere in the back of my mind there was approval of his ideas. I fluttered about him mentally, accepting, withdrawing, irresistibly attracted.

He often referred to *Progress and Poverty*, which I had read at the university. I had laid it aside, saying to myself: "That is the most interesting book on political economy I have ever read. What Henry George says seems to be true. But it must be false. Such a simple explanation of the wrongs of society and the way to correct them cannot be right. If it were, every one would have accepted the reform as soon as the book was published and we should have had the single tax long ago."

I finally called on Mr. Johnson at his office. I wanted to be assured of his sincerity. We talked a long time. Among other things, I told him about reading *Progress and Poverty*, of how I had been unable to answer the arguments but was convinced that it must be wrong.

He smiled and told me his own story.

"Years ago," he said, "when I was a young man just getting started in the street-railway business, I was coming up from Indianapolis to Cleveland on the Big Four Railroad. The "butcher"—as they called the man who sold books on the train—came along with a bundle of books on his arm. The conductor passed at the same moment, and taking a book from the pile, he said: 'Mr. Johnson, I think you would like this book. It is called *Social Problems*, by Henry George.'

"I looked at the book and returned it. Thinking it was a treatise on prostitution, I said I was not interested in social problems.

" 'It isn't that kind of book,' the conductor said. 'It deals with your kind of business—with street-railroads, steam-railroads, and the land question.'

"I bought the book and read it. I read it a second time. Then I took it to Arthur Moxham, my partner in the steel business, and asked him to read it. I said: 'Arthur, you know more about books than I do. I haven't read much. But if this book is right, then your business and mine are all wrong.'

"Some weeks after this, he told me he had read the book; it was interesting but quite wrong. He had marked the passages that were faulty. A short time afterward, I asked again about it. He said he had been rereading the book; it was wrong, but he had rubbed out some of his objections. Finally he came to me and said: 'Tom, I have read that book four times. I have had to rub out every one of my objections. The book is sound. Henry George is right.'

"In the meantime, I had read *Progress and Poverty*. I said to myself: 'If this book is really true, I shall have to give up business. It isn't right for me to make money out of protected industries, out of street-railway franchises, out of land speculation. I must get out of the business, or prove that this book is wrong.' I went to L. A. Russell, my attorney, and said to him:

" 'Here, Russell, is a retainer of five hundred dollars. I want you to read this book and give me your honest opinion on it, as you would on a legal question. Treat this retainer as you would a fee.'

"A few weeks later I got a memorandum from Mr. Russell pointing out the errors of Henry George. I was starting for New York on a business errand and asked Mr. Russell to go with me.

" 'We will talk this thing over in New York,' I said.

"In New York we met Mr. Du Pont, of Delaware, and Arthur Moxham. In the evening we all went to my rooms in the hotel. We took up Russell's objections one by one. We spent the whole night on them. One question after another was disposed of, and finally Russell threw up his hands and said:

" 'I have to admit that I was wrong. The book is sound. This man Henry George, whoever he is, is a wonderful philosopher.'

"All four of us were content with the decision. We were converted to an unnamed philosophy, by an unknown prophet, an obscure man of whom we had never before heard.

· · ·

"Now you know," said Mr. Johnson, "why I am running for mayor. I have been in Congress, but there isn't much to be done there. The place to begin is the city. If one city should adopt the single tax, other cities would have to follow suit. If we are the first to take taxes off houses, factories, and machinery, we will have a tremendous advantage. Factories will be attracted to Cleveland; it will be a cheap city to do business in, cheap to live in. Untaxing the things people use will cheapen them, it will encourage production. And if we tax the land heavily enough we will discourage speculation. With cheap land on the one hand and cheap houses, factories, and goods on the other, Cleveland will be the most attractive city in America."

Mr. Johnson's sincerity was convincing. But I had one more question to put.

"Why don't you cut loose," I asked, "from Charlie Salen and the other politicians whom the people distrust? If you do that, you will make an appeal to all the people I know. You are a business man and we all want a business man's administration. Then you could get the young men of the east end, the business men, the educated classes, to support you."

"No," he replied, "they will never support me. They can't support me. There is nothing I could say and nothing I could do that would make it possible for the 'good people,' as you term them, to support me. This fight cuts too deep. It touches too many interests, banks, business, preachers, doctors, lawyers, clubs, newspapers. They have to be on one side. And it isn't my side. They will be against me. The only people who can be for me are the poor people and the politicians who will have to follow the poor people when they get started."

I had still a moment of hesitation. I did not see clearly enough what he wanted to do. I had never thought of ending poverty through politics. We should always have poverty. I did not believe in working with spoilsmen. I saw that Tom Johnson was fighting his friends, men of his own class, that he took pleasure in the companionship of common people. The people whom I trusted he found untrustworthy.

But suddenly I found myself saying:

"I think I will withdraw from the Republican ticket and come out and support you. I can't do it and remain a candidate. And you can do things I never could do."

"No," he said, "you get elected as a Republican. Parties don't matter. We will work together. If I am elected, I shan't be able to do anything without the council."

As we shook hands he looked at me closely. "You know you will have to pay," he said, "for siding with me."

He was wondering, he later confessed to me, if I would be willing to pay the price.

A RUDE AWAKENING

Tom Johnson was elected mayor on the issue of municipal ownership and a three-cent fare on the street-railways. Along with a number of other men endorsed by the Municipal Association, I was returned to the council, which had enough independent members to be organized on a non-partisan basis. The beginning of the political renaissance had come. Spoilsmen, bosses, grafters would be driven out. Cleveland was to be America's pace-maker.

Mr. Johnson brought to the mayoralty extraordinary business talent and technical ability. He knew mathematics, electricity and power problems. He had been a shrewd monopolist and he knew every foot of the various street-car lines in the city. He had fought many legal battles around the obstacles placed in the laws of the State to shield the companies already in the field. Elected by a large majority, he would put his programme through, it seemed, with ease.

He did a characteristic thing by taking the oath of office as soon as the election returns were officially announced. Mayor Farley, he had discovered, was about to sign an ordinance granting the valuable lake-front property, which had been the subject of twelve years' litigation, to the railroads. To forestall this action Mr. Johnson walked into the mayor's office, and announced that he had been sworn in. In this way he entered dramatically on his ten years' administration.

The conservative press waited. It was puzzled. So were many of Mr. Johnson's old business associates. They were not yet convinced that he had abandoned his business past and had really dedicated himself to the public service.

Not as close to him while I held my Republican seat in the council as I came to be later, but enamored of the dream of a free city, with a master mind and a great idealist as its directing genius, I began to have a rough-and-tumble experience of city politics. Our first job was to clean house, to be rid of the spoilsmen, to drive out the "notorious thirteen." And we had made a beginning by our non-partisan organization of the council. A few weeks after the election I was asked by Mayor Johnson to introduce an ordinance making a grant to a natural-gas company, which proposed to provide light and fuel at thirty cents a thousand cubic feet. Cleveland was then paying eighty cents a thousand for artificial gas. I went over the ordinance with care, as did the city law department. When it was read in council meeting, bearing my name, I noticed that significant looks were exchanged among the notorious thirteen, and I suspected that they would be against it.

The following day a group of business men called on me to discuss the ordinance. Some of them were clients of our law firm. "Natural gas will ruin my business," said a coal merchant, as frankly as if it were obvious that a boon to three hundred thousand people could not be considered by reasonable persons in the face of his personal loss. The Chamber of Commerce came out against the ordinance. A new gas company meant tearing up the streets; it might kill the trees. And it would injure the existing company, which had twelve million dollars invested in the business. This was the nub of the situation. Soon a thoroughly organized campaign was started, backed by the press, the Chamber of Commerce, and by many of my friends. As time went on it became very bitter. I could not understand the opposition; other cities had natural gas, it was safe, convenient, and cheap. The arguments against it seemed trivial. I expected the ordinance to pass by a substantial majority. But it was defeated by one vote. To my surprise a number of reform councilmen voted against it. They gave no reasons; simply voted in the negative.

Immediately after the vote was announced a councilman from the west side named Charlie Kohl rose on a question of personal privilege. Drawing from his inside coat-pocket a package of bank bills, he addressed the president.

"Mr. President, on my way to the council-chamber this evening I was met by Dr. D-----. He asked me if I would vote against the gas ordinance. When I told him I had not made up my mind, he said:

" 'Charlie, I don't want this ordinance to pass. It is a matter of great importance to the old gas company. You and I have long been friends. I helped you to be elected and I judge by what you say that you may vote against the ordinance. Well, here are two thousand dollars. Pay off the mortgage on your house. I thought of giving it to one of the other boys, but I prefer giving it to you.' "

He laid the roll of bills on the clerk's desk. The atmosphere was charged with excitement. Reform councilmen who had voted against the ordinance were white in the face. The "thirteen" sat stolid. The galleries were packed with men from the Chamber of Commerce who were there in opposition to the ordinance and with city employees who favored it. Friends of mine in the audience were opposed to the ordinance. I expected them to protest, to make some kind of demonstration over the disclosure. But they did nothing. They were quiet, apparently unmoved.

I had heard of bribery, but it had never come close to me before. What could be done about it, I thought. Were we bound by a corrupt vote? Was it possible that the city should be denied the boon of cheap gas by such means?

In the suspense Mr. Johnson rose from his chair, apparently quite at ease. Pointing to Dr. D-----, who was moving toward the door, he directed one of the policemen to arrest him and take him to his office. Some one moved a reconsideration of the vote. Here was a way out; the ordinance would surely pass now by an overwhelming vote. I had never made a sustained speech and did not know how to begin. But I got to my feet and blazed out my feelings. I was outraged, and assumed that everybody else was outraged. Here was proof of what the press had been saying, of what the Municipal Association had said, of what we all suspected. Here was proof of how city business was carried on. And the astounding thing was that bribery was not all done by paving contractors and ordinary grafters, but by men of another class. For obviously Dr. D----- was acting for some one higher up. He was acting for the existing gas company. The bills still bore the binders of the bank from which they had come. That shocked me most.

I concluded:

"I have heard complaints about the so-called anarchists who speak on the public square. Anarchy, as I understand it, means the destruction of organized government. What is bribery but the destruction of government? It means substituting money for honest discussion. It means an end to democracy. The anarchists on the public square, if such there be, merely talk about putting an end to government. Here are men who have substituted corruption for discussion, and ours," I said, "is a government by discussion. The real enemies of the State, the most dangerous of anarchists, are the men who have plotted this thing, to subvert the will of the elected representatives of the people."

On the vote the ordinance was adopted by a small majority. The "thirteen" said nothing. Some of the reform councilmen protested their honesty. Except my own, there was little indignation.

I left the council-chamber with a feeling of exaltation. Such disclosures as this would bring home to the people the necessity of putting good men in office, who would stand by the city's interest, men who had the courage to denounce corruption and bribery, no matter from what source it came.

As I went down the stairs I was roughly brushed by two members of the "thirteen." They had voted against the ordinance. I had noticed the expressions of astonishment on their faces when I spoke about the use of money and about the artificial-gas company. They were plainly very angry.

"What do you mean by double-crossing us this way?" they demanded.

"Double-crossing?" I asked. "What do you mean?"

"Oh, you know well enough," they said. "Why did you go back on the rest of us and leave us in the ditch? Why did you double-cross the gas company?"

I was in the dark. I protested that I did not know what they meant.

"Oh, you can't put that stuff over on us," said one. "You know you were nominated and elected by the old gas company in the Fourth District. What d'ye suppose they backed you for? Do you think they put two thousand dollars in your campaign just because you were beautiful? Come along, Mike, he double-crossed them just as he double-crossed us."

A chill of questionings went through me. Was this true? Were the members of the committee who urged me to run not the disinterested citizens I had supposed them to be? Had I been deceived about the moral awakening in my district? Had I been picked out in the belief that because I was a corporation lawyer I could be relied on to serve business interests and to do the bidding of the men who financed my campaign?

There had been no understanding on my part as to how I should vote on any question, and I did not know the business connections of the men who had called upon me. But I soon learned that what Mike and Johnny said was true. One member of my nominating committee was the son of the vice-president of the gas company, while the men who were with him were his associates in various business enterprises.

I was terribly confused. I began to understand much that had been mysterious. I understood where the army of men came from who had been set to work the day my name was entered in the primaries. They were gas-company employees. I understood the lavish expenditure of money and the mysterious smiles of members of the councilmanic ring when I had introduced the natural-gas ordinance. There was some trick in the whole thing, they said to themselves. Of that they were sure. Possibly it was a big shake-down that the old company understood but that they had not been taken in on. I understood the anger of Mike and Johnny as they left the council-chamber. We were all gas-company men. The same men that had financed them had financed me. They had delivered the goods, but I had not. They had stuck to their friends, I had betrayed them. They had been faithful to the only political ideals they recognized, which was to keep your word no matter what it cost and to be loyal to those who were loyal to you. From their point of view I had been guilty of the one offense that could not be forgiven. I had double-crossed the men who had put me in office and who had financed my campaign.

And there was worse to come. The next day a group of business men and bankers called on me. With them was one of the trustees of the Charity Organization Society. He was a man whom I greatly respected, identified with almost every good movement in the city, one of the board of directors of the college settlement where I had lived.

"Fred," he began, "your friends are hurt by the things you said in the council last night. You compared the man who gives a bribe with the anarchists on the public square; you said that he was worse than the grafters in the council, for the grafters were poor and ignorant, some of them had to do what they were told. Of course no one can defend bribery. You know I wouldn't defend it. But you're a corporation lawyer, you ought to understand these things. Public-utility corporations are hounded by politicians; they have millions of dollars invested. They have to protect their investments, there are many widows and orphans. It is unfortunately true that they use money, but they can only get along by the means that you denounced. There isn't any other way for them to do business. They are always being subjected to some striking legislation. They can't get the things they ought to have with straightforward methods."

I was dumbfounded. Here was a new angle of political morality held by respected friends, who had contributed to my election.

"Do you mean," I asked hesitatingly, "that a gas or electric lighting or street-railway company can live only by bribery and corruption? Can private individuals carry on businesses of this kind only by what we all know are criminal means?"

They did not like the way I put it, but they agreed that the situation was, unfortunately, just that. There was no other way, in the present instance, to carry on the gas business. It had to corrupt the government.

"Well," I said, "listen. I don't know whether what you say is true or not but you have all acted as though it were true. I have heard about the 'natural' way of getting a franchise. I know about the contributions made by public-utility corporations to political parties, and about the financial pressure that is brought to bear on councilmen. There's a saying over in the City Hall that the street-railways pick men out of the cradle and train them for the council. But I didn't expect to hear a defense of these practices from men like you.

"I think you have converted me to public ownership. When a private business can live only by bribery, then the logical conclusion is that we can't have that kind of private business. We can fight the spoils system, bad as it is, in the open; it is not nearly so dangerous to democracy as is corruption. For corruption"—I warmed to my theme of the night before—"will destroy responsible government. You gentlemen have made the most convincing argument that could be made for public ownership."

My speech in the council made a difference with some of my friends. That was the thing I was least prepared for. It was not that I had double-crossed my backers, for that was not generally known. It was something deeper than that. Apparently I had touched a herd instinct. The herd was not organized, but subconsciously all its members thought alike. It was afraid. I had justified my election pledges and I expected approval. I was rather eager for it. But I won no approval. Indeed, the reverse was true. I sustained myself by reflecting that some one had to pay in the cleaning-up process. It was rather fine that I was permitted to make the sacrifice. Still, it hurt me that my friends at the club did not come to me and say:

"Fred, that was a fine speech you made at the council meeting on the gas ordinance. Bribery is the worst of all crimes. You're right about its destroying responsible government."

These men had applauded my attacks on Mayor McKisson and the notorious thirteen. Why did they not applaud me when I attacked the men who did the bribing? Was not the giver as bad as the taker—worse, indeed, since he does not need money? Why should not every one see this?

Not long afterward I introduced for Mayor Johnson an ordinance providing for a three-cent fare on the street-railways. This involved bringing in another company and affected the interests of Senator Hanna, of the banks, of many of our clients and the men with whom I was associated. I was conscious of increasing social alienation. At the club I was made to feel uncomfortable. Most of the people I knew were opposed to everything I did. And I began to question my classification of people, which Mr. Johnson had questioned for me in his campaign speeches. Good people, my friends, were unconcerned over bribery; they were not outraged by it when it was done by people they knew. They would not stand by criminal proceedings instituted against bribe-givers. Why, I wondered, this palsy benumbing good people? When the way was pointed out, how could they fail to rise and save the city?

Subsequent experience on the city council increased these doubts. I was interested in playgrounds for children, in public baths and dance-halls, in the opening up of parks and providing recreation for the poor. Here, I thought, is something my friends will surely rally to. Here is a way to beat the saloon, to stop crime at the source, far more efficiently than by raids or regulation. I introduced legislation for these things, showed by the experience of other cities that crime had been reduced where children were taken from the streets and given a place to play, with trained instructors to help them do so.

But my friends did not rally to such measures. On the contrary, a committee of the Chamber of Commerce denounced public baths as socialistic. There was an outcry against the wider use of the parks, especially against taking down the "Keep-off-the-Grass" signs. Reform councilmen protested that these things would increase the popularity of Mayor Johnson and would add to the tax-rate. Such support as came to me came from the old gang. In time the measures came out of the committees where they had lain for weeks and were passed with the aid of the men whom I had previously denounced. The bad men in the council rallied to the children. They knew better than I did where the children lived and where they had to play. On measures where there was no money moving they voted right; while representatives from the east-end wards often voted wrong.

In the end, through the activity of Mr. Johnson, Cleveland acquired a city-wide system of parks, playgrounds, and public baths. On Saturday and Sunday the whole population played baseball in hundreds of parks laid out for that purpose. Cleveland became a play city, and this generous provision for play has declared dividends. Workmen like to live in Cleveland. Workmen are followed by factory-owners. The growth of Cleveland in the last decade is partly traceable to the policy of making the city an attractive place in which to live.

In spite of its initial confusion and in spite of disappointments my term on the city council was one of happy activity. I grew to love the city and the big problems it presented. I visited other cities to study police administration, methods of street-cleaning, the grouping of public buildings. The city appealed to me as a social agency of great possibilities; at an insignificant cost it could fill the lives of people with pleasure. It could protect the poor by more intelligent use of the police force. It could provide things at wholesale; could open playgrounds and public baths. It could develop the lake front into a beautiful, long esplanade. It could take over the charities and run them as public agencies. I no longer believed in private charity. It seemed unfair that men and women who had given their lives to industry should have to rely upon private benevolence when in need. I saw endless possibilities of beauty in Cleveland.

. . .

At the expiration of my term I was ready to run again as an independent candidate. It was obvious that I could not be nominated on the Republican ticket. The party had identified itself with the traction interests and was controlled by Senator Hanna and his associates. I could not stand on the Republican platform even if I were nominated, and I had alienated many friends who had been responsible for my nomination. I declined a place on the Democratic ticket that Mr. Johnson offered me, feeling confident that I could be elected as an independent candidate. The district was an intelligent one, the issues were clear, and the regular party candidates were obviously unfit.

But the ballots did not fall as I had expected. I was a bad third in the race. People were not voting as my pattern of politics led me to believe they would. I got scarcely any support from my own ward, the richest in the city. From that time on I was identified frankly with Mr. Johnson and with the Democratic party. I was appointed chairman of the finance commission of the city, and during the next six years devoted most of my free time to politics, to speaking campaigns, to daily conferences in the City Hall or with the mayor at his home, which became the headquarters of a group of young men attracted, as I had been attracted, by Tom Johnson's personality and programme.

A TEN YEARS' WAR

Mr. Johnson called his ten years' fight against privilege a war for "A City on a Hill." To the young men in the movement, and to tens of thousands of the poor who gave it their support, it was a moral crusade rarely paralleled in American politics. The struggle involved the banks, the press, the Chamber of Commerce, the clubs, and the social life of the city. It divided families and destroyed friendships. You were either for Tom Johnson or against him. If for him, you were a disturber of business, a Socialist, to some an anarchist. Had the term "Red" been in vogue, you would have been called a communist in the pay of Soviet Russia. Every other political issue and almost every topic of conversation was subordinated to the struggle.

The possibility of a free, orderly, and beautiful city became to me an absorbing passion. Here were all of the elements necessary to a great experiment in democracy. Here was a rapidly growing city with great natural advantages and with few mistakes to correct. Here was a wonderful hinterland for the building of homes, a ten-mile water-front that could be developed for lake commerce, a population that had showed itself willing to follow an ideal, and, most important of all, a great leader.

I had an architectonic vision of what a city might be. I saw it as a picture. It was not economy, efficiency, and business methods that interested me so much as a city planned, built, and conducted as a community enterprise. I *saw* the city as an architect sees a skyscraper, as a commission of experts plans a world's fair exposition. It was a unit, a thing with a mind, with a conscious purpose, seeing far in advance of the present and taking precautions for the future. I had this picture of Cleveland long before the advent of city-planning proposals; it was just as instinctive as any mechanical talent. I saw cities in this way from the first lectures of Doctor Albert Shaw at Johns Hopkins; I went to Germany in the summers, especially to Munich, drawn there by orderliness, by the beauty of streets, concern for architecture, provision for parks, for gardens and museums, for the rich popular life of the people. And I studied cities as one might study art; I was interested in curbs, in sewers, in sky-lines. I wrote about cities—articles and books. I dreamed about them. The city was the enthusiasm of my life. And I saw cities as social agencies that would make life easier for people, full of pleasure, beauty, and opportunity. It could be done so easily and at such slight individual expense. Especially in a city like Cleveland that had few mistakes to correct, that was flanked on one side by a lake front which could be developed with breakwaters into parks and lagoons, and with natural parkways extending about it far back into the country.

I had never gotten over this enthusiasm. I never grow tired of city-building, of city enthusiasms, city ideals. And with all of its crudities and failures I have never lost faith that the American city will become a thing of beauty and an agency of social service as yet unplumbed.

The mad king of Bavaria dreamed no more ambitious dreams of city-building than did I of Cleveland. Here democracy would show its possibilities; the city would become our hope instead of our despair, and in a few years' time all America would respond to the movement. The crusade of my youth, the greatest adventure of my life, as great a training-school as a man could pass through—this the decade of struggle in Cleveland from 1901 to 1910 was to me.

The immediate struggle revolved about two main issues: the public ownership of public utilities, especially the street-railways and electric-lighting service, and the reduction of street-railway fares to three cents. Neither of them seemed adequate to explain the bitterness of the conflict and the power which reaction was able to organize to obstruct the movement. These issues mobilized the conservative forces of the city—banks, the Chamber of Commerce, lawyers, doctors, clubs, and churches. The press was partly owned by Mark Hanna, while advertisers were organized to bring pressure on editors and owners. Instinct held the propertied classes together no matter how detached they might be from the interests that were directly menaced. Before the expiration of the first two years of Mr. Johnson's term of mayoralty the city was divided into two camps along clearly defined economic lines. There was bitterness, hatred, abuse. Also social ostracism and business boycott. The press was unscrupulous in its attacks. On the one side were men of property and influence; on the other the politicians, immigrants, workers, and persons of small means. This line of cleavage continued to the end.

And I was not on the side where I would have chosen to be. The struggle brought me into conflict with friends, clients, my class. I preferred to be with them, I liked wealth and the things that went with wealth; I enjoyed dining out, dances, the lighter things of life. I suffered from the gibes of men with whom I had once been intimate, and fancied slights which did not in fact occur. I could not see why men would not treat political differences as natural; why my opinions on municipal ownership should make me any less desirable socially than I had been while living at the settlement engaged in uplift work.

Now, too, I was part of a political machine, was part of the spoils system, was apparently approving of things I had once thought to be the supreme evils in our politics; I was counselling with ward leaders, many of whom were saloon-keepers, none of whom were of my class or had any interest in politics beyond jobs, political power, and such distinction as came through the party organization.

This departure from former ideals did not disturb me as did the loss of old friends. I wanted to live with my class, to enjoy its approval, to exhibit the things I had learned at the university among people who lived in fine houses, who made the social and club life of the city.

Still, I was happy in the fight. It was always dramatic, and I had a passion for the things we were fighting for. I saw that the city must own its transportation system before it could begin to plan anything else; it ought to own its electricity supply; most important of all, it must end class war, which I was beginning to see was caused by the fight for franchise rights of great value involving most of the prominent men in the city. My passion for the city was also a passion for Tom Johnson. And I had come to love him as fervently as I loved the things he promised to achieve.

MELVIN G. HOLLI
Social and Structural Reform

Urban politics in the late nineteenth and early twentieth centuries have been variously interpreted as clashes between bosses and reformers, business-men and reformers, or between "conservatives" and "liberals." In this selection, Melvin G. Holli constructs yet another framework of analysis. Holli contends that the distinction between "social" reform and "structural" reform is crucial to an understanding of urban politics in this period. He begins by summarizing the major accomplishments of Hazen S. Pingree, Detroit's reform mayor from 1890 to 1897. Though originally elected as a "business" candidate, Pingree gradually developed his own brand of urban politics. Though he was a boss in that he headed an effective political organization with considerable grass-roots support, the principal direction of his organiza-tion was toward socioeconomic change.

Does Holli's analysis provide an adequate interpretive framework for an understanding of the issues and personalities we have been concerned with throughout this book? And on the basis of his argument, what can we conclude about the validity of the "boss-reformer" dichotomy, and about the nature of urban reform in the years between 1880 and 1920?

I

Before 1890, there was not a single municipal model after which Pingree could have fashioned his social reform programs for Detroit. Most of the nation's big city reform mayors had been cast from the same mold and had focused the force of their administrations upon cutting taxes, driving out corruption, and bringing honesty into municipal government. Pingree, too, had used the "drive the rascals out" approach but found it wanting at the end of his first administration and turned to fashioning his own brand of reform. "Collision" with the unpleasant facts of city life had stirred the Mayor toward a quest for equality and social justice and transformed Pingree into an urban pioneer in the social reform movement.[1]

During his four terms as mayor Pingree had moved progressively toward a social justice position which had culminated in the Mayor's fight for lower gas, light, telephone, and traction rates. Pingree had reconstructed the sewer system, brought Detroit to the first rank as a well-paved city, inaugurated a conduit system for unsightly and dangerous overhead wires, constructed schools, parks, and a free public bath, exposed corruption in the school board and bribery by a private light company, broken the paving "combine," implemented his equal-tax policies in the city, forced down the cost of ferry, gas, telephone, and streetcar rates, sponsored the entry into the city of a competitive street railway company and a telephone company, established a municipal light plant, forced the adoption of electrified rapid transit, ousted the toll roads, and initiated a work-relief program that had as its goals both aid to the unfortunate and a change in the climate of public opinion toward "paupers." The authority of the mayor in Detroit had, moreover, been tremendously enhanced and enlarged under Pingree's leadership.

In addition to these tangible achievements, Pingree had become a vocal proponent of the abolition of child labor, the popular election of United States senators, the direct primary, the graduated income tax, and municipal ownership; he remained throughout his life both a foe of monopoly and an advocate of state regulation of big business. Moral questions, which civic uplift groups considered paramount, Pingree ignored. The Mayor had no desire to enforce the Sunday saloon-closing law, and prostitution was tolerated by his administration as a "necessary evil." When the school board adopted Bible readings for the curriculum, Pingree vetoed the measure. "I do not believe in stirring up any religious strife among the people," the Mayor asserted. "The Jews, the Catholics, the several thousand atheists among the Germans as well as many Christians of various denominations who are opposed to the introduction of this book are entitled to the same consideration as all the other taxpayers." It would be far better to teach natural history than religion in the public schools, Pingree observed. In his personal religion, Pingree became a practical social gospeler. After having watched a Salvation Army soup kitchen distribute its limited resources to those in distress, he declared: "This is my kind of religion—divide and help your neighbor."[2]

Pingree's achievements as Detroit's social reform mayor were impressive and unmatched by those of any reform mayor of the nineties. "Men who are willing to fight corporate wealth at the present time are rare," B. O. Flower, an editor, told the Mayor in 1896. "I thank you for the work you have done for the people." In the wake of the presidential election that year, Professor Richard T. Ely advised Henry Demarest Lloyd to come into close personal relations with Pingree while he continued his social reform work to help him avoid any serious mistakes which might count him out as a Presidential nominee in 1900. Lloyd told Samuel "Golden Rule" Jones on the eve of his mayoralty career in Toledo that "Pingree [was] the best Mayor America ever has produced."[3]

Several factors appear to have been influential in shaping Pingree's career. Pingree's tough-minded sense of righteousness, his unflinching view of an honorable businessman's responsibility, the public approval he reaped from the traction controversy, his social ostracism, and his warm compassion for the masses all appear to have had some bearing upon his conception of the role of a responsible urban executive. Several of these elements had been foreshadowed in his life as an entrepreneur. As a shoe manufacturer, he had placed a high premium upon good quality and business integrity. As a successful businessman, he had imposed his will, his discipline, and a rational order on an obsolete shoe-making operation and built it into a million-dollar business. Pingree carried the systematic planning and surveying of customer wants and needs that he had conducted as a sales employee with him into his mayoralty administrations. He analyzed the quality of concrete, made engineering surveys of the sewers and streets, examined franchises, and gathered statistical information from other cities about the price and quality of gas, light, and telephones; and he used all this to support his reform proposals. Rationalizing the business process was clearly a technique that had served him well both as an entrepreneur and as an urban reformer. Yet techniques do not make reformers. New York mayors Abram Hewitt, a successful iron master, and William Havemeyer, a sugar manufacturer, were probably superior to Pingree in rationalizing the business process, but neither became a social reformer.

Pingree was an omnivorous reader of both popular and serious periodicals and quality monthlies. He read the essays and articles of Richard T. Ely, Benjamin O. Flower, Albert Shaw, and Washington Gladden; visited and corresponded with John R. Commons, William T. Stead, and Henry Demarest Lloyd; associated with Edward W. Bemis; and knew of the work of Professor Frank Parsons and Governor John Peter Altgeld. He eclectically took bits of the ideas, notions, and social attitudes of these men. However, none of these men held a major municipal office and thus they were not able to provide Pingree with a practical blueprint for urban reform. Pingree gained the support of urban populists and labor radicals whom he took into his inner circle. It is doubtful if this radical reform tradition ultimately explains Pingree, for part of this intellectual legacy was just as available to New York's Seth Low, San Francisco's James D. Phelan, and dozens of other mayors, but they failed to heed it or to initiate programs of social reform in their cities.

The sociological concept of a "status revolution" appears even less satisfactory in explaining the Mayor. Pingree's background was not that of a middle class professional or a genteel small businessman who reacted with fear to the rise of a newly rich, uncultured, industrial class and thus stumbled into reform. Pingree was part of that postwar generation which rose from humble origins to wealth and a comfortable station in life.[4] The same was true of later reformers who followed the social reform tradition that Pingree helped to establish: "Golden Rule" Jones, a Welsh-born oil field roustabout and Tom L. Johnson, a newsboy who came from a poor Southern family, had come up through inventions and sharp deals, and then embarked upon urban reform careers. If anything, mid-western urban reform seemed more related to the dynamics of that class of newly arrived, scantily educated, urban capitalists than to the status anxieties of upper class patricians or middle class professionals.

Fundamentally Pingree was an economic empiricist who drew his conceptions and built his programs from his own experiences. Despite the fact that he was a capitalist, he accepted the labor theory of value during his mayoral years, and he argued that labor deserved greater consideration because it was the creator of all value. The idea was hardly novel during the 1890's, nor was it to be found exclusively in the province of social theorists: it was as much a part of the popular philosophy of the urban working classes as it was the agrarian philosophy of the populists.

Although Pingree's untutored brand of political economy sounded Marxist to some, Pingree's ideas were a product of his own observations of industrial life and the class structure of Detroit. He had seen Detroit transformed from a wayfarer's station into an industrial center in the brief span of twenty-five years. He had observed how new industrial wealth had taken over control of the city and state G.O.P., and how it controlled access to the highest offices the party had to offer. The old political regime which supported powerful bosses like Zachariah Chandler, a dry goods merchant, had been superseded by the new order of G.O.P. sachems such as James McMillan who stood at the very pinnacle of industrial, commercial, and business affluence and power in Michigan. In Detroit Pingree had personally observed traction, light and gas interests exercise their economic sway over councilmen and city officials in the process of buying valuable franchises and monopolies. Pingree himself had been offered a bribe of $50,000 to permit certain franchises to pass and another of $75,000 to take the pressure off the Citizens' Street Railway Company. What Pingree had personally experienced in Detroit confirmed his views about the national scene.[5]

Economic determinism was a strong article of faith for Pingree, who believed that every man had his price. When challenged on his social theory and asked why, if that were the case, had he not sold out, Pingree's reply was that no one had yet met his price. Pingree firmly believed that the social and political structure of society reflected the wishes, desires, and aspirations of those who controlled and owned the means of production.[6]

II

Pingree's brand of social reform—whose objective was to lower utility rates for the consumer and which attempted to place a larger share of the municipal tax burden on large corporations—was not the prevailing mood of urban reform in late-nineteenth and early-twentieth-century America. Far more prevalent in the programs of large-city mayors who earned the epithet "reformer" was the effort to change the structure of municipal government, to eliminate petty crime and vice, and to introduce the business system of the contemporary corporation into municipal government. Charter tinkering, elaborate audit procedures, and the drive to impose businesslike efficiency upon city government were the stock-in-trade of this type of urban executive. Mayors of this kind of reform persuasion could be found in New York, Brooklyn, Buffalo, San Francisco, and countless other cities.

Although most of these structural reformers did not articulate their positions as eloquently as Seth Low or attempt to install business methods as ruthlessly as John Purroy Mitchel, they all shared a certain style, a number of common assumptions about the cause of municipal misgovernment, and, in some instances, a conviction about which class was best fitted to rule the city. Few of them were as blatantly outspoken in their view of democracy as Samuel S. McClure, the publisher of the leading muckrake journal. He instructed Lincoln Steffens to prove that popular rule was a failure and that cities should be run by a dictatorship of wise and strong men, such as Samuel S. McClure or Judge Elbert Gary. Similarly New York's former reform mayor, Abram Hewitt asserted in 1901 that "ignorance should be excluded from control, [and] the city business should be carried on by trained experts selected upon some other principle than popular suffrage."[7]

None of the structural reformers had the unqualified faith in the ability of the masses to rule themselves intelligently that social reformers Hazen S. Pingree, Samuel "Golden Rule" Jones, or Tom L. Johnson did. "I have come to lean upon the common people as the real foundation upon which good government must rest," Pingree told the Nineteenth Century Club in 1897. In a statement that represented more than a rhetorical flourish, "Golden Rule" Jones chastised Reverend Josiah Strong for his distrust of the masses and told him that the "voice of the people is the voice of God." Tom Johnson, asserted Brand Whitlock, knew that "the cure for the ills of democracy was not less democracy, as so many people were always preaching, but more democracy." When Johnson was defeated by the Cleveland electorate at the very pinnacle of one of the most productive urban reform careers in the nation, he told Whitlock "The people are probably right."[8]

The structural reform movement was in sharp contrast to the democratic mood of such a statement. It represented instead the first wave of prescriptive municipal government which placed its faith in rule by educated, upper class Americans and, later, by municipal experts rather than the lower classes. The installation in office of men of character, substance, and integrity was an attempt to impose middle class and patrician ideals upon the urban masses. The movement reached its height in the second and third decades of the twentieth century with the city-manager and city-commissioner forms of government, which called for the hiring of nonpartisan experts to decide questions hitherto viewed as resolvable only by the political process. Like the structural reform movement of the late-nineteenth-century, the city-manager movement reflected an implicit distrust of popular democracy.[9]

New York's Mayor William F. Havemeyer was a prototype of the twentieth-century structural reformers. Having inherited a substantial fortune, he retired from the sugar refining business at the age of forty and devoted most of his career to public service. Elected mayor in 1872 during the public exposure of the Tweed Ring, Havemeyer was a reformer who championed "clean government," "economy," and the business class point of view. Obsessed with tax cuts and retrenchment, he and his fiscal watchdog, city Treasurer Andrew H. Green, cut wages on public works and demanded elaborate procedures to account for all petty expenditures of public funds. Green's painstaking scrutiny of every claim snarled the payroll so badly that the city's laborers rioted when their pay checks got lost in an administrative tangle.[10]

To practice economy, Havemeyer sacrificed important public services and, in the process, "crippled downtown development." During a three-month period in 1874 the Mayor vetoed more than 250 bills related to street grading, paving, and widening, board of education contracts, and appropriations intended for public charities. In justifying his liquidation of work relief, Havemeyer told the Harvard Association that contributions of private individuals and Christian and charitable associations were generous enough to meet the needs of the poor. According to Seymour Mandelbaum, the lower classes and the promoters of new areas of the city suffered most from Havemeyer's policies.[11]

During his second year in office, the aging Mayor fought with the city council and accomplished nothing of lasting importance. Havemeyer and the New York Council of Political Reform were so obsessed with "honest, efficient and economical government" that they indicted every public improvement as a "job" and labeled every politician who supported such measures as an "exponent of the class against which society is organized to protect itself." The Mayor's death in 1874 mercifully ended the agony of a reform administration which was strangling the city with red tape generated by its own economy programs. Ironically, Havemeyer helped to perpetuate the widespread belief that reformers were meddling, ineffectual reactionaries, or, as George Washington Plunkitt charged, "morning glories" who wilted in the heat of urban politics.[12]

Buffalo's "fighting mayor," Grover Cleveland, 1882, was another one of the progenitors of the structural reform tradition. Preoccupied as much as Havemeyer with cutting taxes and municipal expenditures, Cleveland had no positive programs to offer, with one notable exception: he fought and won authorization for a massive interceptor sewer system to diminish the dumping of refuse into the Erie Canal. He made his mark in Buffalo by the veto of a corrupt street cleaning contract, the "most spectacular single event" of his administration in Allan Nevins's view. In addition, Cleveland fought to stop the constant proliferation of city jobs, exercised a Havemeyer type of vigilance over all claims made against the city treasury, and directed city employees to stop closing their offices at 4:00 p.m. and to perform a full day's work. His inflexible drive for economy and efficiency and his contempt for the dishonesty of city machines won him a reputation as a rugged veto and reform mayor.[13]

Seth Low, a wealthy merchant, philanthropist, and university president, was mayor of Brooklyn (1882-85) and later of New York (1902-03).

Perhaps more than any other American mayor, he possessed the qualities of a high-minded, nonpartisan structural reformer who attempted to infuse a large dose of businesslike efficiency into municipal government. He was widely recognized by his generation as one of the most prominent practicing reformers on the urban scene, but he also built a considerable reputation as a scholar of municipal affairs. In countless addresses, Low argued that the answer to urban problems was charter reform to bring nonpartisanship and a centralized administration into city government. Reform of this sort would arouse a new civic consciousness and create a cohesive corporate government that could be run along business lines, free from outside influences.[14]

Under the aegis of a silk-stocking Citizens' Committee, Low, with his refined eloquence and business support, had waged an effective campaign against political spoilsmanship and partisanship and won Brooklyn's mayoralty election in 1881. Low disregarded political affiliation and based his appointments on ability and merit. Although his two terms proved to be unspectacular, Low had advanced what he considered the cardinal principles of municipal reform: he had reduced the city's debt, tightened up the tax system, and conducted a vigorous campaign at Albany to stop special state legislation from interfering in Brooklyn's affairs. Such social questions as tenement house reform and aid to the aged, the poor, or workingmen were for Seth Low but special benefits which could not be considered until local partisanship had been wiped out and municipal government had been reorganized along the lines of authority and responsibility. Low's name had become synonymous with efficiency, responsibility, and clean government.[15]

After a particularly flagrant period of municipal corruption under Tammany Hall, a reform-minded Citizens' Union, which counted J. Pierpont Morgan and Elihu Root among its founders, asked Seth Low to enter the lists as an independent candidate for mayor of New York against the Tammany favorite in 1901. Low ran on a platform of home rule and nonpartisanship, avoided the social-welfare planks endorsed by the Citizens' Union, and discussed honesty, economy, and responsibility in his speeches. Low was known to the voters because he had assisted in drafting the first charter for Greater New York, which consolidated hundreds of small towns and three large cities into one unit. Low's victory in 1901 was probably less an endorsement of his brand of reform than a public reaction against the excesses of Tammany.[16]

As New York's mayor, Low brought in experts to operate the various departments, pared away Tammany's payroll padding, and set himself up as the businessman in office. He cut salaries, increased the length of the working day for municipal employees, and reduced the city's annual budget by $1,500,000. In the public transit and utility field, Low saw to it that franchises were carefully drafted to safeguard the city's interests and to provide for additional revenue. He failed to press for lower rates, to agitate for a public rate-making body, or to instruct his district attorney to investigate the corrupt alliances between private business and politicians. He balked at appointing one of the best-qualified housing reformers, Lawrence Veiller, to head the tenement house commission, apparently because Low did not wish to disturb the conservative real estate interests. Low was willing, however, to use the full force of law against Sunday drinking, petty gambling, and prostitution, which were commonly found in the immigrant and lower class sections of the city. The Bureau of Licenses also cracked down on the city's 6,000 pushcart peddlers who were operating without licenses, and the Department of Law prosecuted residents whose tax payments were delinquent. With similar zeal, the Department of Water raised nearly $1,000,000 in income from overdue water bills.[17]

Low's tinkering with the machinery of government, his charter revision and rewriting, his regularization of tax collections, his enforcement of the city statutes, his appointment of men of merit, and his reduction of city expenditures were laudable actions by almost anybody's test of good government. Unfortunately, these measures bore most severely upon the lower classes. Low's structural reforms were also very impolitic, as his defeat in the election of 1903 demonstrated. Low never seemed to realize that his municipal reform had nothing to offer the voters but sterile, mechanical changes and that fundamental social and economic conditions which pressed upon the vast urban masses of immigrants and poor could not be changed by rewriting charters or enforcing laws.[18]

San Francisco's reform mayor James D. Phelan, a wealthy banker and anti-Bryan Democrat who held office from 1897 to 1902, was also a structural reformer like his model, Seth Low, whom Phelan frequently quoted. Phelan's program for reform included the introduction of efficiency and economy to ensure "scientific, systematic and responsible government," which was also the goal of the San Francisco Merchants' Association. Franchise regulation, lower traction rates, municipal ownership, and equal taxation were not part of Phelan's design for a better San Francisco. The distinguishing mark of the Phelan administration was its sponsorship of a strong mayor, and a short ballot charter that provided rigid fiscal controls over expenditures, city-wide elections for the council, and a merit system. Known as a "watchdog of the treasury," Mayor Phelan supported a low tax rate that forced the city to withhold schoolteachers' salaries, suspend many of the essential functions of the city health department, subject patients at the city hospital to inadequate care, and turn off the street lights at midnight. Phelan crippled his administration when he permitted the president of the police commissioners (who was also president of the Chamber of Commerce) to protect strikebreakers and club pickets during a teamsters' and a dock-workers' strike against the open shop. Although the 18 unions lost their strike, they retaliated by forming their own political party and defeating the reformers in 1901. In the famous graft prosecutions after 1901, Phelan continued to act like a "member of his class" or, as Fremont Older put it, "a rich man toward a great business in which he is interested."[19] Like Low, Phelan failed to attack what social reformers recognized as the basic problems confronting the city.

Equally ineffectual in his attempt to make New York the best governed city in the nation was Mayor John Purroy Mitchel, who served from 1914 to 1917. He was an "oddly puritanical Catholic" who represented the foibles and virtues of patrician class reform. Mitchel's election in 1913 was the result of voter reaction to a decade of brazen looting by Tammany Hall. Like his reform predecessors, Mitchel was responsible for little of lasting importance and did not generate enthusiasm among the large mass of voters with his structural reforms.[20]

Mitchel's failure was due to his misconception that city government could be conducted by the "ledger book ethics of the corporation accountant." So dedicated was Mitchel to budgetary cutbacks that he adopted the Gary Plan of education, which enabled New York City to cram more children into the existing schools. He decreased appropriations for the city's night schools, thus seriously hampering the entire program; for the summer program, Mitchel asked the teachers to volunteer their services without remuneration. Mitchel also appointed cost-cutting charity agents who began either to return feeble-minded children to their parents or to threaten to charge the often hard-pressed parents if their children were kept in public supported institutions. In addition, he instituted an investigation of the city's religious child care organizations, hoping thus to cut the city subsidy; but this action brought the wrath of the Catholic church down upon him.[21] Mitchel, although well-intentioned, had a kind of King Midas touch in reverse: everything he touched seemed to turn to ashes.

Robert Moses dismissed the Mitchel administration's efficiency drives as "saving rubber bands" and "using both ends of the pencil," but its flaws were much greater. The Mitchel administration and the structural reform movement were not only captives of a modern business mentality but sought to impress middle and upper class social values upon the urban community and to redistribute political power to the patrician class.[22]

Built upon a narrow middle and patrician class base and a business concept of social responsibility, the structural reform movement, with its zeal for efficiency and economy, usually lacked staying power. As George Washington Plunkitt pointed out, such crusaders were usually repudiated by lower class voters after a brief tenure in office. Unlike the social reformers, who were also interested in economy, the structural reformers had a blind spot when it came to weighing the human cost of their programs. They failed to recognize that a dose of something as astringent as wage-cutting and payroll audits had to be counterbalanced with social welfare programs if the public were to be served effectively. Too often they blamed the immigrant for the city's shortcomings or directed much of the force of their administrations to exterminating lower-class vices, which they saw as the underlying causes of municipal problems.[23]

Unlike the structural reformers, social reform mayors such as Hazen S. Pingree (1890-97), "Golden Rule" Jones (1897-1903), Tom Johnson (1901-09), Mark Fagan (1901-07), Brand Whitlock (1906-13), and Newton D. Baker (1912-16) began with a different set of assumptions about the basic causes of misgovernment in the cities. They shared the view, which Lincoln Steffens later publicized, that big business and its quest for preferential treatment and special privileges had corrupted municipal government. The public service corporations, the utilities, the real estate interests, and the large industrial concerns all had vested interests in urban America. They sought special tax advantages, franchises which eliminated competition, and other municipal concessions. They bought aldermen, councilmen, and mayors to protect these interests and, in the process, demoralized urban politics and city government. Mayor Tom Johnson's aide Frederic C. Howe was shocked when he was berated by his upper class friends for opposing a franchise steal; they explained that the public utilities have "millions of dollars invested" and had to "protect their investments." "But I do say emphatically," declared Mayor Pingree in 1895, ". . . better take [the utilities] out of private hands than allow them to stand as the greatest corruptors of public morals that ever blackened the pages of history."[24]

The programs of the social reform mayors aimed at lower gas, light, telephone, and street railway rates for the community and higher taxes for railroads and business corporations. When they were unable to obtain the regulation of public utilities, these mayors fought for municipal ownership, the only technique to redistribute economic power available to them as urban executives. Establishment of free public baths, expansion of parks, schools, and public relief were similarly attempts to distribute the amenities of middle class life to the masses. The social reformers recognized that the fight against crime, in its commonly understood sense (i.e. rooting out gambling, drinking, and prostitution) was an attempt to treat the symptoms rather than the disease itself and that such campaigns would burn out the energies of a reform administration and leave the fundamental problems of the urban masses untouched. Pingree, like Jones and Johnson, believed that such binges of "Comstockery" were irrelevant to municipal reform. "The good people are always insisting upon 'moral' issues," asserted Toledo Mayor Brand Whitlock, "urging us to turn aside from our large immediate purpose, and concentrate our official attention on the 'bad' people—and wreck our movement."[25]

The saloons where drinking, gambling, and other vices flourished, Pingree, Jones, and Johnson agreed, were but poor men's clubs and offered the workers but a few of the comforts that most rich men enjoyed. "The most dangerous enemies to good government are not the saloons, the dives, the dens of iniquity and the criminals," Pingree told the Springfield, Massachusetts, Board of Trade. "Most of our troubles can be traced to the temptations which are offered to city officials when franchises are sought by wealthy corporations, or contracts are to be let for public works." For refusing to divert public attention from the "larger and more complex immoralities" of the "privileged" interests, as Brand Whitlock put it, to the more familiar vices, the social reformers earned the bitter censure of the ministerial and "uplift" groups.[26]

The whole tone of the social reform movement was humanistic and empirical. It did not attempt to prescribe standards of personal morality nor did it attempt to draft social blueprints or city charters which had as their goals the imposition of middle class morality and patrician values upon the masses. Instead, it sought to find the basic causes of municipal misgovernment. Pingree, the first of the broad gauged social reformers, discovered the sources of municipal corruption in his day-to-day battle with the light, gas, telephone, and traction interests, the latter represented at the time by Tom Johnson. Johnson, like Mayor Newton D. Baker, knew from his own experience as a utility magnate why municipal government had been demoralized. Mayor Mark Fagan discovered that Jersey City could neither regulate nor tax the utilities and the railroads because both parties were dominated by these interests.[27]

In attempting to reform the city, Pingree, Jones, Johnson, and Whitlock lost upper class and business support and were forced to rely upon the lower classes for political power. The structural reformers, on the other hand, were frequently members of and sponsored by the very social and economic classes which most vehemently opposed social reform. "If we had to depend upon these classes for reforms,'' Pingree told the *Outlook* in 1897, "they could never have been brought about.'' "It is not so much the undercrust as the upper crust,'' asserted Professor Edward Bemis, who served as a Pingree aide, "that threatens the interests of the people.''[28]

The inability of the structural reformers to pursue positive programs to alter the existing social and economic order was probably a reflection of their own business and class backgrounds. Their high regard for the sacrosanct nature of private property, even if obtained illegally, limited them to treating but one aspect of the municipal malaise, and then only when corruption by urban machines reached an intolerable point. This half-way attempt at urban reform prompted Brand Whitlock to observe in 1914: "The word 'reformer' like the word 'politician' has degenerated, and, in the mind of the common man, come to connotate something very disagreeable. In four terms as mayor I came to know both species pretty well, and, in the latter connotations of the term, I prefer politician. He, at least, is human.''[29]

III

The structural reform tradition drew much of its strength from a diverse group of theorists composed of good government people, spokesmen for the business community, civic uplifters, representatives of taxpayers' associations, editors, and college professors. The most prominent and influential spokesmen of this persuasion were the Englishman James Bryce, college professors Frank J. Goodnow and William B. Munro, and the editor and scholar Albert Shaw. These theorists diagnosed problems of the city differently from the social reformers. Of fundamental importance to the models they formulated to bring about better city government was their view of the basic causes of the urban malaise. New York's problems, according to Professor Frank Goodnow, had begun in 1857, when the "middle classes, which had thus far controlled the municipal government, were displaced by an ignorant proletariat, mostly foreign born.'' Three decades later, James Bryce, who dealt with the problems of the city in one of the most influential books of his age, observed that the same "droves of squalid men, who looked as if they had just emerged from an emigrant ship" were herded by urban bosses before magistrates to be enrolled as voters. Such men, said Bryce, were "not fit for suffrage" and "incompetent to give an intelligent vote.'' Furthermore, their odious habits and demeanor had driven "cultivated" and "sensitive" men out of political life and discouraged the business classes from assuming their share of civic responsibility. One of the most able students of comparative municipal government, Albert Shaw, agreed with Bryce and Goodnow and concluded that the foreign-born had provided the opportunities for the "corruptionist and the demagogue,"[30] who had demoralized city government and lowered the tone of civic responsibility. The immigrant was central to the analyses of the theorists: although a few of them admitted other contributing factors, it is doubtful that any of them believed that the quality of civic responsibility, the level of public morality, and the honesty of urban administrations could have sunk as low had not the immigrant been present in overwhelming numbers in American cities.

Unlike the immigration restrictionists, the theorists did not distinguish between the new and old immigrants but lumped them together with the urban lower classes and attacked the political agencies that had facilitated the rise to power of these new groups. Even the newcomers from Northern Europe "know nothing of the institutions of the country, of its statesmen, of its political issues," Bryce argued. "Neither from Germany nor from Ireland do they bring much knowledge of the methods of free government." Lower class representatives from the wards were not welcome in municipal circles, for presumably the district system produced "inferior men" of "narrowed horizons," or as Alfred Conkling put it, permitted the balance of power to be held by the "worst class of men." "Wards largely controlled by thieves and robbers," Cornell's Andrew D. White warned, ". . . can control the city." Harvard's Professor Munro argued that the ward system elected councils that only wasted time and money in "fruitless debate" and sent to councils men "whose standing in the community is negligible." The ward system of representation was denounced by Professors Goodnow and Munro and Delos F. Wilcox for producing the worst representatives in the city. The National Municipal League's model charter called upon municipalities to abolish local representation. In Goodnow's view there were no local interests worthy of political representation anyway.[31]

In building their case against the ability of a mass urban electorate to rule itself, the theorists also drew upon psychology and history. The "craving for excitement" and the "nervous tension" of the city had a degenerative effect, Delos F. Wilcox argued, for "urban life tends to endanger the popular fitness for political power and responsibility." City populations were "radical rather than conservative," and "impulsive rather than reflective," asserted Goodnow, and far less inclined than rural populations to have "regard for the rights of private property." This was caused in part by the fact, Goodnow continued, that urban residents, unlike rural, had "no historical associations" with the cities in which they lived and thus had a poorly developed "neighborhood feeling." The elective system that depended upon familiar relationships and a cohesive community for its success was thus a failure in the city. Goodnow was also disturbed by his study of the larger contours of Western municipal history which convinced him that when city populations had been permitted to develop free of outside control, they evinced an "almost irresistible tendency to establish oligarchical or despotic government." American cities that were under Boss rule, in his opinion, showed similar tendencies.[32]

The first solutions proposed by many spokesmen of reform were hardly original. Outright disfranchisement had been suggested frequently since the end of the Civil War. Some cities had enacted stiffer registration requirements to pare down the vote of the unwashed, and some states had followed the pattern of Michigan, which revoked the alien franchise in 1894. Just as effective, although less direct, was the 1876 recommendation of the New York commissioners for the creation of an upper house with control over money bills in New York City, which was to be elected by propertied voters.[33]

The theorists, however, appear to have been inspired by a contemporary historical event. Drawing upon the Southern experience of disfranchising the Negro, Albert Shaw and Frank Goodnow suggested that such a measure might be applied to Northern cities. The "grandfather clause" apparently convinced Goodnow that the nation was not irrevocably committed to universal suffrage: once the people became convinced that "universal suffrage inevitably must result in inefficient and corrupt government, it will be abandoned," he predicted. The safeguards of suffrage, Fourteenth and Fifteenth Amendments, did not pose insurmountable obstacles, argued Goodnow. He dismissed the Fourteenth Amendment as merely an appeal to Congress, and he pointed out that the Fifteenth left room for educational and property qualifications.[34]

Accepting the Southern solution as reasonable, Shaw argued that the franchise in the North should be "absolutely" restricted to those who could read English, and "in the case of the foreign-born, to those showing positive fitness for participation in our political and governmental life." Furthermore Shaw argued that European immigrants should be directed southward where they would provide competition for Negroes which would result in a beneficial "survival of the fittest." In order to upgrade the quality of the urban electorate, Professor Munro recommended that the literacy test for the franchise should be extended throughout the nation. Universal suffrage was a "sacrifice of common sense to abstract principles," Bryce asserted. "Nobody pretends that such persons [immigrant voters] are fit for civic duty, or will be dangerous if kept for a time in pupilage, but neither party will incur the odium of proposing to exclude them."[35]

Although demands to purge the unfit elements from urban voting lists were often voiced during the 1890's, it became apparent that such a solution was too drastic. Few civic federations and even fewer politicians picked up the suggestion. Despite the prestige and influence of the theorists, it was evident that disfranchisement was unacceptable to the American public as a way to solve its urban problems. Clearly, less abrasive and more refined techniques would have to be found.

The theorists often spoke of installing into office the "better" classes, the "best" citizens and civic patriots. Excluded were labor, ethnic, or lower class representatives. As Goodnow put it, their choice was "men engaged in active business" or professionals, presumably associated with the business community. The theorists did not distinguish between big and small businessmen, or between entrepreneurs and financiers. What they wanted, as Conkling expressed it, was "any business or professional man . . . who has been successful in private life" and who was reasonably honest. As Richard T. Ely observed, the battle cries of the good government crowd in the 1890's had been: "Municipal government is business not politics." "Wanted, A municipal administration on purely business principles." If one accepted the premise it followed logically, as Ely noted, that businessmen were the "natural and inevitable directors of local affairs."[36]

The theorists argued that the business of city government was business and not politics. The "purely administrative functions—that is to say business functions—outweighed the political functions nine to one," declared Walter Arndt. They extensively used the modern business corporation as a model in their discussions of city government; some called the citizens "stockholders," and others referred to the council as the "board of directors" and the mayor as the "chairman of the board." They spoke of the pressing need for efficiency, the complexity of urban problems, and favored the use of experts to replace elected amateurs. Goodnow argued that a clear distinction must be drawn between legislative and administrative duties and that municipal departments must be staffed by experts. Munro warned that public opinion was the "worst" enemy of the expert and therefore should be rendered less influential in municipal decision-making. In short, the theorists were arguing that the role of public opinion and political expression should be substantially reduced in governing the modern city.[37]

In urging the reconstruction of city government, the theorists called for far-reaching changes in city charters. They advocated a strong mayor system, which accorded with what most of them knew about New York City politics: at least once during each decade since the end of the Civil War, "reformers" had been able to win the mayoralty, although they repeatedly failed to control the city council. The theorists also recommended that the mayor be given complete authority to appoint members to the various municipal boards. Board members, they argued, should serve without pay since this would remove the mercenary motive that prompted professional politicians to serve and, incidentally, would eliminate most of those without substantial wealth as well. If those who got their "living out of their salaries" could be excluded from municipal office, Goodnow argued, the way would be open for the "business and professional classes" to assume control of the city.[38] At the lower levels of municipal administration, Shaw, Goodnow, and Munro recommended a thoroughgoing application of the civil-service system, which also tended to eliminate ethnic and lower class representatives. A professional civil service at the lower grades, the theorists argued, would create a good technical and supportive staff and, as Goodnow put it, "make it possible for the business and professional classes of the community to assume the care of public business without making too great personal sacrifices."[39]

The recommendations of the theorists aimed at weakening popular control over the legislative arm of government, the city council. Goodnow was convinced that the council system, since it provided so many "incompetent if not corrupt men," should not be a powerful force in municipal government. Goodnow was more favorably impressed by municipal arrangements in Berlin, Germany, where a propertied electorate comprising less than 10 per cent of the voters elected two-thirds of the city council. "This gives to the wealthier class the directing voice in municipal affairs," commented Professor Leo S. Rowe with approval. Andrew D. White argued that men of property should be represented by a board of control, "without whose permission no franchise should be granted and no expenditure should be made." The English system which in effect disfranchised most lower class slum residents also met with Goodnow's favor. Councils elected by a nonpropertied franchise disturbed Goodnow, for such bodies often prodded cities into "undertakings which are in excess of the city's economic resources." Evidently pessimistic about changing the basis of municipal suffrage to one of property, Goodnow reversed the formula and suggested that to extend the tax-paying obligation to more citizens might produce better councils. That failing, he supported state intervention to limit taxing and spending of municipal governments. "The trouble with leaving our cities to govern themselves, at least along purely democratic lines," argued C. E. Pickard, is "that they are utterly unworthy of trust."[40]

The theorists also argued for fewer elective offices and smaller city councils. "Men of little experience and less capacity have found it easy to get themselves elected to membership in large city councils," asserted Munro. Smaller councils would presumably concentrate responsibility and produce better men. The at-large election was a favorite device of the theorists and one of the most important structural changes they proposed. City-wide elections to the council, in their opinion, could be won only by men of commanding presence and city-wide prominence. Obviously the lower class politician or the ethnic representative who served his ward well would come out second best if pitted against a prominent businessman or professional. Not until late in the Progressive period, after the at-large system began to elect the "better classes" into office, did the theorists return to decentralizing authority and to expanding the powers of councilmen who then would be known as city commissioners. The ideas of the theorists make it difficult to quibble with Frederic C. Howe's observation: "Distrust of democracy has inspired much of the literature on the city."[41]

Agencies to regulate utility rates, to investigate tax inequities, or to foster and advance social reform were not on the drawing boards of the theorists. Few of them focused their wrath and moral indignation upon the corrupting influence of privately owned utilities and the real estate interests on city councils. They were less bothered by the businessman who bribed the city council than by the machine politician who accepted the bribe. Yerkes and Whitney seldom warranted their attention in the way that Tweed did. They chose instead to focus responsibility upon the individuals who sat on councils and the political systems that elected them rather than upon the business interests that sought favorable franchises, tax favoritism, and city services, such as paving, sewers, and water, which enhanced the value of their enterprises.

The ideas of the theorists were not lost upon the practitioners and designers of good city government. The structural reformers began to design new forms of urban organization and to codify the ideas of the theorists into new city charters. Two decades of searching and theorizing produced the city commissioner and later the city manager systems.

The theorists provided the rationale for the most radical departure the American city took in all its history. The widespread adoption of the commissioner and manager systems late in the Progressive period brought about what one scholar called a "revolution in the theory and practice of city government." Although the commissioner system had its origins in an accident of nature, it and the manager plan soon became the favored devices for achieving what the old political system could not—namely, the large scale movement of businessmen and business-minded representatives into public office. Both systems were patterned after the modern business corporation and rapidly adopted its ideals. Henry Bruère, a director of the New York Bureau of Municipal Research, boasted that commission governments were often made a "part of the progressive programs of 'boosting' commercial organizations." "Money saving and efficiency" were pursued as key objectives under the manager plan. The "Godfather of City Managerism," Richard S. Childs, observed that the city managers at their fourth annual conference could "unblushingly point with pride" to an average savings of 10 per cent in tax levies in the cities under his brain child. The first city manager of the publicized "Dayton Plan," Henry M. Waite, admitted that the "main thing" the nation's fifty manager towns had accomplished up to 1917 was a "financial saving." "Economy, not service," James Weinstein correctly asserted, was the "basic principle" of both the commissioner and manager systems. As Harold A. Stone has suggested, and Weinstein has demonstrated, no important reform movement of the Progressive period was more peculiarly the captive of organized business than the commissioner and manager movements.[42]

Although the commissioner and manager systems achieved their greatest success in middle-sized and smaller cities, they represented the ultimate ideal of the earlier theorists (whose major concern had been large American cities). Commissioner and manager reorganization brought about in its finished form the structural arrangements that facilitated the movement into office of that class of people whom Bryce, Goodnow, Munro, and Shaw believed best fitted and qualified to rule the city. Chambers of commerce and the dominant business groups were the main force behind the movement, and, as James Weinstein and Samuel P. Hays have demonstrated, these new forms facilitated the inflow of the commercial and upper class elements into the centers of municipal power at the price of ethnic and lower class representation.[43] The business model of municipal government would eventually spread to nearly one-half of our cities, and the structural-reform persuasion would dominate the main stream of urban reform thought in the twentieth century.[44] This extension of the instruments and the ideology of the business world would help to return to power men with the temperaments of Havemeyer, Cleveland, and Low and considerably diminish the electoral prospects for men like Pingree, Jones, and Johnson—as well as like Tweed.

The conservative revolution in city government would also help to end the process whereby astute politicians and socially-conscious reformers used the political system to ease the shock of assimilation for newcomers into American life. The political machine may have been one of the most important institutions not only for acknowledging the immigrant's existence but for interpreting a new environment to him and helping him to adjust to a bewildering new society.

By concentrating on the mechanistic and bureaucratic aspects of city government and by throwing the weight of their influence behind the election of businessmen, the theorists grossly oversimplified the problems of the city. Wiping out lower class and foreign-born corruption unfortunately took precedence in their minds over the social needs of the city. The theorists confined themselves to dealing with the plumbing and hardware of city government and finally became narrow administrative reformers. In the process, they deceived themselves and helped to mislead a generation of reformers into thinking that they were dealing with the fundamental problems of the city, when in reality they were retooling the machinery of urban government to fit the needs of the business world.

Characteristically, the manager and commissioner movement, which represented the greatest achievement of the structural-reform tradition, experienced its greatest success during the twilight of the Progressive period and during the nineteen twenties,[45] when great expectations for social reform were withering and receding. This late triumph of good government reform was not an accident of historical timing. It was not a case of cultural lag, nor can it be attributed to a late blooming of the urban Progressive spirit. If anything, new concepts and systems of organization usually appeared sooner at the urban level than at the national. The victory of the manager-commissioner system during the age of Harding and Coolidge was an historical acknowledgement of the basically conservative nature of the structural-reform tradition. The nation had finally tailored the urban political organization and molded reform thought to respond to the most powerful economic forces in the city. In this instance it was not free silver but the chamber of commerce that became the cowbird of reform. This should not be surprising, for the chamber of commerce and its affiliates had also proved to be the greatest obstacle to social reform in Pingree's Detroit.

NOTES

[1] Henry Demarest Lloyd to Richard T. Ely, November 16, 1896, Lloyd Papers; Samuel M. Jones to Hazen S. Pingree, August 4, 1899. Jones Papers.

[2] Pingree quoted in Detroit *Free Press:* November 27, 1896 and Detroit *Evening News:* March 17, 1897, P.S.

[3] B. O. Flower to Hazen S. Pingree, February 1, 1896, Pingree Papers; Richard T. Ely to Henry Demarest Lloyd, November 12, 1896; Henry Demarest Lloyd to Samuel M. Jones, May 23, 1897, Lloyd Papers.

[4] Richard Hofstadter, *The Age of Reform: From Bryan to F.D.R.* (New York, 1960), pp. 135-48.

[5] Hazen S. Pingree address to Detroit Chamber of Commerce, November 2, 1895, Pingree Papers; Hazen S. Pingree, *Facts and Opinions* (Detroit, 1895), pp. 85-86; Pingree quoted in New York *Journal:* December 8, 1896, P.S.

[6]Detroit *Tribune:* May 1, 1899, P.S.
[7]Lincoln Steffens, *The Autobiography of Lincoln Steffens* (New York, 1931), pp. 374-75; Hewitt quoted in *Pilgrim*, III (December, 1901), 4.
[8]Hazen S. Pingree, "Address to the Nineteenth Century Club of New York," November 11, 1897, p. 7; S. M. Jones to Josiah Strong, November 15, 1898, Jones Papers; Brand Whitlock, *Forty Years of It* (New York, 1914), pp. 172-74.
[9]Frederic C. Howe, *The City: The Hope of Democracy* (New York, 1913), pp. 1, 2. For the elitist views of reformers who overthrew Boss Tweed, see Alexander B. Callow, Jr., *The Tweed Ring* (New York, 1966), pp. 69-71, 265-67. Charles R. Adrian, "Some General Characteristics of Nonpartisan Elections," Robert C. Wood, "Nonpartisanship in Suburbia," both in *Democracy in Urban America*, ed. Oliver P. Williams and Charles Press (Chicago, 1964), pp. 251-66. For an exposition of the views regarding municipal government of one of the most prominent twentieth-century "structural" reformers, see Richard S. Childs, "The Faith of a Civic Reformer," *ibid.*, pp. 222-24. The "elitist commitments" of the city manager system (as prescribed in city government textbooks) can also be seen in Lawrence J. R. Herson, "The Lost World of Municipal Government," *American Political Science Review*, LI (June, 1957), 330-45.
[10]Howard B. Furer, *William Frederick Havemeyer: A Political Biography* (New York, 1965), pp. 14, 144-54, 160; Seymour J. Mandelbaum, *Boss Tweed's New York* (New York, 1965), pp. 91, 97, 108, 111; Callow, *The Tweed Ring*, pp. 253-86.
[11]Mandelbaum, *Boss Tweed's New York*, pp. 98-100, 111; Furer, *William F. Havemeyer*, pp. 156, 158, 160-61, 169.
[12]*Ibid.*, p. 161; Mandelbaum, *Boss Tweed's New York*, pp. 112-13; William L. Riordin, *Plunkitt of Tammany Hall* (New York, 1963), p. 17.
[13]Allan Nevins, *Grover Cleveland, A Study in Courage* (New York, 1941), pp. 61-62, 83-94.
[14]Harold Coffin Syrett, *The City of Brooklyn 1865-1898, A Political History* (New York, 1944), p. 134; Steven C. Swett, "The Test of a Reformer, A Study of Seth Low," *New York Historical Society Quarterly*, XLIV (January, 1960), pp. 8, 9; Lincoln Steffens, *The Shame of the Cities* (New York, 1966), p. 201.
[15]Syrett, *Brooklyn*, pp. 104-6, 109-19, 134; Swett, "Test of a Reformer," pp. 7-9.
[16]Albert Fein, "New York City Politics From 1897-1903: A Study in Political Party Leadership" (M.A. thesis, Columbia University, 1954), pp. 19-20; Swett, "Test of a Reformer," pp. 10-14, 16-18.
[17]*Ibid.*, pp. 21-23, 26-31, 35-36; Roy Lubove, *The Progressives and the Slums, Tenement House Reform in New York City, 1890-1917* (Pittsburgh, 1962), pp. 153-54.
[18]Swett, "Test of a Reformer," pp. 6, 32, 35-36, 38-41; Wallace S. Sayre and Herbert Kaufman, *Governing New York City Politics in the Metropolis* (New York, 1960), p. 695.
[19]James D. Phelan, "Municipal Conditions and the New Charter," *Overland Monthly*, XXVIII (no. 163, 2nd series), pp. 104-11, Roy Swanstrom, "Reform Administration of James D. Phelan, Mayor of San Francisco, 1897-1902," (M.A. thesis, University of California-Berkeley, 1949), pp. 77-79, 80, 83, 85, 86; Walton Bean, *Boss Ruef's San Francisco: The Story of the Union Labor Party, Big Business, and the Graft Prosecution* (Berkeley, 1952), pp. 8, 9, 16, 17, 23; George E. Mowry, *The California Progressives* (Chicago, 1963), pp. 23-25; Fremont Older, *My Own Story* (San Francisco, 1919), pp. 27, 31, 65.
[20]William E. Leuchtenburg, Preface to Edwin R. Lewinson, *John Purroy Mitchel: The Boy Mayor of New York* (New York, 1965), pp. 11-13; Lewinson, *Boy Mayor*, pp. 93, 95, 100, 102, 117, 124.
[21]Leuchtenburg, *ibid.*, p. 12; Lewinson, *ibid.*, pp. 18, 151-69, 175-88.
[22]Leuchtenburg, *ibid.*, pp. 11-13; Samuel P. Hayes, "The Politics of Reform in Municipal Government," *Pacific Northwest Quarterly*, LV (October, 1964), pp. 157-69.
[23]Lewinson, *Boy Mayor*, pp. 11-13, 18, 93, 95, 102; Riordin, *George Washington Plunkitt*, pp. 17-20; Swett, "Seth Low," pp. 8, 9; Allan Nevins, *Abram S. Hewitt: With Some Account of Peter Cooper* (New York, 1935), pp. 515-16, 529-30, Seth Low, "An American

View of Municipal Government in the United States," in James Bryce, *The American Commonwealth* (New York, 1893), I, 651, 665.

²⁴Hoyt Landon Warner, *Progressivism in Ohio 1897-1917 (Columbus, 1964), pp. 32,* 70-72; Whitlock, *Forty Years of It*, pp. 211, 252; Clarence H. Cramer, *Newton D. Baker: A Biography* (Cleveland, 1961), pp. 46-47; Steffens, *Autobiography of Lincoln Steffens*, pp. 477, 492-93; Frederic C. Howe, *The Confessions of a Reformer* (New York, 1925), pp. 98, 102-8, Pingree, *Facts and Opinions*, p. 196. For Mark Fagan, see Lincoln Steffens, *Upbuilders* (New York, 1909), pp. 28, 30, 33, 35, and Ransom E. Noble, Jr., *New Jersey Progressivism before Wilson* (Princeton, 1946), pp. 13-42. St. Louis Circuit Attorney Joseph W. Folk (1901-04), who began his career by investigating and prosecuting franchise "grabs," discovered that the real despoilers of municipal government were not minor city officials but promoters, bankers, and corporation directors who profited by misgovernment. After he became governor he dropped his crime-busting and supported progressive and urban reforms. Louis G. Geiger, *Joseph W. Folk of Missouri* (Columbia, 1953), pp. 32, 41, 81, 88, 93, 99-117. Robert Wiebe's assertion that the "typical business ally of the boss, moreover, was a rather marginal operator, anathema to the chamber of commerce" is at variance with what is known about the political influence wielded in Detroit by urban capitalists such as the Hendries, McMillans and Johnson or for that matter with the role played by Yerkes and Insull in Chicago, Mark Hanna in Cleveland and the Huntington interests in Los Angeles, just to cite a few examples. *The Search for Order, 1877-1920* (New York, 1967), p. 167.

²⁵Steffens, *Upbuilders*, pp. 3-45; Warner, *Progressivism in Ohio, 1897-1917*, pp. 71, 74; Cramer, *Newton D. Baker*, pp. 50-52; Howe, *Confessions of a Reformer*, pp. 90-93, 108-9; Carl Lorenz, *Tom L. Johnson, Mayor of Cleveland* (New York, 1911), p. 152; Steffens, *Autobiography of Lincoln Steffens*, p. 480; Detroit *Free Press*, March 14, 1896, P.S.; Samuel M. Jones to Henry D. Lloyd, April 16, 1897, Lloyd Papers; Samuel M. Jones to James L. Cowes, April 27, 1897; Tom L. Johnson to S. M. Jones, May 3, 1902, Jones Papers; Harvey S. Ford, "The Life and Times of Golden Rule Jones" (Ph.D. thesis, University of Michigan, 1953), pp. 185, 284-85, 330; Whitlock, *Forty Years of It*, p. 212. William D. Miller has argued that "Boss" Edward H. Crump, who was Memphis mayor from 1910 to 1916, stands with "Golden Rule" Jones and Tom L. Johnson as a typical progressive of the period, but an examination of Miller's book raises serious doubts about that judgment. Although Crump occasionally employed reform rhetoric, established a few milk stations for the poor, and put screens on public school windows, he used most of the energy of his administration to enforce the laws and instill efficiency into the municipal government in the structural-reform tradition. Crump wiped out "policy" playing by Negroes, eliminated loafing by the garbage collectors and street pavers, forced the railroads to construct eleven underpasses, lowered city taxes, reduced waste in municipal government by extending audit procedures even to the purchase of postage stamps, and increased city income by selling empty bottles, feed sacks, and scrap. William D. Miller, *Mr. Crump of Memphis* (Baton Rouge, 1964), pp. 79-113. Brooklyn's Mayor Charles A. Schieren (1894-95), who gained some stature as a reformer by defeating a venal Democratic machine, also followed a well-trodden path of cleaning out "deceit and corruption" and installing "integrity, nonpartisanship, and routine efficiency." Like most of the reform mayors of his period, Schieren failed to advance or support social reform programs. Harold C. Syrett, *The City of Brooklyn, 1865-1898, A Political History* (New York, 1944), pp. 218-32. Geoffrey Blodgett has tried to show that Boston became for "a brief time the cutting edge of urban reform in America" under Mayor Josiah Quincy (1896-1900), who established a publicly owned printing plant and expanded the city's playgrounds. Although the Dover Street Bath House may have been a "monument to municipal socialism" as Blodgett contends, Mayor Quincy stopped his programs short of anything that would have threatened the vested interests in the traction and utility business. Geoffrey Blodgett, *The Gentle Reformers: Massachusetts Democrats in the Cleveland Era* (Cambridge, 1966), pp. 240-61. For Quincy's absurd notion that regular bathing would cause the "filthy tenement house" to disappear, crime and drunkenness to decrease and the death rate to drop, see Josiah Quincy, "Municipal Progress in Boston," *Independent*, LII (February 15, 1900),

424. Henry Demarest Lloyd was critical of Mayor Quincy's failure to resist the traction interests and referred to the Mayor's public baths as Quincy's "little sops." H. D. Lloyd to Samuel Bowles, December 13, 1898, Lloyd Papers.

[26]Ford, "Golden Rule Jones," pp. 151, 166, 339; Samuel M. Jones to Dr. [Graham] Taylor, October 5, 1897; S. M. Jones to L. L. Dagett, April 17, 1899, Jones Papers; Hazen S. Pingree address to Springfield, Massachusetts Board of Trade, March 3, 1894, Ralph Stone Scrapbook; Whitlock, Forty Years of It, pp. 252, 254.

[27]Robert H. Bremner, "The Civic Revival in Ohio: The Fight Against Privilege in Cleveland and Toledo, 1890-1912," (Ph.D. thesis, Ohio State University, 1943), p. 25; Hazen S. Pingree, "The Problem of Municipal Reform. Contract by Referendum," Arena, XVII (April, 1897), 707-10; Cramer, Newton D. Baker, p. 46; Steffens, Upbuilders, pp. 28-30, 33, 35; Noble, New Jersey Progressivism before Wilson, pp. 25-26, 35, 38.

[28]Tom L. Johnson, My Story (New York, 1911), p. 113; Ford, "Golden Rule Jones," pp. 136-37, 170, 339; Hazen S. Pingree, "Detroit: A Municipal Study," Outlook, LV (February 6, 1897), 437; Bemis quoted in Detroit Evening News: June 21, 1899, Stone Scrapbook; Whitlock, Forty Years of It, p. 221.

[29]Whitlock, Forty Years of It, p. 221.

[30]Frank J. Goodnow, "The Tweed Ring in New York City," in James Bryce's The American Commonwealth (London, 1888), II, 335; Bryce, ibid., p. 67; Bryce, ibid., I, 613; Albert Shaw, Political Problems of American Development (New York, 1907), p. 66. According to Edwin L. Godkin, New York City's problems began with the establishment of universal suffrage in 1846 which coincided with the beginning of the great Irish migration. Edwin L. Godkin, Problems of Modern Democracy, ed. Morton Keller (New York, 1896, Cambridge, 1966), p. 133.

[31]Bryce, American Commonwealth, II, 67; William B. Munro, The Government of American Cities (New York, 1913), pp. 308-9, 310, 312; Andrew D. White, "The Government of American Cities," Forum, X (December, 1890), 369; Alfred R. Conkling, City Government in the United States (New York, 1899), p. 49; Frank J. Goodnow, Municipal Problems (New York, 1897), pp. 150-53; Delos F. Wilcox, The Study of City Government (New York, 1897), p. 151; "Report of the Committee on Municipal Program," Proceedings of the Indianapolis Conference for Good City Government and Fourth Annual Meeting of the National Municipal League (Philadelphia, 1898), p. 11 (hereafter cited Proceedings for Good City Government).

[32]Wilcox, The Study of City Government, pp. 237-38; Frank J. Goodnow, Municipal Government (New York, 1910), pp. 39, 149, 378-79; James T. Young, Proceedings for Good City Government, 1901, p. 230.

[33]Michigan Legislative Manual and Official Directory 1899-1900 (Lansing, 1899), p. 322; Report of the Commission to Devise a Plan for the Government of Cities in the State of New York (New York, 1877), pp. 35-36.

[34]Goodnow, Municipal Problems, pp. 148-49.

[35]Shaw, Political Problems of American Development, pp. 65-67, 82, 125; Munro, Government of American Cities, pp. 120-21; Bryce, American Commonwealth, II, 67.

[36]Goodnow, Municipal Problems, p. 278; Conkling, City Government in the United States, p. 34; Richard T. Ely, The Coming City (New York, 1902), p. 29.

[37]Walter T. Arndt, The Emancipation of the American City (New York, 1917), p. 12; Frank M. Sparks, Government As a Business (Chicago, 1916), pp. 1, 7; Goodnow, Municipal Government, pp. 150, 381-82; Munro, Government of American Cities, p. 306; William H. Tolman, Municipal Reform Movements in the United States (New York, 1895), p. 34.

[38]Conkling, City Government in the United States, pp. 6, 32; Goodnow, Municipal Problems, pp. 262-65.

[39]Ibid., pp. 204-5, 265; Munro, Government of American Cities, pp. 241, 279-80; Albert Shaw, "Civil Service Reform and Municipal Government," in Civil Service Reform and Municipal Government (New York, 1897), pp. 3-7.

[40]Goodnow, *Municipal Government*, pp. 142-46, 385-86, and *Municipal Problems*, pp. 66-67; Leo S. Rowe, "City Government As It Should Be And May Become," *Proceedings for Good City Government, 1894*, p. 115; White, "The Government of American Cities," p. 370; John Agar, "Shall American Cities Municipalize?" *Municipal Affairs*, IV (March, 1900), 14-20; C. E. Pickard, "Great Cities and Democratic Institutions," *American Journal of Politics*, IV (April, 1894), 385. The Boston mayor Nathan Mathews, Jr., asserted that the proposal to restrict municipal suffrage to the propertied classes was one of the most common remedies for the evils of city government of his age. Nathan Mathews, Jr., *The City Government of Boston* (Boston, 1895), p. 176.

[41]Munro, *Government of American Cities*, pp. 294, 308-10; Goodnow, *Municipal Problems*, pp. 150-53; Leo S. Rowe, "American Political Ideas and Institutions in Their Relation to the Problem of the City," *Proceedings for Good City Government, 1897*, p. 77; William Dudley Foulke, *ibid.*, *1898*, p. 137; Frederic C. Howe, *The City, The Hope of Democracy* (New York, 1913), p. 1.

[42]Henry Bruère, "Efficiency in City Government," *Annals* of the American Academy of Political and Social Science, XLI (May, 1912), 19; Richard S. Childs, "Now that We Have the City Manager Plan, What Are We Going to Do With It," *Fourth Yearbook of the City Managers' Association* (Auburn, 1918), pp. 82-83; Henry M. Waite, *ibid.*, pp. 88-89; Harold A. Stone, Don K. Price and Kathryn H. Stone, *City Manager Government in the United States* (Chicago, 1940), pp. 25-27; James Weinstein, "Organized Business and the City Commissioner and Manager Movements," *Journal of Southern History*, XXVIII (May, 1962), 166, 179.

[43]*Ibid.*, p. 173; Samuel P. Hayes, "The Politics of Reform in Municipal Government in the Progressive Era," *Pacific Northwest Quarterly*, LV (October, 1964), 157-69.

[44]Edward C. Banfield and James Q. Wilson, *City Politics* (New York, 1963), p. 148.

[45]The peak period for the spread of the city commissioner and the city manager system was 1917-27. Leonard D. White, *The City Manager* (Chicago, 1927), p. 317; Harold Zink, *Government of Cities in the United States* (New York, 1939), p. 301.

Suggestions for Further Reading

The historical literature dealing with the issues covered in this book is quite extensive, and continues to grow as historians investigate new approaches and seek out new evidence. This bibliography is, of necessity, highly selective, and is principally devoted to secondary works concerning urban politics and reform in the period from 1880 to 1920. For a recent, but unannotated, bibliography see Arthur S. Link and William M. Leary, Jr., *The Progressive Era and the Great War, 1896–1920* (1969). For the Gilded Age, see John A. Garraty, *The New Commonwealth, 1877–1890* (1968).

The best single historical survey of the period from 1880 to 1920 is Robert H. Wiebe's excellent *The Search for Order, 1877–1920* (1967). Other surveys of the period include Samuel P. Hays, *The Response to Industrialism, 1885–1914* (1957); Richard Hofstadter, *The Age of Reform: From Bryan to F.D.R.* (1955); Eric Goldman, *Rendezvous With Destiny* (1953); Thomas H. Greer, *American Social Reform Movements: The Patterns Since 1865* (1949); Ray Ginger, *Age of Excess: The United States From 1877 to 1914* (1931); and Bruce M. Stave, ed., *Urban Bosses, Machines, and Progressive Reformers* (1972).

The best recent source on reform in the Gilded Age is John G. Sproat, *"The Best Men": Liberal Reformers in the Gilded Age* (1968). The movement for civil service reform is treated in Ari Hoogenboom, *Outlawing the Spoils: A History of the Civil Service Reform Movement, 1865–1883* (1961); Hoogenboom, "An Analysis of Civil Service Reformers," *The Historian*, XXIII (November, 1960); Hoogenboom, "Civil Service Reform and Public Morality" in H. Wayne Morgan, ed., *The Gilded Age* (rev. ed., 1970). Views of the Mugwump include Lorin Peterson, *The Day of the Mugwump* (1961); Allan Nevins, *Grover Cleveland, A Study in Courage* (1932); Carleton Putnam, *Theodore Roosevelt: The Formative Years, 1858–1886* (1958); David S. Muzzey, *James G. Blaine, A Political Idol of Other Days* (1934). See the previously cited works by Hoogenboom for an application of the status revolution thesis to reform in the Gilded Age, and for a contrasting interpretation see John N. Ingham, "Robber Barons and the Old Elites: A Case Study in Social Stratification," *Mid-America*, LII (July, 1970).

Various aspects of reform thought and ideology in the Gilded Age are covered in Paul F. Boller, Jr., *American Thought in Transition: The Impact of Evolutionary Naturalism, 1865–1900* (1968); Geoffrey Blodgett, "Reform Thought and the Genteel Tradition" in Morgan, ed., *The Gilded*

Age; Blodgett, "The Mind of the Boston Mugwump," *Mississippi Valley Historical Review*, XLVIII (March, 1962); Arthur Mann, *Yankee Reformers in the Urban Age 1880–1900* (1954); Philip S. Benjamin, "Gentlemen Reformers in the Quaker City, 1870–1912," *Political Science Quarterly*, LXXXV (March, 1970); E. Digby Baltzell, *Philadelphia Gentlemen: The Making of a National Upper Class* (1958); Gerald W. McFarland, "The New York Mugwumps of 1884: A Profile," *Political Science Quarterly*, LXXVIII (March, 1963); Thomas J. Condon, "Politics, Reform and the New York City Election of 1886," *New York Historical Society Quarterly*, XLIV (October, 1960); Joseph O. Baylen, "A Victorian's 'Crusade' in Chicago, 1893–1894," *Journal of American History*, LI (December, 1964). For analyses of individual reformers, see David P. Thelen, "Rutherford B. Hayes and the Reform Tradition in the Gilded Age," *American Quarterly*, XXII (Summer, 1970) and Gerald W. McFarland, "Partisan of Non-partisanship: Dorman B. Easton and the Genteel Reform Traditions," *Journal of American History*, LIV (March, 1968).

The literature on the growth of the city between 1880 and 1920 is substantial. The best brief survey is Charles N. Glaab and A. Theodore Brown, *A History of Urban America* (1967). Other useful surveys include Blake McKelvey, *The Urbanization of America, 1860–1915* (1963), which contains an excellent bibliography; Constance M. Green, *The Rise of Urban America* (1965); Arthur M. Schlesinger, Sr., *The Rise of the City, 1878–1898* (1933); and Adna F. Weber, *The Growth of Cities in the Nineteenth Century* (1899). The best bibliographic essays on materials related to urban history are Charles N. Glaab, "The Historian and the American City: A Bibliographic Survey" in Philip M. Hauser and Leo F. Schnore, eds., *The Study of Urbanization* (1965), and Dwight W. Hoover, "The Diverging Paths of American Urban History," *American Quarterly*, XX (Summer Supplement, 1968). Also see Blaine A. Brownell, "American Urban History: Retrospect and Prospect," *Proceedings of the Indiana Academy of the Social Sciences* (1970). On municipal reform in this period, see C. W. Patton, *The Battle For Municipal Reform* (1940), and Frank Mann Stewart, *A Half-Century of Municipal Reform: A History of the National Municipal League* (1950).

On the rise of the city boss and the urban political machine, see Harold Zink, *City Bosses in the United States* (1939); Edward C. Banfield and James Q. Wilson, *City Politics* (1965); Robert K. Merton, *Social Theory and Social Structure* (1957); Fred Greenstein, *The American Party System and the American People* (1963); Harold F. Gosnell, *Machine Politics:*

Chicago Model (1936); Oscar Handlin, *The Uprooted* (1951); Theodore J. Lowi, "Machine Politics—Old and New," *Public Interest* (Fall, 1967); and Moisei Ostrogorski, *Democracy and the Organization of Political Parties* (1902), Vol. II. For a contemporary view of the urban political machine, see Lincoln Steffens, *Autobiography of Lincoln Steffens* (1931). See also: James Bryce, *The American Commonwealth* (1893) and Steffens, *The Shame of the Cities* (1904). The relationship between corruption and urban politics is examined in James C. Scott, "Corruption, Machine Politics, and Political Change," *American Political Science Review*, LXIII (December, 1969); J. S. Nye, "Corruption and Political Development: A Cost-Benefit Analysis," *American Political Science Review*, LXI (June, 1967); and Eric McKitrick, "The Study of Corruption," *Political Science Quarterly*, LXXII (December, 1957).

Studies of urban politics in specific cities are especially abundant. For Chicago, see Lloyd Wendt and Herman Kogan, *Bosses in Lusty Chicago: The Story of Bathhouse John and Hinky Dink* (1967, orig. pub. 1943); Wendt and Kogan, *Big Bill of Chicago* (1953); Alex Gottfried, *Boss Cermak of Chicago* (1962); Joel A. Tarr, *A Study of Boss Politics: William Lorimer of Chicago* (1971); and Gosnell's *Machine Politics: Chicago Model*. On New York, see Nancy Weiss, *Charles Francis Murphy, 1858–1924: Respectability and Responsibility in Tammany Politics* (1968); Alexander B. Callow, Jr., *The Tweed Ring* (1966); Seymour J. Mendelbaum, *Boss Tweed's New York* (1965); Theodore J. Lowi, *At the Pleasure of the Major: Patronage and Power in New York City, 1898–1958* (1964). Other studies include George M. Reynolds, *Machine Politics in New Orleans, 1897–1926* (1936); William D. Miller, *Memphis During the Progressive Era, 1900–1917* (1957); James B. Crooks, *Politics and Progress: The Rise of Urban Progressivism in Baltimore, 1895–1911* (1968); Zane L. Miller, *Boss Cox's Cincinnati: Urban Politics in the Progressive Era* (1968); Lyle W. Dorsett, *The Pendergast Machine* (1968); Walton E. Bean, *Boss Ruef's San Francisco* (1952); Melvin G. Holli, *Reform in Detroit: Hazen S. Pingree and Urban Politics* (1969); and Jack Tager, *The Intellectual as Urban Reformer: Brand Whitlock and the Progressive Movement* (1968).

General views of reform in the Progressive Era include Dewey W. Grantham, Jr., "The Progressive Era and the Reform Tradition," *Mid-America*, XLVI (October, 1964); Andrew M. Scott, "The Progressive Era in Perspective," *Journal of Politics*, XXI (November, 1959); Peter G. Filene, "An Obituary for 'The Progressive Movement'," *American Quarterly*, XXII (Spring, 1970); Daniel Levine, *Varieties of Reform*

Thought (1964); John Braeman, "Seven Progressives," *Business History Review*, XXXV (Winter, 1961); and John D. Buenker, "The Progressive Era: A Search for Synthesis," *Mid-America*, LI (July, 1969).

Contemporary views of reform can best be seen in Herbert Croly, *The Promise of American Life* (1909); Harold L. Ickes, *The Autobiography of a Curmudgeon* (1943); William A. White, *The Autobiography of William Allen White* (1946), Steffens, *Autobiography of Lincoln Steffens* (1931); Robert M. La Follette, *La Follette's Autobiography* (1911); Walter E. Weyl, *The New Democracy* (1912); and Jacob A. Riis, *The Making of An American* (1901).

For favorable views of the status revolution thesis, see George É. Mowry, "The California Progressive and His Rationale: A Study in Middle Class Politics," *Mississippi Valley Historical Review*, XXXVI (September, 1949); Mowry, *The California Progressives* (1951); Mowry, *The Era of Theodore Roosevelt and the Birth of Modern America, 1900–1912* (1958). A comprehensive but extreme interpretation of status anxieties and class conflict is contained in Hofstadter's *Age of Reform*. For supporting evidence, see Alfred D. Chandler, Jr., "The Origins of Progressive Leadership" in Elting Morison, ed., *The Letters of Theodore Roosevelt* (1951–1954), Vol. VIII, Appendix III; Russell B. Nye, *Midwestern Progressive Politics* (1959); and Robert Maxwell, *La Follette and the Rise of the Progressives in Wisconsin* (1956). Evaluations of the status anxiety concept can be found in the following: Seymour Martin Lipset and Reinhard Bendix, "Social Status and Social Structure: A Re-Examination of Data and Interpretations," *British Journal of Sociology*, II, (June, September, 1951); Lipset and Bendix, eds., *Class, Status, and Power: A Reader in Social Stratification* (1953); and Harold M. Hodges, *Social Stratification in America* (1964). The best review of the sociological and psychological literature dealing with the status revolution theory is David P. Thelen, "Social Tensions and the Origins of Progressivism," *Journal of American History*, LVI (September, 1969).

Studies which have found "anti-reform" or "anti-progressive" groups to be also middle class in character include Jack Tager, "Progressives, Conservatives and the Theory of Status Revolution," *Mid-America*, XLVIII (July, 1966); Richard B. Sherman, "The Status Revolution and Massachusetts Progressive Leadership," *Political Science Quarterly*, LXXVIII (March, 1963); E. Daniel Potts, "The Progressive Profile in Iowa," *Mid-America*, XLVII (October, 1965); William T. Kerr, Jr., "The Progressives of Washington, 1910–1912," *Pacific Northwest Quarterly*, LV (January, 1964); Bean, *Boss Reuf's San Francisco*; Benjamin, "Gentlemen Reformers in the Quaker City"; and Norman M. Wilensky, *Conservatives in the Progressive Era: The Taft Republicans of 1912* [Florida] (1965).

A number of recent studies have emphasized the contributions of immigrant, new-stock elements to reform, rather than the middle class. See J. Joseph Huthmacher, "Urban Liberalism and the Age of Reform," *Mississippi Valley Historical Review*, XLIX (September, 1962); Huthmacher, "Charles Evans Hughes and Charles Francis Murphy: The Metamorphosis of Progressivism," *New York History*, XLVI (January, 1965); Huthmacher, *Senator Robert F. Wagner and the Rise of Urban Liberalism* (1968). John D. Buenker arrived at similar conclusions in a number of articles, including, "Cleveland's New Stock Lawmakers and Progressive Reform," *Ohio History*, LXXVIII (Spring, 1969); "Urban Immigrant Lawmakers and Progressive Reform in Illinois" in Donald F. Tingley, ed., *Essays in Illinois History: In Honor of Glenn Huron Seymour* (1968); "Urban, New Stock Liberalism and Progressive Reform in New Jersey," *New Jersey History*, LXXXVII (Summer, 1969). Other works which note the contributions of immigrants to reform include Philip Gleason, "An Immigrant Group's Interest in Progressive Reform: The Case of the German-American Catholics," *American Historical Review*, LXXIII (December, 1967) and Gleason, *The Conservative Reformers* (1968). For a study of California progressivism and the immigrant, see Michael P. Rogin, "Progressivism and the California Electorate," *Journal of American History*, LV (September, 1968). Concerning the immigrant and woman suffrage, see Joseph F. Mahoney, "Woman Suffrage and the Urban Masses," *New Jersey History*, LXXXVII (Autumn, 1969).

Although the "Progressive Movement" is usually considered an anti-business phenomenon, a number of historians have drawn attention to the role of businessmen in various reform efforts of the period. See Robert H. Wiebe, "Business Disunity and the Progressive Movement, 1901–1914," *Mississippi Valley Historical Review*, XLIV (March, 1958); Wiebe, *Businessmen and Reform: A Study of the Progressive Movement* (1962); Gabriel Kolko, *The Triumph of Conservatism: A Re-Interpretation of American History, 1900–1916* (1963); Kolko, *Railroads and Regulations, 1877–1916* (1965); James Weinstein, "Organized Business and the City Commission and Manager Movements," *Journal of Southern History*, XXVIII, (May, 1962); Weinstein, *The Corporate Ideal in the Liberal State: 1900–1918* (1968); James J. Lorence, "Business and Reform: The American Asiatic Association and the Exclusion Laws, 1905–1907," *Pacific Historical Review*, XXXIX (November, 1970); Spencer Olin, *California's Prodigal Sons: Hiram Johnson and the Progressives, 1911–1917* (1968); Gerald D. Nash, *State Government and Economic*

Development: A History of Administrative Policies in California, 1895–1933 (1964); and Roy Lubove, *The Struggle For Social Security 1900–1935* (1968).

Some recent studies which stress the importance of rural areas in the progressive reform effort include Kerr, "The Progressives of Washington, 1910–1912"; Charles N. Glaab, "Failure of North Dakota Progressivism," *Mid-America*, XXXIX (October, 1957); Genevieve B. Gist, "Progressive Reform in a Rural Community: The Adams County [Ohio] Vote-Fraud Case," *Mississippi Valley Historical Review*, XLVIII (June, 1961); and Michael P. Rogin, *The Intellectuals and McCarthy: The Radical Specter* (1967). For a suggestion that the urban-rural dichotomy between the Populists and the Progressives is exaggerated, see Wayne E. Fuller, "The Rural Roots of the Progressive Leaders," *Agricultural History*, XLII (January, 1968).

Other significant articles on progressivism that indicate directions for future research include Robert W. Doherty, "Status Anxiety and American Reform: Some Alternatives," *American Quarterly*, XIX (Summer, 1967); Herbert Janick, "The Mind of the Connecticut Progressive," *Mid-America*, LII (April, 1970); Thelen, "Social Tensions and the Origins of Progressivism"; Hays, "The Social Analysis of American Political History, 1880–1920"; G. Edward White, "The Social Values of the Progressives: Some New Perspectives," *South Atlantic Quarterly*, LXX (Winter, 1971).

Analyses of the impact of the settlement house on reform movements and the relationship between settlement workers and the urban political machine are Allen F. Davis, *Spearheads For Reform: The Social Settlements and the Progressive Movement, 1890–1914* (1967); Davis, "Social Workers and the Progressive Party, 1912–1916," *American Historical Review*, LXIX (April, 1964); Davis, "Jane Addams vs. the Ward Boss," *Journal of the Illinois State Historical Society*, LIII (Autumn, 1960); Humbert S. Nelli, "John Powers and the Italians: Politics in a Chicago Ward, 1896–1921," *Journal of American History*, LVII (June, 1970); George Cary White, "Social Settlements and Immigrant Neighbors," *Social Science Review*, XXXIII (March, 1959).

Studies of women and their relationship to politics include Eleanor Flexner, *Century of Struggle: The Women's Rights Movement in the United States* (1959); William O'Neill, *Everyone Was Brave: The History of Social Feminism in America* (1969); J. F. Mahoney, "Woman Suffrage and the Urban Masses"; John D. Buenker, "The Urban Political Machine and Women Suffrage: A Study in Political Adaptability," *The Historian*, XXXIII (February, 1971); Anne Firor Scott, *The Southern Lady,*

1830–1930 (1970); Roy Lubove, "The Progressive and the Prostitute," *The Historian*, XXIV (May, 1962); Egal Feldman, "Prostitution, the Alien Woman, and the Progressive Imagination, 1910–1915," *American Quarterly*, XIX (Summer, 1967).

For conflicting views of prohibition and reform sentiment, see James H. Timberlake, *Prohibition and the Progressive Years*, 1900–1920 (1963) and Joseph R. Gusfield, *Symbolic Crusade: Status Politics and the American Temperance Movement* (1963). Individual state studies include Norman H. Clark, *The Dry Years: Prohibition and Social Change in Washington* (1965); Gilman M. Ostrander, *The Prohibition Movement in California, 1848–1933* (1957); John D. Buenker, "The Illinois Legislature and Prohibition, 1907–1919," *Journal of the Illinois State Historical Society*, LXII (Winter, 1969); Paul E. Issac, *Prohibition and Politics: Turbulent Decades in Tennessee, 1885–1920* (1965); James B. Sellers, *The Prohibition Movement in Alabama, 1702–1943* (1943); and Daniel Jay Whitener, *Prohibition in North Carolina, 1715–1945* (1946).

A number of local and regional studies have expanded considerably our understanding of progressivism and reform. On the South, see Arthur S. Link, "The Progressive Movement in the South, 1870–1914," *North Carolina Historical Review*, XXIII (April, 1946); Anne Firor Scott, "A Progressive Wind from the South, 1906–1913," *Journal of Southern History*, XXIX (February, 1963); Sheldon Hackney, *Populism to Progressivism in Alabama* (1969); Herbert J. Doherty, "Voices of Protest from the New South, 1875–1910," *Mississippi Valley Historical Review*, XLII (June, 1955); C. Vann Woodward, *Origins of the New South, 1877–1913* (1951); George B. Tindall, *The Emergence of the New South, 1913–1945* (1967); and Raymond Pulley, *Old Virginia Restored: An Interpretation of the Progressive Impulse, 1870–1930* (1968). The basic history of progressivism in the Middle West is Nye's *Midwestern Progressive Politics*, and other works include Joel A. Tarr, "William Kent to Lincoln Steffens: Origins of Progressive Reform in Chicago," *Mid-America*, XLVII (January, 1965); Sidney I. Roberts, "The Municipal Voters' League and Chicago Boodlers," *Journal of the Illinois State Historical Society*, LIII (Summer, 1960); Herbert Margulies, *The Decline of the Progressive Movement in Wisconsin, 1890–1920* (1968); Maxwell, *La Follette and the Rise of the Progressives in Wisconsin*; and Hoyt Landon Warner, *Progressives in Ohio, 1897–1917* (1964). For the East, see Robert F. Wesser, *Charles Evans Hughes: Politics and Reform in New York State, 1905–1910* (1967); Wesser, "Charles Evans Hughes and the Urban Sources of Political Progressivism," *New York Historical Society Quarterly*, L (October, 1966); Ransom E. Noble, Jr., *New Jersey Progressivism Before Wilson*

(1946); Richard M. Abrams, "A Paradox of Progressivism: Massachusetts on the Eve of Insurgency," *Political Science Quarterly*, LXXV (September, 1960); Abrams, *Conservatism in a Progressive Era: Massachusetts Politics, 1900–1912* (1964); and Winston Allen Flint, *The Progressive Movement in Vermont* (1941). On California and the West Coast, see Mowry, "The California Progressive and His Rationale: A Study in Middle Class Politics"; Mowry, *The California Progressives*; Kerr, "The Progressives of Washington, 1910–1912"; Olin, *California's Prodigal Sons: Hiram Johnson and the Progressives, 1911–1917*; Michael P. Rogin, "Progressivism and the California Electorate," *Journal of American History*, LV (September, 1968).

Other interesting views of the progressive reform impulse can be found in Paul W. Glad, "Bryan and the Urban Progressives," *Mid-America*, XXXIX (July, 1957); Stanley K. Schultz, "The Morality of Politics: The Muckraker's Vision of Society," *Journal of American History*, LII (December, 1965); Samuel Haber, *Efficiency and Uplift: Scientific Management in the Progressive Era, 1890–1920* (1964); Daniel Aaron, *Men of Good Hope: A Story of the American Progressive* (1964); Charles Forcey, *The Crossroads of Liberalism: Croly, Weyl, Lippmann and the Progressive Era, 1900–1925* (1961); Herbert Margulies, "Recent Opinion of the Decline of the Progressive Movement," *Mid-America*, XLV (October, 1963).

For material on the role of the urban boss in reform in the years from 1880 to 1920, see the previously cited works by John D. Buenker and J. Joseph Huthmacher. Also see Warner, *Progressivism in Ohio, 1897–1917*; Holli, *Reform in Detroit: Hazen S. Pingree and Urban Politics*; Arthur Mann, *La Guardia Comes to Power: 1933* (1965); Robert Moses, *La Guardia, A Salute and a Memoir* (1957); Mark Foster, "Frank Hague of New Jersey: The Boss as Reformer," *New Jersey History*, LXXXVI (Summer, 1968); Oscar Handlin, *Al Smith and His America* (1958); Miller, *Boss Cox's Cincinnati: Urban Politics in the Progressive Era*; Tager, *The Intellectual as Urban Reformer: Brand Whitlock and the Progressive Movement*; and Lyle W. Dorsett, "The City Boss and the Reformer: A Reappraisal" (unpublished paper presented to the annual meeting of the Organization of American Historians, Los Angeles, California, April, 1970).